CONVERSATIONS WITH DENIS KITCHEN

Conversations with Comic Artists M. Thomas Inge, General Editor

Conversations with Denis Kitchen

Edited by Kim A. Munson

University Press of Mississippi / Jackson

The University Press of Mississippi is the scholarly publishing agency of the Mississippi Institutions of Higher Learning: Alcorn State University, Delta State University, Jackson State University, Mississippi State University, Mississippi University for Women, Mississippi Valley State University, University of Mississippi, and University of Southern Mississippi.

www.upress.state.ms.us

The University Press of Mississippi is a member of the Association of University Presses.

All images courtesy of Denis Kitchen except figure 14, Steven Grant; figure 22, Johan de Neef; figure 26, Tea Krulos; figure 31, John Lind.

Publisher: University Press of Mississippi, Jackson, USA
Authorised GPSR Safety Representative: Easy Access System Europe –
Mustamäe tee 50, 10621 Tallinn, Estonia, *gpsr.requests@easproject.com*

Library of Congress Cataloging-in-Publication Data

Names: Munson, Kim A. editor | Salkowitz, Rob, 1967– author of foreword
Title: Conversations with Denis Kitchen / Kim A. Munson, Rob Salkowitz.
Other titles: Conversations with comic artists
Description: Jackson : University Press of Mississippi, 2025. | Series: Conversations with
    comic artists series | Includes bibliographical references and index.
Identifiers: LCCN 2025025207 (print) | LCCN 2025025208 (ebook)
    | ISBN 9781496859495 hardback | ISBN 9781496859501 trade paperback |
    ISBN 9781496859518 epub | ISBN 9781496859525 epub |
    ISBN 9781496859532 pdf | ISBN 9781496859549 pdf
Subjects: LCSH: Kitchen, Denis, 1946—Interviews | Comic Book Legal Defense Fund—History |
    Kitchen Sink Press—History | Cartoonists—United States—Interviews |
    Comic books, strips, etc.—Publishing | Comic books, strips, etc.—Influence
Classification: LCC PN6727.K59 C66 2025 (print) | LCC PN6727.K59 (ebook)
LC record available at https://lccn.loc.gov/2025025207
LC ebook record available at https://lccn.loc.gov/2025025208

British Library Cataloging-in-Publication Data available

Selected Works by Denis Kitchen

Underground Comix

Mom's Homemade Comics #1–3 (1969–1971)
Teen-Age Horizons of Shangrila #1 (1970)
Bizarre Sex #1 (1972)
Snarf #1 (1972)
Comix Book #1–5 (1974–1976)
Weird Trips #1 (1974)
Jim Spencer's *Major Arcana* (album cover, 1975)
Mondo Snarfo #1 (1978)
Energy Comics #1 (1980)

Books

Playboy's Little Annie Fanny (2001)
Lil' Abner: The Frazetta Years (2003)
Al Capp's Complete Shmoo (2008)
Underground Classics: The Transformation of Comics to Comix (with James Danky, 2009)
The Art of Harvey Kurtzman: The Mad Genius of Comics (with Paul Buhle, 2009)
The Oddly Compelling Art of Denis Kitchen (2010)
Denis Kitchen's Chipboard Sketchbook (2011)
Al Capp: A Life in the Contrary (with Michael Schumacher, 2013)
Best of Comix Book: When Marvel Comics Went Underground (with John Lind, 2013)
Trump: The Complete Collection (with John Lind, 2016)
Everything Including the Kitchen Sink: The Definitive Interview with Denis Kitchen (Jon B. Cooke, 2016)
Will Eisner: A Centennial Celebration—1917–2017 (2017)
A Contract with God: Curator's Edition (with John Lind, 2018)
Madness in Crowds: The Teeming Mind of Harrison Cady (with Violet Kitchen, 2020)
Creatures from the Subconscious (2022)

Art Exhibitions

Cartoon-O-Rama. Priebe Galley, University of Wisconsin–Oshkosh (1976)
Original Comic Art by Denis Kitchen. Reeve Memorial Union, University of Wisconsin–Oshkosh (1978)

Denis Kitchen. Ripon Center for the Arts, Ripon College, Ripon, Wisconsin (1990)

Curated *Harvey Kurtzman: Retrospective of a MAD Genius* at the Cartoon Art Museum, San Francisco, California (1995)

Curated *Harvey Kurtzman* at the Society of Illustrators, New York, New York (2004)

Curated *Will Eisner: A Retrospective*, which originated at MoCCA, New York, New York, and continued to Utah Valley State College, Orem, Utah, and the University of Massachusetts, Amherst, Massachusetts (2005)

Cocurated *Underground Classics: The Transformation of Comics to Comix* at the Chazen Museum of Art, Madison, Wisconsin (with James Danky, 2009)

The Oddly Compelling Mini-Retrospective of Denis Kitchen, MoCCA, New York, New York (2010)

Cocurated *The Living Spirit of Will Eisner* for Rio Comicon, Rio de Janeiro (with Marisa Furtado, 2012)

Cocurated *The Art of Harvey Kurtzman*. Society of Illustrators, New York (with Monte Beauchamp, 2013)

Cocurated *Robert Crumb and the Underground*. Kunstmuseum, Lucerne, Switzerland (with James Danky, 2013)

The Oddly Compelling Art of Denis Kitchen, August 1–October 8, at the Fine Arts Gallery, University of Wisconsin–Parkside (2014)

The Oddly Compelling Art of Denis Kitchen, Scott Elder Gallery, Brooklyn, New York (2016)

Curated *Will Eisner: A Brief Retrospective*. Geppi's Entertainment Museum, Baltimore, Maryland (2015)

Curated *Will Eisner: 75 Years of the Spirit*. Jewish Museum, Munich, Germany (2015)

Cocurated *Will Eisner: The Centennial Celebration* at the Society of Illustrators, New York, New York, and Amador, Portugal (with John Lind, 2017)

Curated *Will Eisner: A Centennial Celebration* at Le Musée de la Bande Dessinée, Angouleme, France (2017)

Strange & Captivating: The Work of Denis Kitchen at Amerikahaus Munchen, part of the Munich Comics Festival, Munich, Germany (2017)

Cocurator *Wisconsin Funnies: 50 Years of Comics*. The Museum of Wisconsin Art, West Bend, Wisconsin (with James Danky, 2020)

Curated *A Serious Look at the Funnies*, Ewing Gallery of Arts, University of Tennessee–Knoxville (2022)

Creatures from the Subconscious. The Stadtbibliothek, in conjunction with the biennial Munich Comics Festival (2023)

CONTENTS

Denis Kitchen. 2020. "Dream of Nancy & Sluggo in the Orkneys." Published in *Roarin' Rick's Rare Bit Fiends* #24.

Denis Kitchen: An Appreciation

ROB SALKOWITZ

Artist, publisher, comics historian, entrepreneur, artists' representative, civil liberties advocate, curator, connector—there are so many ways to view the career of Denis Kitchen that it has almost become a cliché to enumerate them all. But to that already long list I would append at least one more item: evangelist. By melding his deeply informed love of comics history with a keen eye for the new and exciting, Kitchen helped promote an unusually expansive vision of the potential of comics—one that stretched from masterful classics of the 1920s, '30s and '40s through the undergrounds of the 1960s and '70s, and onward into the ambitious creator-owned and independent comics of the '80s and '90s—at a critical moment when the medium was gaining new cultural status. In so doing, he influenced the tastes of two generations of readers, including many who went on to become scholars, critics, and professionals.

I was one of those readers. When I was a kid in the mid-1970s, my father realized that I wasn't going to "outgrow" comics, so he decided that if you can't beat 'em, join 'em. One day, he came home with a stack of magazines he'd picked up at a secondhand store and said, "If you're going to read comics, at least read good ones." What he gave me were reprints of a newspaper strip he remembered reading with *his* father back in the 1940s involving a certain masked detective: Will Eisner's *The Spirit*.

I was hooked from the first story and devoured the stack of pulpy old magazines. Hunting for new issues, I discovered *The Spirit* had just moved over to Kitchen Sink Press (KSP), a publisher I'd never heard of. The Kitchen Sink *Spirit* magazines featured better paper, clearer reproduction, more coherent selection of stories, and a more authoritative editorial tone. Since mainstream comics in this era were at their absolute nadir of production value as publishers cut every corner to keep costs down, KSP's approach was a breath of fresh air. Whoever put this magazine out genuinely loved comics enough to present them with quality and respect.

The KSP issues also featured another difference from the previous publishers. Instead of ads for old horror movies, toys, and tchotchkes, Kitchen Sink advertised independent comics; naughty-looking comics about sex, drugs, and rock and roll; various art portfolios; and some of the very first graphic novels, including Eisner's *A Contract with God and Other Tenement Stories*. Not all of these were published by Kitchen Sink, but their presence in such a quality publication suggested they were at least worthy of my consideration.

Through the pages of the Kitchen Sink Spirit magazines, my provincial tastes in superhero comics were expanded in all kinds of new directions. I discovered the genre-defining visual storytelling of Milton Caniff's *Steve Canyon* and *Terry and the Pirates*, the sophisticated social observations and progressive politics of Eisner's one-time assistant Jules Feiffer, the radical visions of the underground creators, and more challenging mainstream-style work coming from the independent presses who followed in Kitchen Sink's footsteps.

The caliber of KSP's taste and judgment can be seen in the titles he brought forth in the 1980s as it became a bigger player in the direct market. Mark Schultz, Charles Burns, Don Simpson, Reed Waller, Kate Worley, Howard Cruse, Dave McKean, Scott McCloud, James O'Barr, Dan Burr, and James Vance were some of the talents whose career-shaping works first appeared under the Kitchen Sink imprint. The company also saw earlier than most the potential of comics on the bookshelf, becoming a leading publisher of archival and original graphic novels.

By the time I met Denis in person in the late 1990s, I was barely conscious of the extent to which my early exposure to KSP's output in the previous twenty-five years had shaped my tastes and understanding of American comics. We connected over my particular point of entry, the work of Eisner, who was still alive, well, and actively working with Denis on a number of projects. It quickly became clear that one of the things that had so impressed me about Eisner—his combination of creative talent and entrepreneurial skills—was also present in Denis, to an extent that may have deprived us of seeing more of Denis's own wonderful artwork and storytelling over the course of his career.

Over the next twenty years, we became close friends and occasional business associates. In 1979, Denis had run the only letter to the editor I ever wrote to a comic book company, which was the first time I saw my name in print. More than thirty years later, as my agent, he helped get my 2012 book *Comic-Con and the Business of Pop Culture* published by McGraw-Hill.

Eventually, I made the pilgrimage to his expansive compound in rural western Massachusetts, where I witnessed firsthand how the eclectic tastes Denis exhibited as a publisher were only the tip of the iceberg in terms of his personal interests, collections, and fascinations. In a way, his entire career can be seen as an effort to share his boundless passion for the clever, quirky, individually expressive, well-crafted, and sometimes unjustly overlooked masterpieces of popular culture with the wider world, grabbing us all by the lapels and saying, "Isn't this *great*?"

Through the interviews and articles collected in this book, I hope the rest of the world can get the same sense of Denis Kitchen the artist, the storyteller, activist, entrepreneur, historian, and all the other hats he wears. But above all, I hope readers can appreciate his pivotal role in shaping our understanding of the breath, depth, and historical expanse of twentieth-century comics. Today it is commonplace to consider all genres and styles of comics as facets of a single medium and to view the industry as a patchwork of formats and distribution methods ranging from handmade zines to deluxe trade books. But to embrace that conception of comics as far back as the 1960s, and to continually bet the fortunes of your business on it through a fifty-year career, takes an extraordinary combination of vision and pure chutzpah. That describes Denis Kitchen to a T. He is truly comics' indispensable man, and this deep dive into his career is both welcome and necessary.

Rob Salkowitz
Seattle, WA, August 2023

Rob Salkowitz is senior media/entertainment contributor for *Forbes*; author or editor of five books, including *Comic-Con and the Business of Pop Culture* (McGraw-Hill, 2012); and senior affiliate instructor at the University of Washington Graduate School of Communication.

INTRODUCTION

At San Diego Comic-Con 2009, comics historian and journalist Michael Dooley began the *Spotlight on Denis Kitchen* panel by unspooling a long roll of paper that spilled over the table down to the floor, joking that the man of the hour had worn so many hats and survived so many changes in his career and in the comics industry that Dooley needed a ten-foot roll of paper to cover it all. Everyone in the audience laughed knowingly. Denis Kitchen (b. August 17, 1946) has had one of the most accomplished and tumultuous careers in comics.

A Wisconsin native, Kitchen's professional career began with *Mom's Homemade Comics* #1, an underground style comic that he self-created and sold for forty-nine cents a copy to spectators at the 1969 Great Schlitz Circus Parade in Milwaukee. From that humble beginning, Kitchen has built an incredibly diverse career as a publisher of underground comix, classic reprints, graphic novels, art books, trading cards, and novelties for both Kitchen Sink Press (KSP, 1969–1999) and Kitchen Sink Books (KSB, with Dark Horse, 2013–); a writer; an editor; the founder of the Comic Book Legal Defense Fund (CBLDF, 1986–); a curator; an art and literary agent; and the job he loves most and never seems to have time for—cartoonist.

Kitchen enters all of these ventures and collaborations with the same creative passion as his artwork. Throughout his career, he has woven a dense web of connections with artists both well-known and undiscovered. With a nose for talent and keen interest in a good story, he revitalized the careers of mentors like Will Eisner and Harvey Kurtzman and gave many new artists the forum they needed to grow. In the chronology of his career following this introduction, I've listed not only key life events, publications, artwork, and exhibitions, but also the dates of the first KSP publications with creatives like Eisner, Kurtzman, Robert Crumb, Trina Robbins, Howard Kruse, Milton Caniff, Mark Schultz, Charles Burns, and others. Although this book focuses on Kitchen and his business relationships, the importance of family—his siblings, wives, and daughters—is another important undercurrent throughout these interviews.

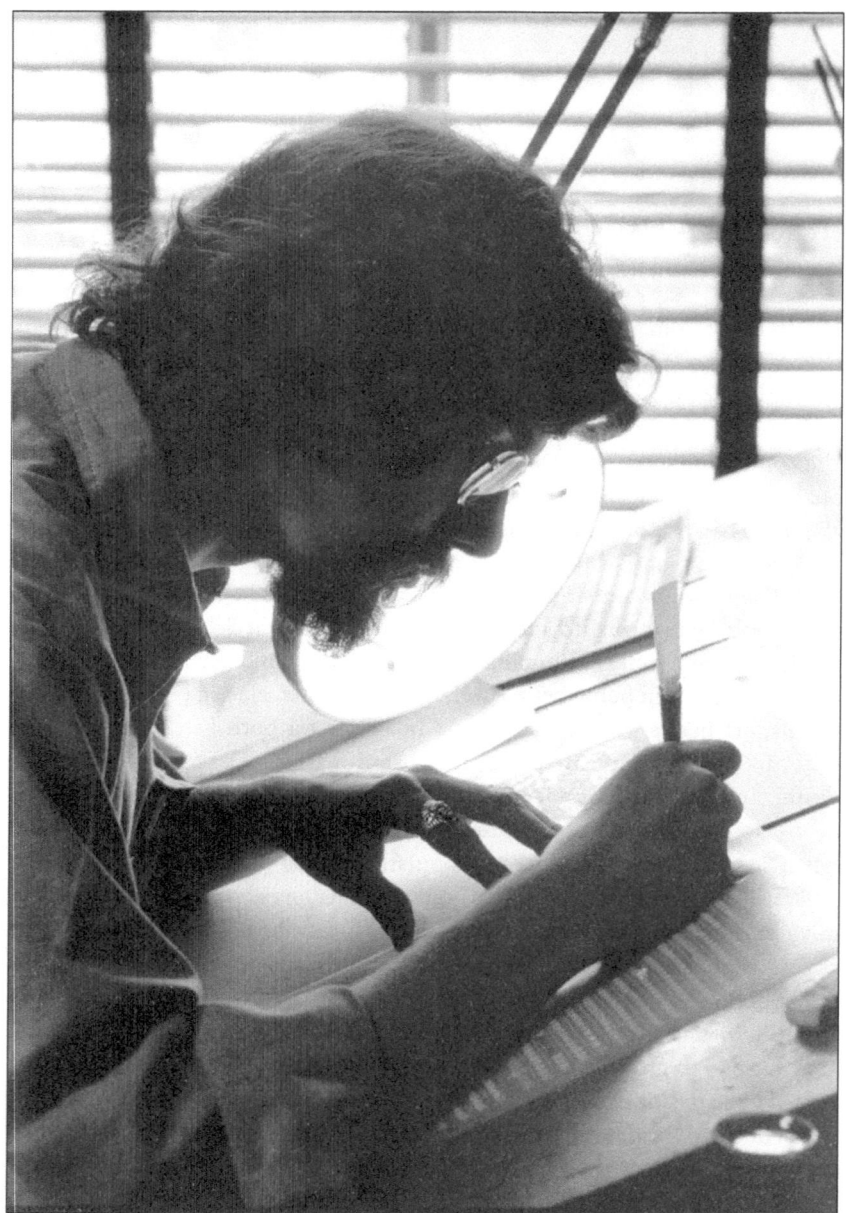

Denis Kitchen at his drawing board, 1975.

Several book-length publications look at Kitchen's life and career in depth. *Everything Including the Kitchen Sink* by Jon B. Cooke (TwoMorrows Publishing, 2016) is a lushly illustrated book-length interview with a journalist–author that knows him well. *The Oddly Compelling Art of Denis Kitchen*, with an introduction by Neil Gaiman and an in-depth essay by Charles Brownstein, is a coffee table art book that reproduces artwork from 1953 (second grade) to 2009. For insight into KSP's publications, successes, and failures, I highly recommend *Kitchen Sink Press: The First 25 Years*, by KSP editor Dave Schreiner, published to celebrate KSP's twenty-fifth anniversary in 1994. It provides a year-by-year checklist and summary of important events, as well as short interviews with key artists, employees, and business connections. In 2023, Lars Ingebrigtsen completed his survey of all KSP's comics titles from 1969 to 1999. The result is *The Entire Kitchen Sink Redux* website, containing a cover photo of each KSP publication, along with a short review and photos of each issue.

Building on all of these reference works, this book allows Kitchen to tell his story in his own words as it was happening, era by era. It includes interviews from mainstream news outlets, fanzines, comics news websites, exhibition catalogs, industry trades, and other publications. In some cases, Kitchen has provided me with unpublished source interviews used as background information for articles on specific topics, such as the development of *Gay Comix*, his interactions with Harlan Ellison, and the controversial life of Al Capp.

One can think of the arc of Kitchen's career in three big chunks: his beginning with Krupp Comic Works, Inc., and his central role as a publisher and cartoonist in 1970s and '80s underground comix; the height of Kitchen Sink Press in the 1990s, ending with the disastrous Tundra merger and the painful loss of the company at the end of the decade; and his successful self-reinvention as an agent, publisher, artist, and entrepreneur.

Following this introduction is the entire penultimate issue of *Klepto* (#24, 1963). Kitchen was raised in Caledonia, a suburb of Milwaukee, Wisconsin, and cut his teeth as a cartoonist and publisher at the tender age of thirteen with a monthly dittoed gossip sheet–humor zine called *Cleptomaniac*, which he continued publishing as *Klepto* at Horlick High School, charging ten cents for a six-page zine. In *Klepto*, with its balloon characters and cheesy midwestern humor, we can see the seeds of Kitchen's work in *Mom's #1*.

The main content of this book begins with three interviews given between 1972 and 1981 that show the evolution of KSP from its beginning—publishing and distributing a handful of popular underground titles—to the rapidly expanding self-described "hippie empire" with a wide range of underground

Cover, *The Oddly Compelling Art of Denis Kitchen* (Dark Horse, 2010).

titles, new work, and publications from comics icon Eisner, as well as a vast distribution network in the US and internationally. I am pleased to include Kitchen's first interview, in the fanzine *The Vault of Mindless Fellowship* #2 (1972), which has not previously been reprinted.

Six articles written between 1992 and 2000 cover the height of KSP and its demise in 1999 following KSP's 1993 merger with Kevin Eastman's Tundra

Publishing. The entry from 1992 features Kitchen's predictions about the future of the comics industry at an industry roundtable organized by Capital City Distribution, including his remarks on the early cases of the CBLDF and its progress. In these interviews he discusses the success of James O'Barr's *The Crow*, creating the animated cartoon series *Cadillacs and Dinosaurs* (based on *Xenozoic Tales* by Schultz), working with figures like Stan Lee and the Grateful Dead, his commitment to reprint the entire run of Al Capp's *Li'l Abner*, and other projects. I have made an exception to the "interviews only" format to include an in-depth contemporaneous article from *BusinessWest*, a regional Massachusetts business magazine, about the actions by business consultant Don Todrin that pushed Kitchen out of his own business and resulted in the end of KSP, as well as Todrin's attempt to spin off KSP's novelties arm as a stand-alone candy company named True Confections.

Following the death of KSP, Kitchen quickly reinvented himself with new roles as an agent, estate representative, author, curator, and a new publishing imprint with Dark Horse, Kitchen Sink Books. This book concludes with a group of interviews conducted between 2001 and 2022 in which Kitchen not only promotes new projects, but he also talks about key relationships with creators like Capp, Kurtzman, Crumb, Kruse, Ellison, and his evolving relationship with Eisner as publisher, editor, and eventually as the art agent for his estate.

After a period of intense activity with Dark Horse, in recent years Kitchen has found more time to curate exhibitions (chiefly Eisner's work and his own); develop books about forgotten cartoonists with his youngest child, Violet Kitchen; and to do more cartooning, with an emphasis on his surreal chipboard drawings and 3D art. Also claiming some of Kitchen's attention is the dangerous upswing in the censorship of comics and graphic novels from the extreme ends of the political left and right. CBLDF is again at the forefront of defending authors and artists from these attacks. This book concludes with a 2022 discussion about this issue and the importance of cultivating intellectual and artistic curiosity throughout his life and career.

KM

6 PAGES

KLEPTO

A

10 CENTS

MAY

SPECIAL SPRING ISSUE

Chock full of things totally unrelated to Spring

POLITICAL ENEMIES BLAST EACH OTHER

ALL OF BERLIN TAKEN BY REDS

"ROCKEFELLER IS STUPID", SAYS GOLDWATER

"GOLDWATER IS DISTASTEFUL", SAYS ROCKY

Bulletin! All of Berlin was taken by the Reds Monday.

However, doctors said that Irving Berlin, well-known composer, would recover from the measles by Friday.

Hey Boys! Cheesecake pictures on page two!

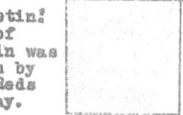

Barry Goldwater, senator from Arizona, member of the space committee, said Sunday, "The aeronautical engineers are debating whether to put pressurized seats or rocking chairs in the space capsule for the astronaut fellas. Well, I think pressurized seats are fine, but to Rock a feller is stupid!"

IN THIS GIGANTIC SIX PAGE SPRING ISSUE:

Photo-Quiz, Pin-Ups, Gossip, World News, Polaris Expose, Love Advise, Autos, Junk

Nelson Rockefeller, governor of New York, told the comissioners of the Public Water Works at a meeting Sunday, "You are going to have to do something about the problem of minerals dissolving in public water. Don't get me wrong; silver water and iron water are okay, but Gold water is distasteful!"

KLEPTO # 24

Written by
Denis Kitchen
Published by
Bob Wilson

Denis Kitchen, 1963. *Klepto* #24. Complete six-page issue. Written and drawn by Denis Kitchen, published by Bob Wilson. Reprinted by permission.

PIN-UP

Guys: Hang up these bewitching pin-ups in your locker, and see your fellow classmates drool with envy.

MISS SPRING 1963

KLEPTO PIN-UP # 1

STATISTICS

Miss Spring is in reality, Miss Joy Venturooni. Her measurements are 38-24-36 (not necessarily in that order). She is 5'3", and weighs a trim 180 pounds. Miss Spring is a big city girl. She was born in Kenosha, where she works as a welder for Nash. There she was chosen Miss Transmission of 1937, and her career has been booming since.

ADVICE TO THE LOVELORN

Dear ABEE,
Recently my 94 year-old cousin moved in with us. Everything was okay, but now he just sits in the corner and never moves. What's wrong? Worried

Dear Worried: It's quite possible your cousin is dead.

Dear ABEE,
My problem is this: I'm so handsome that girls always chase me. In fact, one girl right now is pounding on my bedroom door. What should I do? Handsome

Dear Handsome: Let her out of your bedroom.

Dear ABEE,
What can I do? My mother won't let me buy Klepto. She says it's just a bunch of trash. Neglected

Dear Neglected: Listen to your mother. She knows the value of a dime.

Dear ABEE,
Please help me. I'm in love with a boy who doesn't know I'm alive. What can I do ? Diane

Dear Diane: Why don't you show him your birth certificate.

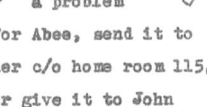 If YOU have a problem for Abee, send it to her c/o home room 115, or give it to John Burgeson in person.

What is a barfafone? You have probably been lying awake nights asking yourself that. For the startling answer, see page three.

Denis Kitchen, 1963. *Klepto* #24. Page two of six.

KLEPTO PHOTO-QUIZ

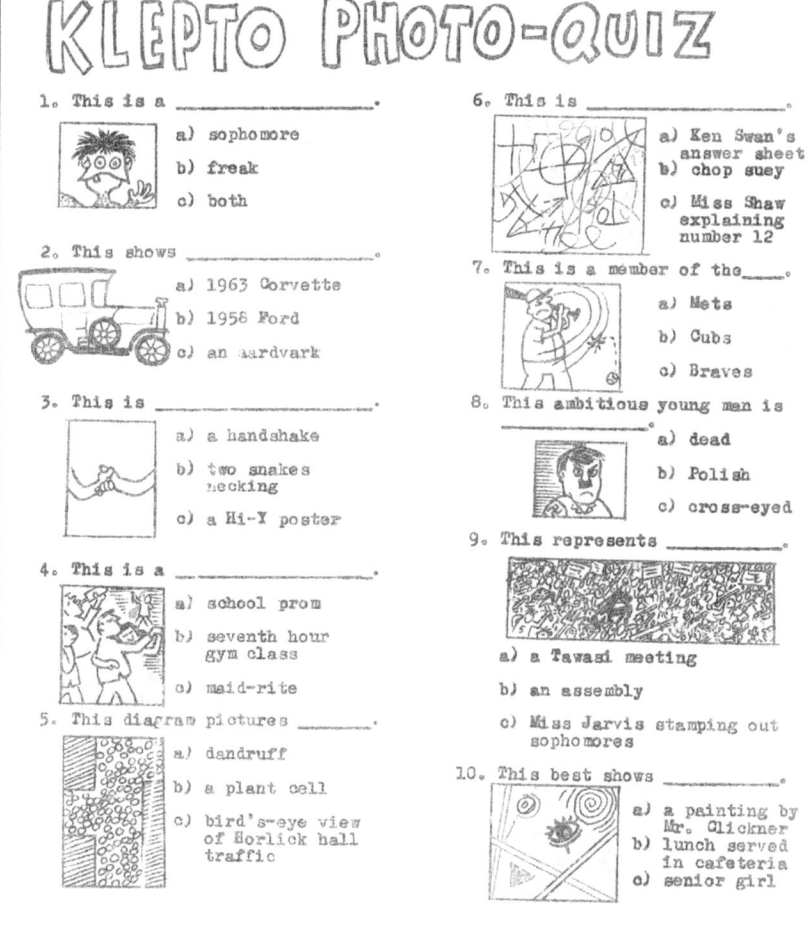

1. This is a _____.

   a) sophomore

   b) freak

   c) both

2. This shows _____.

   a) 1963 Corvette

   b) 1958 Ford

   c) an aardvark

3. This is _____.

   a) a handshake

   b) two snakes necking

   c) a Hi-Y poster

4. This is a _____.

   a) school prom

   b) seventh hour gym class

   c) maid-rite

5. This diagram pictures _____.

   a) dandruff

   b) a plant cell

   c) bird's-eye view of Horlick hall traffic

6. This is _____.

   a) Ken Swan's answer sheet

   b) chop suey

   c) Miss Shaw explaining number 12

7. This is a member of the____.

   a) Mets

   b) Cubs

   c) Braves

8. This ambitious young man is _____.

   a) dead

   b) Polish

   c) cross-eyed

9. This represents _____.

   a) a Tawasi meeting

   b) an assembly

   c) Miss Jarvis stamping out sophomores

10. This best shows _____.

    a) a painting by Mr. Clickner

    b) lunch served in cafeteria

    c) senior girl

Denis Kitchen, 1963. *Klepto* #24. Page three of six.

KLEPTO CLASSIFIED ADS
USED CARS

1954 Chevy two door coupe with bucket seats, Corvette engine, full race cam, FM radio, floor shift, rolled and pleated leather interior, candy apple red. 45,000 miles. A real bargain. Only one owner; an old grandma who only drove it to church on Sundays.
Midnight Motors. 2542 Douglas.

1952 Plymouth 2 door sedan; 59,000 original miles, with blue and white racing stripe, powered by '62 Ram Charger with 3 duces. Contact Bob Wilson.

ROLLS ROYCE $180

1961 Rolls-Royce coupe only $180. Has '49 Studebaker body, '52 Kaiser engine, and '40 LaSalle transmission. Rolls-Royce hub caps.

CUSTOMIZED

1956 Ford four door Customized; chromed oil pan, full race valve covers, louvered gas tank, Frenched motor mounts, mounted rust. A deal at $95.
Albert Kokke Used Cars. Racine.

1958 Oldsmobile, with Chevy 409 h/p dragster engine; 4 speed floor shift and optionals: dice or booties dangling from rear view mirror, mud flaps, monotone radio.
See Mr. Curtis, Driver Ed teacher.

1960 DeSoto sedan $1100

1922 Model T Ford, convertible.

1954 road grader.   Shulman Motors

1956 Cadillac - a real honey! 2 miles to the gallon. Bloody pontoons and three notches on steering wheel.

1929 Essex original - completely restored. White wall tires, color TV, transistorized ignition, heater, fins, Chrysler grill, 2-tone.

1958 Dodge four door coupe. White enamel finish. Pictured below. One defect — cracked front headlight.

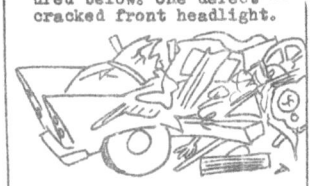

GO MAN!

Denis Kitchen, 1963. *Klepto* #24. Page four of six.

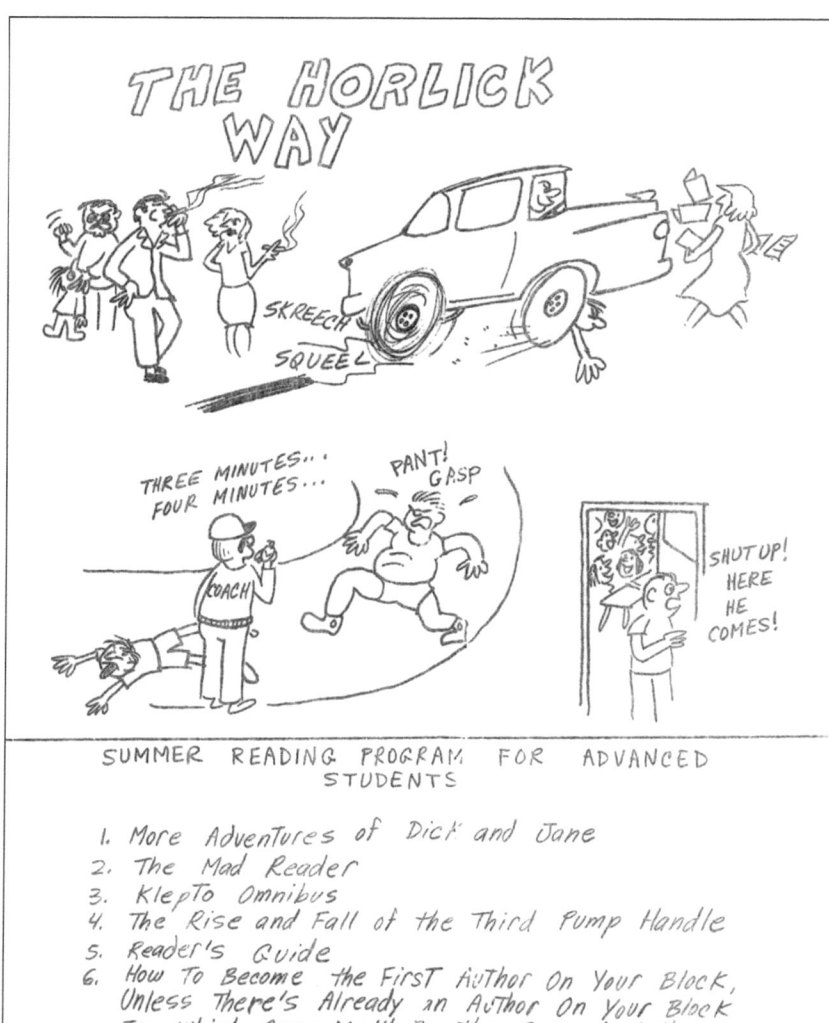

Denis Kitchen, 1963. *Klepto* #24. Page five of six.

GOSSIP
BY MISS X

Ethel R, how many days?.... John B finally got his license.... I hear Lois D is quite a mover....Does Marilyn C really weigh 145 pounds? Wow!... What's this false rumor about Barb W? ....Gen S, Do you like rabbits?.... Helen H, you switch often, don't you? ....Diane F, what's the lawyer for?.... Bob G, Boy, that's mellow. What does he mean, Helen?.... Those senior girls will do anything to go to prom, won't they, senior boys? ....Are Dick D and Barb B really going out on the sly?.... Not everyone can lock their keys in the trunk, can they, Mick....Rick C going to be best man? Somebody tell him the truth....Does Sandy J always say such things in math class ....Who is the senior girl who had a little trouble on the four mile road last week?.... I understand Gerd H is going to have quite a vocabulary to take home....   con't

....Is Ted E still trying to sell his notebook for $2?.... Sue B can hit pretty hard!....Does Gary P enjoy losing miniature golf to girls?....Why is Steve K called "pinky"?....Dick S had quite a time at the last card game....Anyone have any tape for John B's Skoda?.... that conceited junior girl is the belle of the town, but she shouldn't have been tolled....   Miss X

WANT-ADS

Job Opening— need a thermo-nuclear physicist, familiar with lunar-cyst radiation & dynamated perm-isophere reaction. No experience necessary.

Contents of typical Horlick student's purse (girl's):

What's missing? Best answer wins.

FREE Emergency Pass Slip
Compliments of Klepto (They'll never know the difference)

PASS SLIP

Pass issued by Harold R. Mila
Date Mar 4 1963
Period 4
Destination Gr cope
Student
. . . .
Time of leaving 1.5.16
Teacher in charge MES
. . . .
Time 5-26
Teacher in charge Wm. A. Schlegen.
— please excuse this student.

Denis Kitchen, 1963. *Klepto* #24. Page six of six.

Denis Kitchen, 1969.

CHRONOLOGY

1946   Born August 27, to WWII veteran Benjamin Kitchen, a factory worker, and Margaretha Margert. He was the oldest of their three children, with a middle brother, James, and a younger sister, Gayle. The family settled into a prefabricated home in Caledonia, a suburb of Milwaukee.

1959   While in grade school, Kitchen wrote, illustrated, and sold *Cleptomaniac*, a three-page gossip and humor zine printed on a Ditto machine. When it continued publication into William Horlick High School (Racine, Wisconsin), he expanded the zine to six pages and renamed it *Klepto*. Ultimately it ran for twenty-five issues.

1967   Cofounded *Snide* as a student at the University of Wisconsin–Milwaukee (UWM). It was UWM's first campus humor magazine. Kitchen also contributed a weekly strip, "Sheepshead U," for the *UWM Post* while majoring in journalism.

1968   Kitchen graduated from UWM with a BS in journalism in June. He was drafted and inducted into the military but was sent home after twenty-two days with a temporary medical discharge. He received a high draft number and was not called to serve again.

1969   Created and self-published *Mom's Homemade Comics* #1, which was first sold for forty-nine cents at the Great Schlitz Circus Parade in Milwaukee, with the remainder of the first printing sold at local head shops, drugstores, and Gary Arlington's San Francisco Comic Book Company. A reprint of *Mom's* #1 and the new *Mom's* #2 were published by the Print Mint in San Francisco. A group of like-minded Milwaukee artists formed around him, including Don Glassford, Jim Mitchell, Bruce Walthers, and Wendel Pugh.

1970   The success of *Mom's* drew encouraging letters from Harvey Kurtzman, Stan Lee, and Robert Crumb, people who would be future collaborators. It also gained the attention of Jay Lynch, whose *Bijou Funnies* was also doing well for Print Mint. Unhappy with the business practices at Print Mint, Kitchen decided to take *Mom's* back and self-publish. He agreed to publish *Bijou Funnies* too, and Krupp Comic Works, Inc., was born. It quickly evolved into Kitchen Sink Enterprises and later into Kitchen Sink Press (KSP), the long-running publishing imprint (1969–1999). The "arms" of the Krupp octopus were:

· Strickly Uppa Crust, a Milwaukee comics and head shop.
· The Cartoon Factory, a commercial art studio that supplied art to the Schlitz Brewing Co., *The Chicago Sun-Times*, and other clients.
· Ordinary Records, a label formed to produce music by Crumb.
· Krupp Cards (irreverent Christmas and all-season greeting cards).
· Krupp Mail Order (spun off to partner Tyler Lantzy in 1975).
· Krupp Distribution, which distributed comics and related items internationally (sold to Capital City Distribution in 1980).

Aside from *Mom's*, Kitchen published *Bijou Funnies* #5, *Hungry Chuck Biscuits Comics & Stories*, *Quagmire*, and *Smile* #1. He contributed the five-page story "I Was a Teenage Hippie" to *Teenage Horizons of Shangrila* #1. Kitchen unsuccessfully ran for lieutenant governor of Wisconsin as the candidate of the Socialist Labor Party. He founded the *Bugle-American*, a weekly regional alternative newspaper that ran until 1977. Kitchen contributed color covers, comic strips, illustrations, and custom ads while commuting twice a week between Madison and Milwaukee. Glassford, Mitchell, Walthers, and Pugh also contributed covers and comics. There was a short-lived attempt to syndicate the weekly comics created for the *Bugle* to underground and college newspapers.

1971   Married Irene Nonnweiler (divorced 1974; children Sheena and Scarlet). Crumb's *Home Grown Funnies*, containing the story "Whiteman Meets Big Foot," became Kitchen Sink Enterprise's first best seller, eventually selling over 160,000 copies. For *Mom's Homemade Comics* #3, Kitchen contributed the cover, "Ingrid the Bitch," and "Them Was the Days," and he contributed to "The Kumquat Jam" along with Glassford, Mitchell, Walthers, Pugh, Crumb, Dale Kuipers, Pete Poplaski, Jay Lynch, Dave Dozier, and Dennis Brul. For *Hungry Chuck Biscuits* #1, Kitchen drew the three-page story "Fred the Louse" and contributed to the "Let's Be Realistic" jam with Walthers, Crumb, Mitchell, Lynch, Glassford, Jay Kinney, and Skip Williamson. Kitchen began his lifelong fascination with 3D comics with a story for *Deep 3-D Comix,* and he contributed the two-page story "Juan Cristobal Valdez de ProJunior Explorer" to

Projunior, an anthology that included several popular San Francisco artists, among them Kinney, S. Clay Wilson, Art Spiegelman, Justin Green, Trina Robbins, and Bill Griffith. Comics historian Maurice Horn introduced Kitchen to Will Eisner at a Phil Seuling Comics Convention in New York, New York. Eisner was curious about the underground's direct market business model but taken aback by the uncensored content in some of the comics. Kitchen gradually won him over, which was the beginning of a lifelong professional relationship.

1972   KSP published *Snarf* #1 with a cover and lead comic featuring Kitchen's character Rex Glamour, Process Server, based on his longest-running strip for the *Bugle*. *Snarf* #2 included the one-page Kitchen comic "Let's Be Honest." *Snarf* #3 boasted an Eisner cover and included Kitchen's comic *Ramshackle & Slumlord Realty* (written by Ed Goodman). Kitchen created his most notorious cover, "The Giant Penis That Invaded New York," for *Bizarre Sex* #1, and contributed a cartoon about the values of grass to the *Great Marijuana Debate* minicomic. For *The Milwaukee Journal*, he drew the four-page story "Denis Kitchen, Star Reporter, Visits Milwaukee's Underground," and created the cover for the May 7 issue of *The Journal's Insight* magazine. Krupp's Ordinary Records released a ten-inch disc by R. Crumb and His Keep-on-Truckin' Orchestra, the first 78 rpm record issued in over twenty years. The songs were "River Blues" and "Wisconsin Wiggles." Crumb also created *XYZ Comics*.

1973   In *Miller v. California*, the Supreme Court upheld the prosecution of a California publisher for the distribution of obscene materials. In doing so, it established the test used to determine whether expressive materials cross the line into unprotected obscenity (content that lacks "serious literary, artistic, political, or scientific value"). Since the first test left it to "the average person, applying contemporary community standards" to decide whether the work, "taken as a whole, appealed to the prurient interest," stores throughout the US, especially in conservative states, quickly discontinued all comix that could get them in trouble, disrupting the chain of distribution underground comix depended upon. Kitchen and his family moved from Milwaukee to a farm in Princeton, Wisconsin. Eisner's *The Spirit* #1 and #2 are published, combining old and new material. *Bijou Funnies* #8 featured a Kurtzman cover and included Kitchen's "Hungry Irving Biscuits," a three-page parody of the popular title. He also contributed a *Nancy* parody to *Snarf* #3 (Eisner cover) and "The Underground Cartoonist" (text) to *Snarf* #4. Krupp produced a puzzle game named *Libido* that was prominently plugged in *Playboy*, only to find out that another company owned a trademark for the name. Virtually all copies of the puzzle were destroyed as part of the financial settlement.

1974   Kitchen entered into a short-lived experiment with Lee to edit *Comix Book* for Marvel. Kitchen contributed introductions to issues #1 and #2 and a one-page story, "The Birth of Comix Book" to #1. *Comix Book* #2 also featured the first short story version of Art Spiegelman's *Maus*, which would develop into a Pulitzer Prize–winning graphic novel. The series was canceled after issue #3 in 1975, and Kitchen negotiated the publication of two final issues, #4 and #5, in 1976. For KSP, he also created the cover for *Weird Trips* #1 and the comic strip parodies "B**tle Bailey" and "Bl*ndie and D*gwood" for *Snarf* #5 (Kurtzman cover).

1975   Kitchen contributed the comic "Stranded in Geek Town" to *Arcade* #3. He also created the cover for *Comix Book* #3 and contributed to jam covers for *Consumer Comix* and *Bizarre Sex* #4 (with Poplaski and Peter Loft). *Consumer Comix* contained the two-page Kitchen story "Mail Order Blues." Howard Cruse began his solo series with *Barefootz Funnies* #1. Kitchen created the surreal album cover for Jim Spencer's psychedelic folk rock album *Major Arcana*. Over fifty artists contributed self-portraits to the *Famous Cartoonist Series*, which Kitchen colored with hand-cut overlays and then manufactured as buttons with a manual punch press.

1976   Cofounded *The Fox River Patriot*, a weekly rural Wisconsin newspaper, with Mike Jacobi. Kitchen, Poplaski, and Crumb created covers for it until Kitchen left the paper in 1980. He participated in the art exhibition *Cartoon-O-Rama*—an event including a one-man show of Kitchen's art, additional art from his collection, a chalk talk by editorial cartoonist Bill Sanders, talks by Kurtzman and Dale Messick, a concert by R. Crumb and the Cheap Suit Serenaders, and a film festival—held at the Priebe Gallery, University of Wisconsin–Oshkosh (February 5–28). He contributed "Life in the Ice & Salt Works" (script by Dave Schreiner) to *Snarf* #5 (this Crumb cover was later reused as the cover for *Underground Classics*) and text to *Comix Book* #4 and #5. This year had a bumper crop of books by individuals: *An Army of Principles* by Leonard Rifas, *Artistic Comics* and *The People's Comics* by Crumb, *Barefootz Funnies* #2 by Cruse, *The Compleat Fart and Other Body Emissions* by Lee Marrs, *Kurtzman Komics* by Kurtzman, and *Trina's Women* by Robbins, who also edited *Wet Satin: Women's Erotic Fantasies*, as well as drawing the cover and the five-page story "Rawhide Revenge."

1977   Crumb scored another best seller with *Mr. Natural* #3. Kitchen contributed the cartoon "Outlawed Comics" (script by Rifas) to *Corporate Crime Comics*.

1978   The solo exhibition *Original Comic Art by Denis Kitchen* took place at Reeve Memorial Union at the University of Wisconsin–Oshkosh campus, January 30–February 28. Kitchen created the cover and the three-page story "Major Arcana" to *Mondo Snarfo*, continuing his fascination with surrealist art. KSP also published *Dope Comix* #1 and #2 with covers by Leslie Cabarga and John Pound. *The Spirit Magazine* #17 included "The Interview," a one-page Kitchen–Eisner jam. Kitchen also contributed a story to Jay Lynch's *Nard & Pat* #1. He also created the cover for *Alcohomics* ("straight from the vat") for International Health Projects and a *Nancy* parody strip for *Playboy*.

1979   In addition to the now biweekly *Patriot*, Kitchen and Mike Jacobi acquired *Yesteryear*, a midwestern antiques newspaper. KSP continued *The Spirit Magazine*, now edited by Cat Yronwode. Issues #20–22 reprinted Eisner's story "Life on Another Planet," and #22 included the one-page Eisner–Kitchen jam "Eisner Vault." Kitchen contributed the one-page story "Topps Stays on Top of Gum Card Business" for *Corporate Crime Comics* #2. Another significant book in 1992 was *Power Pak Comics* #1 by Aline Kominsky-Crumb.

1980   Married Holly Brooks (divorced 1987). KSP published *Gay Comics* #1 edited by Cruse (cover by Rand Holmes) and continued the serialization of Eisner's "Life on Another Planet" in *The Spirit Magazine* #23–26. Kitchen created the cover for Rifas's *Energy Comics* #1 (EduComics). Kitchen and Jacobi end their partnership, with Kitchen keeping control of KSP and Krupp and Jacobi taking full control of the two newspapers, *The Patriot* and *Yesteryear*.

1981   "Omaha the Cat Dancer" by Reed Waller debuts in *Bizarre Sex* #9. Crumb's "A Short History of America" is printed in poster form (colored by Poplaski). Kitchen contributes the one-page story "And She Gives Good Head, Fred" to *Snarf* #9. *The Spirit Magazine* #27–29 and #31–32 continues reprints and new work from Eisner. *TSM* #30 was a special issue with a jam cover by Eisner, Poplaski, Kitchen, Milton Caniff, John Pound, Richard Corben, and Leslie Cabarga. Inside were reprints and a new Spirit jam by a stellar cast, including Eisner, Poplaski, Kitchen, Corben, Cabarga, Robbins, Cruse, Kurtzman, Yronwode, Mike Newhall, Fred Hembeck, Denis McFarling, Michael T. Gilbert, Alan Weiss, Fershid Bharucha, Tom Orzechowski, Marshall

Rodgers, Steve Leialoha, Mike Barr, Joe Staton, Bob Smith, Todd Klein, Denny O'Neill, Frank Miller, Terry Austin, Archie Goodwin, George Pratt, Sharon Rappaport, Alan Kupperberg, Len Wein, Ernie Colon, Peter Sanderson, Brent Anderson, Bob Wiacek, Terry Beatty, Ken Stacey, Max Allan Collins, Dean Motter, Roger Stern, Jim Engel, Keno Don Rosa, Mike Tiefenbacher, Chuck Fiala, Chris Claremont, Bill Sienkiewicz, Brian Bolland, John Byrne, and Joe Rubenstein. KSP partnered with a Danish publisher to produce their first squareback, hardbound book, the *Will Eisner Color Treasury*, with new and old work by Eisner and running text by Yronwode.

1982   *The Art of Will Eisner*, an illustrated history of Eisner's creative career edited by Yronwode, was published in a signed and numbered hardcover edition and in paperback.

1983   KSP published the *Kitchen Sink Pipeline*, an adjustment to the new direct market system that required finished covers and a set price three months before publication, a big change from the more casual way of doing business the company was accustomed to. The head shop market was quickly disappearing, and KSP began experimenting with full-color comics to compete in this changing market. Caniff's *Steve Canyon Magazine* launched with #1–4, chronologically reprinting the *Steve Canyon* strips, with covers by Caniff and Poplaski. Books by Eisner continued to sell well, *The Spirit Magazine* #39–40 was joined a new full-color book, *The Spirit* #1 and #2, *Will Eisner Quarterly* #1, *The Outer Space Spirit*, and *Signal from Space*, a hardcover collection of Eisner's "Life on Another Planet." "Safe Sex" by Cruse, the first comics story to directly address AIDS, was published in *Gay Comix* #4.

1984   Two long-running KSP series ended, *Dope Comix* #5 (Charles Burns cover) and *Gay Comix* #5, which would continue after #5 with a publisher specializing in the gay market. *Goodman Beaver* by Kurtzman and Will Elder was published in hardback and softcover. *Megaton Man* #1, a superhero parody by Don Simpson, is a surprise hit.

1985   KSP published Eisner's *A Contract with God*, a long-out-of-print story originally published by Baronet in 1978, and *Will Eisner's New York Stories*. KSP revived the horror, adventure, and sci-fi title *Death Rattle* as a full-color series, featuring a Corben cover and stories by Burns, Holmes, and Charles Dallas in the first issue.

1986   In 1986, Friendly Frank's, a comics store in Lansing, Illinois, was busted for selling "obscene" comics, including *Omaha, the Cat Dancer*; *The*

Bodyssey; *Weirdo*; and *Bizarre Sex*. When Kitchen heard from the distributor Frank Mangiaracina that the store owner, Michael Correa, had been convicted for selling comics, including KSP titles, Kitchen was horrified. Feeling that the industry should step up to fight these battles, he raised money and hired *Playboy* counsel Burton Joseph to litigate the case. (Joseph reversed the original conviction on appeal.) Visualizing similar cases arising in the future, Kitchen used the leftover funds from the Correa case to establish the Comic Book Legal Defense Fund. He served as president and board chair through 2004. Kitchen won the Inkpot Award for "Outstanding Achievements in Comic Art" at San Diego Comic-Con International. KSP published *The Dreamer*, *Hawks of the Seas*, and *New York: The Big City* by Eisner, as well as Kurtzman's *Jungle Book*. Schultz made his KSP debut with the story "Xenozoic" in *Death Rattle #8*.

1987   KSP published *The Steve Canyon 40th Anniversary Special* and *Male Call* by Caniff, *The Collected Omaha* by Reed Waller and Kate Worley, and *The Building* by Eisner. Schultz launched the successful *Xenozoic Tales #1–4*. Dipping back into audio, KSP released *The Spirit Picture Disk*, a 33 1/3 rpm phonograph record with color label illustrated by Eisner, featuring several versions of Eisner's song "Ev'ry Little Bug," and additional music by John Christensen, Artie Barnes, Bill Mumy, and Blackbird McKnight.

1988   KSP begins publishing Al Capp's *Lil' Abner*, with ambitious plans to print fifty-four volumes, and another classic, the 1951 *Flash Gordon* daily strip by Dan Barry, Kurtzman, and Frank Frazetta. Will Eisner's *A Life Force* was released in hardcover and softcover editions. *Kings in Disguise #1–5* by Dan Burr and James Vance debuted, as well as the popular autobiographical adult title *Melody* by Jacques Boivin and Sylvie Rancourt. Kitchen contributed the story "Rural Publishing" (script by Dave Schreiner) to *Twist #2*.

1989   Schultz's *Cadillacs and Dinosaurs* and two collections of Ernie Bushmiller's *Nancy* strip, *Nancy Eats Food* and *How Sluggo Survives*, found success in general bookstores. KSP also issued a set of thirty-six trading cards celebrating their twentieth anniversary. Kitchen contributed the two-page story "Badger Goes Berzerk" (script by Mike Baron) to *Badger Goes Berzerk #1* for First Publishing. He appeared on *Larry King Live* to defend comic books under attack by the later-discredited and imprisoned psychiatrist Dr. Thomas Radecki.

1990   Formed the Denis Kitchen Art Agency to exclusively sell original blue chip cartoon art for clients such as Eisner, Kurtzman, Cruse, Poplaski,

On the front of the card, one of DENIS KITCHEN's surreal comic works. In the early 1960s, the young, starry-eyed Kitchen had a dream. That dream was to perfect his cartoonist art, create a nest of characters, and gather millions of dollars unto himself making people laugh at them. He studied the masters: Capp, Kelly, Bushmiller. He worked on his craft, contributing to any obscure magazine or newspaper that would have him, and getting paid little or nothing for the effort. He moved himself to the cutting edge of technology, discarding his trusty Bic pens in favor of brushes and India ink. He dumped his looseleaf notebook and got a drawing board. Then he created his characters: Little Ingrid, Pooch, the Dread Spud, Mr. Krupp, various geeks, himself, and a star-spangled horde of others. And then he became a publisher. Go figure. Today, Kitchen is gathering millions unto himself by printing the work of others, through Kitchen Sink Press. However, all is not lost. He's kept his cartooning hand limber with work in such titles as MONDO SNARFO, SNARF and TWIST. Soon, his art will be collected in a snazzy volume: THE ODDLY COMPELLING ART OF DENIS KITCHEN. It will include his comics, newspaper, magazine and record album work, and is anxiously awaited by all.

Copyright © 1989 Denis Kitchen

KITCHEN SINK CARDS: 32 of 36

1989 Denis Kitchen card from the KSP twentieth anniversary set (F & B). The first time he used the phrase "oddly compelling" as a self-descriptor.

Miller, Frank Stack, and Gary Hallgren, and later the estates of Eisner, Kurtzman, and Capp. KSP published V. T. Hamlin's *Alley Oop* vol. 1 (1943–1944), Alex Raymond's *Flash Gordon* Sunday pages, Capp's *Fearless Fosdick*, *The Erotic Art of Reed Waller*, and *Batman: The Dailies* vol. 1 and 2. In an arrangement with Rick Marschall and a group of European investors, KSP distributed *The Komplete Kolor Krazy Kat* vol. 1, *The Complete Color Terry and the Pirates* vol. 1, and *The Complete Polly and her Pals* vol. 1. The solo exhibit *Denis Kitchen* took place at the Ripon Center for the Arts, Ripon College, Ripon, Wisconsin.

1991   KSP published *From Aargh! To Zap! Harvey Kurtzman's Visual History of the Comics* and Eisner's *To the Heart of the Storm* and *Grateful Dead Comix* #1–4. Kitchen was a charter inductee into the Underground Comix Hall of Fame, Chicago, IL.

1992   KSP published Burns's *Blood Club*, Kurtzman's *Hey Look!*, Eisner's *Invisible People*, and Crumb's serigraph "A Short History of America." Kitchen contributed the one-page comic "Good Lord! What Ghastly Spawn Have I Unleashed?" to Michael Gilbert's *Mr. Monster's Triple Threat 3-D* (the 3-D Zone).

1993 KSP announced its merger with Eastman's Tundra on April Fool's Day. KSP moved from Princeton, Wisconsin, to Northampton, Massachusetts, to be near Tundra's headquarters. Scott McCloud's *Understanding Comics*, James O'Barr's collected *The Crow*, Alan Moore and Eddie Campbell's *From Hell*, Robbin's *A Century of Women Cartoonists*, and *Melting Pot* by Simon Bisley, Kevin Eastman, and Eric Talbot were published. Larry Welz moved the popular adult title *Cherry* to KSP. *Cadillacs and Dinosaurs*, the animated series, debuted on CBS. It had the misfortune of being scheduled against the year's biggest hit, *Mighty Morphin Power Rangers*, but attracted a toy line from Tyco and several other licensing deals.

1994 O'Barr's graphic novel *The Crow* sold 130,000 copies due to the success of the film, a KSP graphic novel record (by 1998, this number reached 375,000). KSP published *Introducing Kafka* by David Zane Mairowitz and Crumb, as well as *Twisted Sisters*, an anthology of work by women artists edited by Diane Noomin, including Carol Lay, Krystine Kryttre, Mary Fleener, Julie Doucet, Fiona Smythe, and others. In May, the Ocean Capital Group, a Los Angeles-based investment group, bought the controlling interest in KSP, planning to exploit its properties for film, television, and other media. Kitchen and Eastman no longer controlled the company, although Kitchen remained president and publisher. KSP receives thirty-five Harvey Award nominations and wins five, totally dominating that year's award ceremony in Dallas, Texas.

1995 Kitchen announces KSP's strategic alliance (exclusive distribution deal) with Capital City Distribution at San Diego Comic-Con. Curated *Harvey Kurtzman: Retrospective of a MAD Genius* at the Cartoon Art Museum, San Francisco, California. Contributed the one-page story "Square Publisher" to Beauchamp's *Blab* #8. KSP published *Black Hole* #1 by Charles Burns.

1996 Married Stacey Pollard (child Violet). Named Comics Publisher of the Year, the first and only such award presented by *The Staros Report*, Atlanta, Georgia.

1997 Received the Small Press Pioneer Award, a "Barkster" statue presented at a Diamond/Gemstone comics industry event. Facing bankruptcy due to a massive downturn in national comics sales, disappointing sales from the *Crow* sequel, and other problems, Kitchen hired financial consultant Donald Todrin to rescue the company. Todrin convinced the Ocean Group to sell their shares to avoid Chapter 7 bankruptcy, with Fred Siebert of MTV Online owning 60 percent and the Kitchen brothers owning 30 percent.

1999   Kitchen Sink Enterprises ceased publishing and closed. Todrin spun off the candy and novelties business as a new business named True Confections, focusing on chocolate bars featuring licensed characters like Betty Boop. In the wake of the demise of KSP, Kitchen established the following new business entities:

- Kitchen & Hansen Agency, LLC. Kitchen partnered with Judith Hansen to place numerous high-profile graphic novel properties, including *The Book of Genesis* by Crumb (W. W. Norton), Eisner's library of graphic novels and textbook trilogy (W. W. Norton) and *The Spirit* (DC Comics); Schultz's *Xenozoic Tales* (Dark Horse and Flesk); Alissa Torres's *American Widow* (Random House); O'Barr's *The Crow* (Pocketbooks); the *ElfQuest* library (DC Comics); and *Kings in Disguise* and its sequel *On the Ropes* by Vance and Burr (W. W. Norton).
- Denis Kitchen Publishing Co., LLC, a boutique company offering a curated selection of books, art prints and boxed trading cards. DKP published Eisner's final serigraph *River of Crime*; Kurtzman's *The Grasshopper and the Ant*; Crumb's *Mr. Natural Postcard Book* and his four boxed card sets: *Heroes of the Blues, Early Jazz Greats, Pioneers of Country Music*, and the *R. Crumb Trading Cards*; *The Sketchbook Adventures of Peter Poplaski* (with intro by Crumb); *Capitol Hell* by Pete Von Sholly; and the *Reading Comics* postcard book. DKP also published several 3D posters: Kitchen's own *Little Nemo* and *Major Arcana*, as well as Harrison Cady's *Road to Wealth*. This company absorbed the Denis Kitchen Art Agency and Steve Krupp's Gallery and Curio Shoppe, a seller of comix, posters, and novelties.

Kitchen won the Special Harvey Award "in commemoration of Leadership and Service," presented at the Museum of Comics and Cartoon Art (MoCCA) Fest, New York, New York. Chaired the Harvey Awards Committee through 2003.

2001   Created the semiautobiographical six-page story "My 5 Minutes with God" for *Dark Horse Maverick 2001*. Kitchen provided the compilation, introductions, and extensive annotations for the two-volume set *Playboy's Little Annie Fanny*, the first time the complete Kurtzman–Elder color stories were published as a collection (Dark Horse).

2002   Served on Board of Advisors for MoCCA through 2005. Expert witness for plaintiff and writer Neil Gaiman in his successful lawsuit against publisher–artist Todd McFarlane and Image Comics, Federal District Court, Madison, Wisconsin.

2003   Kitchen provided the compilation, introductions, and extensive annotations for the four-volume set *Lil' Abner: The Frazetta Years* (Dark Horse), the first time the Sunday strips Franzetta penciled and inked for Al Capp Studio from 1954–1961 were published as a collection.

2004   Curated the exhibition *Harvey Kurtzman* at the Society of Illustrators, New York, New York.

2005   Received the Defender of Liberty Award, presented by the Comic Book Legal Defense Fund at the Eisner Awards Ceremony, San Diego Comic-Con International. Named to the Board of Advisors for the National Cartoon Museum (formerly the Museum of Cartoon Art) and the Center for Cartoon Studies through 2006. Curated *Will Eisner: A Retrospective*, which originated at MoCCA and continued to Utah Valley State College, Orem, Utah, and the University of Massachusetts, Amherst, Massachusetts. Wrote the foreword for *Comix: The International Revolution* by Dez Skinn (Quality Communications).

2006   Partnered with John Lind to form Kitchen, Lind & Associates, LLC, to represent talent, package books, and oversee the Kitchen Sink Books imprint at Dark Horse Comics. Clients included the Harvey Kurtzman estate, the Al Capp estate (Capp Enterprises, Inc.), the Jerry Robinson estate, Eleanor Davis (*Secret Science Alliance*), Todd Hignite (*The Art of Jaime Hernandez*), Cruse (*Stuck Rubber Baby, Wendel*), Bill Stout (*Legends of the Blues*), Liniers (*Macanudo, Big Wet Balloon*) and others. Published the essay "Man I'm Beat! Harvey Kurtzman's Frustrating Post-Humbug Freelance Career" in *Comic Art* #7 (Todd Hignite Publishing).

2008   Provided the compilation, introductions, and extensive annotations for the two-volume set *Al Capp's Complete Shmoo* for Dark Horse. Contributed comics page to "Milt Gross Homage" in *Arf* vol. 4 (edited by Craig Yoe, Fantagraphics).

2009   Won the Bob Clampett Humanitarian Award, San Diego Comic-Con International. Cocurated *Underground Classics: The Transformation of Comics to Comix* with James Danky, May 2–July 12, at the Chazen Museum of Art, Madison, Wisconsin. Harry N. Abrams published *Underground Classics*, the accompanying catalog. Coauthored *The Art of Harvey Kurtzman: The Mad Genius of Comics* with Paul Buhle, published

Denis Kitchen, 2020. Cartoon logo for Comic Art Productions & Exhibits (CAPE).

by Abrams ComicArts. Appeared as a guest on National Public Radio's "All Things Considered" to discuss Kurtzman. Featured in *Comics in Wisconsin* by Paul Buhle (Borderland Books).

2010   *The Oddly Compelling Art of Denis Kitchen*, a monograph of Kitchen's artistic career, was published by Dark Horse. Kitchen participated in the solo exhibition *The Oddly Compelling Mini-Retrospective of Denis Kitchen*, MoCCA, New York, New York, and the group exhibit *Underground Comix* (one of four featured artists) at Massachusetts College of Liberal Arts Gallery, North Adams, Massachusetts. *The Art of Harvey Kurtzman* won the Eisner award for Best Comics-Related Book, San Diego Comic-Con International, and the Harvey Award for Best Biographical, Historical, or Journalistic work (Baltimore, Maryland). Kitchen formed the short-lived partnership Comic Art Productions & Exhibits (CAPE) with Danky and Kim A. Munson to promote and tour *Underground Classics* and shows featuring art from the Eisner, Kurtzman, and Capp estates. An *Underground Classics* app was created for iPhone and iPad on the Toura platform. It was heavily censored by Apple and ultimately unsuccessful.

2011   *Denis Kitchen's Chipboard Sketchbook* published by Boom! Studios. Coedited *Blackjacked and Pistol-Whipped: A Crime Does Not Pay Primer* with Lind, published by Dark Horse. Appeared as a guest on National Public Radio's "To the Best of Our Knowledge" to discuss underground comix.

2012   Cocurated *The Living Spirit of Will Eisner* with the Brazilian filmmaker Marisa Furtado for Rio Comicon (Rio de Janeiro). The show featured

107 works by Eisner, plus a unique bronze sculpture of the Spirit, sketchbooks, publications, and other materials related to Eisner's life and long career. After Comicon the show moved to the Centro Cultural São Paulo. Kitchen was awarded the Visual Art Lifetime Achievement Award, Wisconsin Academy of Sciences, Arts and Letters and the Wisconsin Museum of Art. Named cochair with Gaiman of the Comic Book Legal Defense Fund Board of Advisors.

2013   Coauthored *Al Capp: A Life in the Contrary* with Michael Schumacher (Bloomsbury). Cocurated *the Art of Harvey Kurtzman* with Monte Beauchamp at the Society of Illustrators, New York. Served as coeditor, introduction author, and artist, *Best of Comix Book: When Marvel Comics Went Underground* with Lind, published by Kitchen Sink Books/Dark Horse. Cocurated the group exhibit *Robert Crumb and the Underground* with Danky at the Kunstmuseum, Lucerne, Switzerland. Participated in the group exhibit, *American Underground Cartoonists*, Valentin Museum, Munich, Germany. Interviewed by *Boing Boing* founder Mark Frauenfelder on *Gweek Podcast*. Appeared as a guest on National Public Radio's "Weekend Edition" to discuss Capp.

2014   Won the Lifetime Achievement Award "in recognition of a career dedicated to promoting and defending the culture of comics," presented at Asbury Park Comicon, Asbury Park, New Jersey. KSB published *Popular Skullture: The Skull Motif in Pulps, Paperbacks, and Comics* by Beauchamp and Steven Heller, and a new edition of *Harvey Kurtzman's Jungle Book* with contributions from Kitchen. Kitchen's work appeared in the solo exhibition, *The Oddly Compelling Art of Denis Kitchen*, August 1–October 8, at the Fine Arts Gallery, University of Wisconsin—Parkside. Contributed the two-page story "The Vexing Thing Upstairs" to Beauchamp's *Blabworld* #2 (Last Gasp). Wrote the introductions to *Eerie Archives*, vol. 17 (Dark Horse) and to *Rocketeer/Spirit* collection (IDW Publishing).

2015   Inducted into the Will Eisner Hall of Fame (San Diego Comic-Con International). Curated *Will Eisner: A Brief Retrospective* at Geppi's Entertainment Museum, Baltimore, Maryland, and *Will Eisner: 75 Years of the Spirit* at the Jewish Museum, Munich, Germany. Wrote and drew a five-page illustrated biography of Dr. Seuss for *Masterful Marks* edited by Beauchamp (Simon & Schuster), which was featured in *The Huffington Post*. Created the cover for *Quarter Moon* #5 (Revenge issue) for Locust Moon Comics. KSB published *Realms: The Roleplaying Game Art of Tony Diterlizzi*. Kitchen held the solo exhibition *The Oddly Compelling Art of Denis Kitchen*, November 6–January 15, 2016, at the Scott Elder Gallery,

Promotional postcard for *The Oddly Compelling Art of Denis Kitchen* exhibit at University of Wisconsin–Parkside (2014).

Brooklyn, New York, and participated in the group exhibition *Little Nemo: Dream Another Dream*, February 10–March 28 at Society of Illustrators, New York, New York. Traveled to the ToonSeum, Pittsburgh, Pennsylvania, the Billy Ireland Cartoon Library and Museum at the Ohio State University, and other locations. Participated in the group exhibition *The Beatles in Comics*, May 7–June 9 at the Valentin-Karlstadt-Museum, Munich, Germany, part of the Munich Comics Festival.

2016   Served as coeditor, contributed an essay, and provided annotations for *Trump: The Complete Collection* (Essential Kurtzman) with Lind, published by KSB/Dark Horse. Miller's *The Hard Goodbye Curator's Collection* Limited Edition Hardcover was the first in the KSB Curator's Collection deluxe books. *Everything Including the Kitchen Sink*, by Jon B. Cooke, is published in book form, based on Cooke's lengthy 1994 interview with Kitchen, originally published in two parts in *Comic Book Creator* magazine. Wrote the introduction for *The Lost Art of Will Eisner* (Beehive Books).

2017   Curated *Will Eisner: A Centennial Celebration* at Le Musée de la Bande Dessinée, Angoulême, France. Cocurated the different but related exhibition *Will Eisner: The Centennial Celebration* with Lind at the Society of Illustrators, New York, New York, continuing to Amador, Portugal. The accompanying catalog, *Will Eisner: The Centennial Celebration*, coedited by Kitchen, Lind, and Paul Gravett, was published in English and French by Kitchen Sink Books/Dark Horse. KSB published Kurtzman's *Marley's Ghost* (an adaptation of Dicken's *Christmas Carol*) as a digital-first title on the comiXology Originals line. Kitchen received the Horlick High School Distinguished Graduate award. Participated in the solo exhibition *Strange & Captivating: The Work of Denis Kitchen* at Amerikahaus Munchen, part of the Munich Comics Festival, Munich, Germany, the group exhibition *Comics! Manga! Graphic Novels!* at the Bundeskunsthall in Bonn, Germany, and the group exhibition *Direct Action Comics: Politically Engaged Comics and Graphic Novels*, February 2–22 at the Herter Gallery, University of Massachusetts, Amherst. *Seltsam & Fesselnd: Das Werk Des Denis Kitchen*, a German translation of *The Oddly Compelling Art of Denis Kitchen* was published with added editorial and visual elements (U-Comix).

2018   Contributed an essay and annotations for the two-volume boxed set *A Contract with God: Curator's Collection*, with Lind, published by KSB/Dark Horse.

2020   Coauthored *Madness in Crowds: The Teeming Mind of Harrison Cady* with Violet Kitchen, published by Beehive Books. Cocurated the

Wisconsin Funnies: 50 Years of Comics with Danky at the Museum of Wisconsin Art, featuring 270 individual pieces of original and published art from thirty-one artists with Badger State ties, including Kitchen. Accompanying catalog published by the museum. Contributed the "Overview" essay to *Comic Art in Museums*, edited by Munson (University Press of Mississippi). Wrote the introduction to *The Return of Hyper Comix* by Steve Stiles (Thintwhistle Books). Wrote the introduction to *Amuzing Stories: Comix for Mature Readers,* by Hallgren (Amazon).

2022   Wrote and drew *Creatures from the Subconscious*, published by Tinto Press. Drew the cover of *Jack the Radio* #2 (George Hage Publishing). Featured in *Maverix and Lunatix: Icons of Underground Comix* by Drew Friedman (Fantagraphics). Participated in the curated exhibition *A Serious Look at the Funnies*, Ewing Gallery of Arts, University of Tennessee–Knoxville.

2023   Wrote the introduction for *Flamed Out: The Underground Adventures and Comix Genius of Willy Murphy* by Mark Burstein (Fantagraphics). Was featured in the solo exhibit *Creatures from the Subconscious*, at the Stadtbibliothek, Munich, Germany, in conjunction with the biennial Munich Comics Festival. Kitchen's "The Giant Penis That Invaded New York" cover of *Bizarre Sex* #1 (1972) is the basis of a new *U-Comix* anthology, *Der riesige Penis, der in New York eindrang*, featuring interpretations of "what came next" by twenty-five German and American cartoonists. An English edition is planned for 2024.

2024   On December 8, Kitchen was awarded the first Underground Visionary Award by the Boston Comic Arts Foundation, given annually at the Massachusetts Independent Comics Expo. Kitchen received an honorary doctorate from the University of Wisconsin–Milwaukee in a ceremony on December 14. This celebration of Kitchen included the exhibit *UWM Underground: The Art of Denis Kitchen* at the Emile H. Mathis Gallery (December 14, 2024–February 20, 2025).

2026   *Depths of Perception*, a book of twenty high-quality 3D images, published by Fantagraphics (expected winter). Director Soren Christiansen launched a Kickstarter in support of *Oddly Compelling: The Denis Kitchen Story*, a documentary he is coproducing with Ted Intorcio (Tinto Press) featuring interviews with Dan Clowes, Carol Tyler, Eddie Campbell, Warren Bernard, Paul Gravett, Joel Christian Gill, Alison Bechdel, Derf Backderf, Karen Green, Jeff Trexler, Noah Van Sciver, MariNaomi, Kim A. Munson, and Emil Ferris.

CONVERSATIONS WITH DENIS KITCHEN

Cover, *The Vault of Mindless Fellow-ship* #2. Fanzine cover art by Mardy Ayers. Courtesy of Steven Grant.

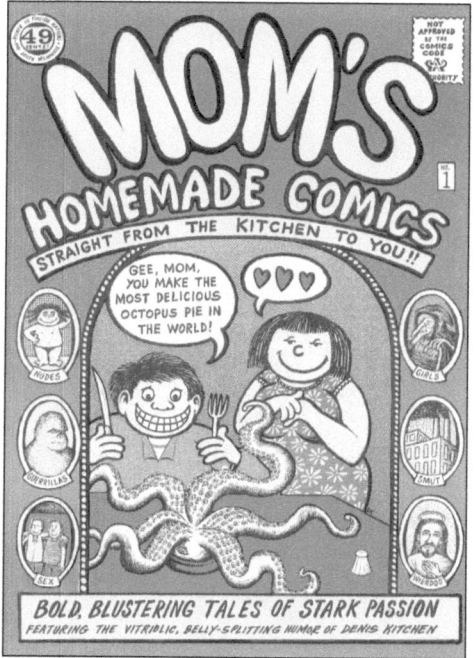

Cover, *Mom's Homemade Comics* #1.

An Interview with Denis Kitchen

BILL CROSS / 1972

From *The Vault of Mindless Fellowship* no. 2 (December 1972). Conducted by Bill Cross on Monday, November 13, at the offices of Krupp Comic Works, Milwaukee, Wisconsin. Reprinted by permission.

Bill Cross: We're talking to Denis Kitchen, the leader of the vast underground publishing cartel known as Krupp Comic Works in Milwaukee. Denis, how did you get started as an underground cartoonist? That's always a good question to begin with.

Denis Kitchen: How did I get started as an underground cartoonist? Well, I started by being a cartoonist, and I kind of got into it accidentally, because I was doing work for the university and I decided to put together a book, and I was totally unaware of what was going on in California that summer—about that time they put out the first *Zap*. I never saw *Zap* until about a year later. I just did a book of my own (*Mom's Homemade Comix*), and somehow, one of the underground publishers at that time, in fact, the only one at that time, the Print Mint, got ahold of a copy and asked if they could reprint it, and that's how I found out that they had this whole thing going with *Zap* and *Bijou* and all the others. You know, Milwaukee, as it is with many things, was way behind the times.

BC: How much trouble did you have getting the first book out?

DK: No trouble at all. Because I found this printer who gave me credit terms. Otherwise, it never would have gotten out.

BC: And from there you graduated to running your own comic book publishing company?

DK: Right. That happened by accident too. I didn't intend to be a publisher by any means. I had gotten ripped off by the Print Mint, and since there was no other publisher around—although there was Rip Off Press, they were financially unsound—so I decided to start a company here.

BC: So how well has it worked out?

DK: Beyond my wildest imagination. Most of my time is now taken up with my duties as a publisher, rather than that of a cartoonist.

BC: Do you find more satisfaction cartooning or running this publishing company?

DK: They're both satisfying. Although I enjoy the publishing, it's nice to draw.

BC: What started as a sort of a sideline to what was happening in the 1960s has now almost become a mainstay as the underground comix. There were a lot of wild speculations about how long they could last and what they could do. Do you have any idea what direction they're going to go? I mean, there was that great burst of energy when they first came out, and then there were the horror books, like *Skull*, and now it seems to be stagnating, and they seem to be looking for a direction. Do you have any idea what this direction is going to be and what it's going to do?

DK: It's really hard to say. I suspect that what will happen is that the underground comix are going to become more traditional and the straight comics are going to become more underground, and there's going to be some point in between where there isn't going to be much difference. I think it all comes down to economics. As long as the undergrounds sell as they're doing right now, they'll stay alive, though no one will really prosper. As for the straight comics, as long as their circulation continues to decline, they're going to try desperate things, and they've already made attempts to make the books more hip and more relevant. They've already gone so far as to use the underground spelling "comix" for several of the Marvel comics. Just a short while ago, Stan Lee called and asked me to edit a book for him that would be semiunderground in the sense that it would be, I think the terms he used were *irreverent* and *iconoclastic*, though not explicit.

BC: Do you see yourself as the new Harvey Kurtzman?

DK: As a matter of fact, he [Stan Lee] made that comparison, although I think it was an attempt to flatter me. At any rate, I turned it down, primarily because it's a lot more fun to call all the shots on a small scale than to be just another editor in a big operation.

BC: A few minutes ago, you said that the straight comics rely on a large mass circulation to survive. If you have a higher cover price and you don't have the same circulation as the straight comics, how do you survive?

DK: The cover price, of course, is fifty cents, and the costs are still kind of high, but if we can sell, say, twenty thousand of a title, then it's still worth our while, and in most cases, that's pretty easy now. There's a lot of trash coming out, I hope by mostly other publishers. I've tried to put out a good quality series, but there have been times when things have slipped through that haven't been that great, and though you try to put out quality books, sometimes the bad books sell well and vice versa. As long as you can keep the cover price at fifty cents and sell a sufficient number of copies, well, that's it.

BC: What about the experiments in color now being conducted in underground comix? When they first came out they were all in black and white, and now they're doing color, such as Richard Corben's *Fantagor*. Are you planning to do anything in color?

DK: Yes. As a matter of fact, we were slow to explore color, because it's an expensive process, and I'm not convinced that it's worth the trouble, because it takes more time with color separation and all, and the higher cover price. Our first color book is going to *Bijou* #9, it's going to be *Tales Calculated to Drive You Bijou*. It's going to be a parody on several levels. First of all, we're going to have underground cartoonists doing parodies of each other. Jay Lynch is going to do "Those Furshlugginer Hairy Geek Brothers," Skip Williamson is going to parody Crumb, I'm doing "Hungry Irving Biscuits," and we're going to be doing it in the old *MAD* style, as you could probably tell by the name Hungry Irving. It's always Irving or Melvin or something. We're going to try to get the look and typography of the early *MAD*s. In addition to parodying Clyne when I do "Hungry Irving Biscuits," I also have to parody Elder or Davis or Wood. So I hope it comes off. It's kind of a big undertaking.

BC: You used to have some contact with Harvey Kurtzman, who used to edit the early issues of *MAD* magazine. Does he have any plans to do anything in the underground?

DK: I'm glad you asked that question. He's doing the cover for *Snarf* #5.

BC: Will he be doing anything else?

DK: I hope so. I'm trying to get him to do things, but it's kind of hard to outbid Hugh Hefner.

BC: Do you know what kind of contract he has worked out with Hefner?

DK: Well, I know he has to do six *Annie Fanny*s a year, and he gets a pretty substantial salary for doing that. He's free to do anything, but he doesn't have much time, and that's why he isn't doing any underground stuff. He knows what's going on, he thinks it's a very exciting field, and he wishes he were younger and less tied down, because he finds himself caught in the middle class trap, and he's got to maintain a standard of living that he can't risk losing, and if he suddenly jumped into the underground, I have no doubt he would lose it.

BC: What is Krupp doing outside of the conventional underground comix? I know you just put out a 78 record by Robert Crumb. Are there any other projects in addition to the record?

DK: Well, we intend to do a series of 78s. You may see the poster on the wall there, advertising giant comic covers. That's our next project. We're doing a magazine called *Inside Dirt*, which is a parody of the old men's magazines, with cheap pulp pages, and articles which have to do with the subculture.

BC: I understand you're planning to publish more or less legitimate artists. I understand that you have the rights to *The Spirit* by Will Eisner.

DK: Well, no one has defined underground yet, and I don't feel that I should limit the books to just young cartoonists. I'd like to use the facilities we have to just get some good books out and leave it up to the readers and critics to define them as underground or not. I'm very happy to have the rights to Eisner's stuff. I think it's classic material, and most people in my generation aren't familiar with it, except for a few comic book freaks like yourselves, and so I found out that Eisner is really excited, for example, about the new comics and about doing new stories, because he's been out of it for twenty years.

BC: Are you planning to do anything along those lines outside of *The Spirit*?

DK: Sure. I have lots of plans . . . whether or not they materialize, I can't say.

BC: You used to be connected with the *Bugle-American*. What happened with that? Are you still connected with that paper?

DK: Not really. I was one of the founders of the paper, and for about six months, three days a week, I worked for them without any kind of pay. At the same time, Krupp was forming, and it wasn't paying either, and I was just about literally starving for a while. One of them had to go, and I decided to stick with Krupp. So I gave up my shares in the *Bugle*, and I occasionally do a guest thing for them, because they're friends, but there's no way I can devote time to both of them.

BC: What happened to those weekly strips you did for it?

DK: Well, what happened with those was, the five cartoonists who were doing them, we decided to each do a strip each week, partly just for our own benefit. We wanted to help out the *Bugle*, and we wanted to do something similar to the daily papers, but with a new approach, and in the back of our minds, we thought we could maybe do some kind of syndication. We tried it with the university papers, and it was a kind of discipline we needed badly, because we were basically lazy, and in many cases our styles hadn't really developed, and we were forced to draw a strip a week at a time when many weeks would go by, and we couldn't draw a thing.

BC: So you stopped drawing them when you thought you'd gone as far as you could go?

DK: As with most things, it stemmed from economics. The *Bugle* at that time had still not reached the breakeven point; and it was barely surviving, mostly due to not paying contributors. Since the syndicate wasn't paying off, where were we going to go from here? We were spending at least a day a week doing our daily strips, and once we finished the strips, we'd go down and help lay out the *Bugle*, and do illustrations and covers, and we found that that kind of investment was no longer tolerable, so we just had to go our own ways. Emotionally, we would have liked to keep doing it. We decided to spend the time on comic book pages, which at least pay a nominal rate.

BC: We've been talking quite a bit about the financial side of this. How is Krupp set up financially? Out of the fifty-cent cover charge, who gets what?

DK: We have the highest royalty setup for any publisher today, which is 12 percent. The next highest rate is 10 percent. So out of a fifty-cent book, six cents goes to the artist. Another seven to eight cents goes to the printer, and most of the rest goes to the distributor, who buys in volume, and gets between 40 and 60 percent off. Between the artist, printer, and distributor, that leaves about six cents per copy for us.

BC: What kind of distribution does the underground have? Is it very well organized among all the companies to get the books out on the stands?

DK: We have deals with the West Coast publishers, primarily with Last Gasp and Rip Off Press, primarily so we can get our books into the Bay Area, and they can get theirs here, but we primarily rely on our own system, which is independent distributors all over the country, and there are strong distributors and weak distributors, and it's hard to gauge just how together we are.

BC: Suppose someone wanted to do an underground comic, how would they go about doing it? Would they just bring you art samples?

DK: Yes. It's a lot harder now, because our standards are getting higher and higher, but basically that's how it works. There are a lot of people who walk in, who send their stuff through the mail, that just aren't anywhere near publishable. Occasionally, someone will come up with something, and if it meets certain criteria, it'll get published. There's no real hassles. I don't sit on things for months or anything.

BC: So you're also more or less the creative director of Krupp?

DK: Yeah. I try to keep the editing minimal. Mostly the editing I do is in multi-artist books. In *Snarf*, for instance, we have six to eight artists per book, and I coordinate the lengths of the pages and the general subject matter, but generally I try to keep it more aesthetic than story-wise. I pretty much let the artists do what they want. I think that the best product comes out when the artist does his own editing.

Interview with Denis Kitchen

JUDY JACOBI / 1975

From *Bugle-American* (September 17, 1975): 24. Reprinted by permission.

Interview with Denis Kitchen

In the following interview judy Jacobi asked Denis Kitchen a few questions. He chose, characteristically, to answer in cartoon form.

Q. Now that you're rich and famous, why do you still do Bugle work?

Q: In the early months of the *Bugle's* existence you used to drive the paste-up from the Madison office to the Milwaukee printer at dawn, after working all night. Several times you fell asleep at the wheel and had "near misses." What went through your mind as you saw disaster staring you in the face?

Q: In retrospect, do you think the original Bugle founders were naive??

Q. If you had to choose between reliving that first year on the Bugle and receiving a 1951 Hudson Hornet in mint condition, which would you do?

Q: Describe your sex life in detail during the *Bugle's* second year.

Q: Did you ever rely on drugs to help you meet deadlines, or use them for inspiration?

Q: Do you feel you've grown as an artist from the first issue of the *Bugle* five years ago? Give us an example of a 1970 Kitchen drawing and a contemporary one.

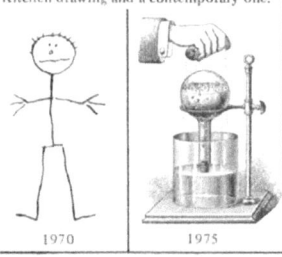

Q. Is the Bugle really a staff-run cooperative?

Q: The *Bugle* for the first year or two had the unique feature of a regular comix page drawn by several local cartoonists. What happened to all those artists, and what are you doing these days?

A: I guess I'll have to deviate from pictures for this one. Don Glassford, who did the "Studley" strip is still in Milwaukee doing nice T-shirt designs that are distributed nationally. Bruce Walthers, who did "Oscar Kabibbler," now lives near Boston, freelances, and daydreams a lot. Wendel Pugh ("Fenster Sitzen") left for Colorado three years ago. The last I heard he was living on a mountaintop. Jim Mitchell ("Smile") is a tragic case. He was busted in Mexico almost two years ago on a drug charge (with circumstantial evidence). He has been languishing in a Mexico City prison cell ever since, and has yet to be tried or sentenced. The level of corruption there is incredible. As for myself, I'm living in the country and still publishing and drawing underground comix, although I am told they died two summers ago.

Page 24   © 1975 Kitchen   September 17, 1975

Denis Kitchen, 1975. Interview included in the *Bugle-American*'s fifth anniversary issue.

Interview with Denis Kitchen

ARTIE E. ROMERO / 1979

From *Cascade Comix Monthly* no. 13 (March 1979). Reprinted by permission.

Cascade: Tell us about yourself, where you're from, and so forth.

Denis Kitchen: I was born in Milwaukee in 1946 and, except for a few childhood years in Texas, have always lived in Wisconsin, for better or worse. I have two daughters [Sheena and Scarlet] and live with them, my fiancé Holly Brooks, and eighteen old jukeboxes in an old farmhouse four miles outside the metropolis of Princeton [Wisconsin, population 1,400].

Cascade: When and how did you get involved with comics?

Kitchen: As early as second grade I wrote and illustrated stories that my teachers let me read in front of class. In eighth grade I created a small publication called *Cleptomanic*. This time the teacher banned it, so I went "underground." *Klepto*, as it became known, lasted twenty-five issues, well into high school. In college I helped create *Snide*, a humor-slash-satire magazine, and decided in 1968 when I became editor to turn it into a comic book. The magazine died, but the idea didn't. After graduation and a brief army stint [see *Snarf* #14], I discovered *Bijou Funnies* #1, the first underground comic I ever saw. This inspired me to create *Mom's Homemade Comics* #1 in 1968.

Cascade: Why did you decide to become an underground comix publisher?

Kitchen: Well, it gets complicated here. I learned the fundamentals of getting a book printed and locally distributed with *Mom's*. But when the Print Mint offered to become my publisher in 1969, I was elated. I would have loved to draw full time and leave the business to them. But they treated me poorly, I felt, and I broke with them. At that time Rip Off Press was just starting and short on cash, so there was no alternative but to publish myself again. I formed Kumquat Productions, which published two books and fizzled and then reorganized as Krupp Comic Works, Inc., in 1970. I guess I had a kind of flair for the business. And I've had a couple of good partners. Some key artists

Denis Kitchen, 1979. A dual self-portrait created for the cover of *Cascade Comix Monthly* #13.

entrusted books to me, and things steamrolled. It's hard to believe Krupp is starting its tenth year.

Cascade: How has publishing affected the amount of comics you draw?

Kitchen: I like to think I'm an artist first. But in reality, the great majority of my time is consumed by Krupp responsibilities. In addition, I'm involved with a separate business, the Fox River Publishing Company, which produces a rural newspaper, *The Fox River Patriot*. So the publisher-slash-editor side of me has to order the artist to draw a page now and then, or I'd never find the time. I do quite a few *Patriot* covers, pages for some Kitchen Sink books, and some freelance work. I even sold a color cartoon to *Playboy* recently. But it's frustrating not doing what I love to do most. I have a bulging idea file. I keep thinking that when the company grows large enough, I can relinquish the day-to-day responsibilities to assistants and draw comics. But that may be pure and simple fantasy. Actually, I do enjoy the creativity of publishing too. I kind of like wearing all these hats.

Cascade: If you could choose any profession other than cartooning, what would it be?

Kitchen: A professional baseball player, I think. More realistically, film-making, maybe, or painting.

Denis Kitchen in his Princeton, WI office, 1978.

Cascade: What goes on at Krupp Comic Works on a typical day?

Kitchen: I go through the morning stack of mail, pawning off as much as possible to Leonard Rifas, my assistant editor, or Sue Schmidt, our secretary. I answer the most important business mail and most of the correspondence with artists. On some days I'll type thirty or thirty-five letters. I'll be on the phone throughout the day, talking to distributors and shops and artists. I may devote some time to designing our newest wholesale catalog, planning new books, or trying to motivate Peter Poplaski, our artist-in-residence, who is always a week or a month behind schedule. I may help unload a freight shipment or type invoices or try to collect from a deadbeat account. Two days a week my daughters stay at the Krupp Day Care Center. I harass our printer about late books. I have frequent meetings with my principal partner Mike Jacobi. And once in a while I'll play with some of the old arcade machines or jukeboxes in the office.

Cascade: From your point of view, how healthy is the comix biz right now?

Kitchen: Very healthy. The business has been steadily growing for us. We grossed a quarter of a million dollars last year and have just set four record months in a row. And my publication chart for upcoming books has never been so cluttered.

Cascade: What kind of comics do you like?

Kitchen: Most of the stuff I publish—though not all. I laugh hardest at Joel Beck, Steve Stiles, and Gilbert Shelton. Robert Crumb I admire greatly. Spiegelman consistently impresses me. The detailed work of Rick Griffin, Robert Williams, and Jay Lynch bowls me over. I think Howard Cruse deserves a much bigger following. For covers I'm hot on Bill Stout, John Pound, and Leslie Cabarga. I could go on about a lot of contemporaries I like. Of the previous generation of cartoonists, Al Capp is tops in my book, despite his obvious decline in later years.

Cascade: You have said that you didn't expect *Mondo Snarfo* to sell well. Why did you publish it?

Kitchen: Good surrealistic comix appeal to me personally. And other artists were excited by the project. But *Mondo Snarfo* is too esoteric or too weird to appeal to a wide audience. But Krupp has reached a point where it can sustain a loss on a book now and then and not worry. There are lots of offbeat comix that need publishing. Profitable books like *Dope Comix* and *Bizarre Sex* help subsidize less popular titles. But the less popular books are frequently the most satisfying personally.

Cascade: What do you consider to be your greatest accomplishment as a cartoonist?

Kitchen: Well, offhand, I'd say my *Mondo Snarfo* pages. But I have a couple stories in the works that I consider my best yet. A German publisher is doing a collection of my work this spring, with sixteen or so pages in color. Looking at all that stuff at once may be the best incentive to produce better stuff and at a better pace.

Cascade: As a publisher?

Kitchen: That's harder. The Crumb books, especially *Home Grown*. The *Bijou* series. *Corporate Crime*. Recent *Snarf*s. And it's been particularly gratifying to publish comics by Will Eisner and Harvey Kurtzman.

Cascade: Although you have certain stock cartoon "types" which recur in your comix, you've not to my knowledge created any characters for continued use. Any particular reason why not?

Kitchen: Stupidity maybe. It pays to have regular characters to develop a popular following. But some artists get away without it. Art Spiegelman has no real regulars. And Crumb drops his if they become too popular. A regular character can be a yoke around your neck. I think if I had to draw a daily strip around the same characters day after day, I'd get bored stiff. Maybe not. Actually, I have plans for using the character Steve Krupp frequently in coming strips [see *Snarf* #15]. I think most underground cartoonists are interested in the possibilities of the medium more than creating commercial properties.

Denis Kitchen, 1978. Cover art, *Mondo Snarfo* #1.

It's one element that differentiates us from other cartoonists. But it's hard to generalize about this. . . .

Cascade: Who was that lady I saw you with last night?

Kitchen: That was no lady. That was a Princeton transvestite.

Cascade: What are your plans or goals?

Kitchen: Eeek! At the risk of sounding tedious, I truly believe the comics medium is just realizing its potential. As much as I can, I want to help it grow. I want to offer a forum for the best contemporary comic artists, develop new artists, and widen our alternative distribution system to reach a greater audience so royalties become more respectable. On a personal level, I want to refine my style and create stories that meet my highest standards. My other goal is to retire on Tahiti.

From the Heartland of America:
An Interview with Krupp Comic's Denis Kitchen

BILL SHERMAN / 1981

From *The Comics Journal* no. 63 (May 1981). Reprinted by permission.

Denis Kitchen, the force behind Wisconsin's Krupp Comic Works, has been part of the underground comix scene since its earliest days. The artist-publisher made his first appearance with *Mom's Homemade Comics* #1 (1969), a solo collection of cartoony blackouts and jokey Milwaukee references that Jay Kinney has called "one of the corniest and cleanest undergrounds ever." *Mom's* was one of the first comix titles to break away from the California/East Village bias that the majority of undergrounders maintained at the time. Chicago's *Bijou* may have been written around the Windy City, but only Kitchen's *Mom's* actively reveled in the basic (and frequently dumb) differences between the Midwest and the coasts. To many midwestern comix readers, already tired of the excessive media attention that the West Coast was receiving in those days, the book was a revelation. *Mom's* was no *American Splendor*—much of its humor seemed more suited to the earlier days of college humor magazines than to the world of *Zap*—but it ultimately provided a base for Kitchen to build his empire. Subsequent issues saw less Kitchen artwork (replaced by some eminently forgettable amateur comix artists) as he increasingly involved himself in the role of publisher–editor. Occasional bursts of Kitchen art have since appeared in various anthology titles, but that first *Mom's* has the distinction of being the only full book of Kitchen.

By 1971, the Krupp line had expanded to include titles like *Home Grown*, the newest issue of *Bijou*, and anthology books like *Teen-Age Horizons of Shangrila*. The early Krupp line was variable: As in those later issues of *Mom's*, Kitchen was trying to flesh out his line with local comix artists of widely disparate talent and credibility. But the era was a flush one for comix publishers, and Krupp

Denis Kitchen, 1972. "Let's Be Honest" from *Snarf* #2.

managed to grow sufficiently to attract more attention from artists outside the Midwest. R. Crumb's solo *Home Grown*, appearing at the height of the artist's underground popularity, was a major coup for the line, and (despite some resistance to the idea of an underground line from—of all places—Wisconsin) more artists eventually followed. Krupp may have lost its initial midwestern feel in the process, but the contents' overall quality was improving.

By 1974, Kitchen had managed to work out an arrangement with Marvel Comics for the distribution of a new comix anthology magazine, *Comix Book*. The title, edited by Kitchen, contained new and reprint work by underground mainstays like Skip Williamson, Trina Robbins, Justin Green, and Art Spiegelman. Produced and distributed for a general magazine market, *Comix Book* was never quite as freewheeling as some comix fans might have wished, but even so, it was apparently too much for Marvel. The company never fully backed the book and after receiving the premiere's initial sales figures decided to drop it. *Comix Book* saw three issues under Marvel's distribution banner; two additional issues, completed before Marvel's decision to drop the title, eventually appeared as Krupp comix.

In the meantime, Kitchen was working on expanding the base of his readership, turning to mainstream comic book artists that he himself liked. In the early 1970s, Kitchen had convinced both Will Eisner and Harvey Kurtzman to produce covers for *Snarf*, a catch-all comix humor book, and in 1973 Krupp produced two comixsized collections of *Spirit* reprints that also contained Eisner updates on the series characters. Following a series of Warren *Spirit* reprints, Eisner returned to Krupp as editor-in-chief of *The Spirit*, a handsome quarterly of reprints that—unlike Warren's magazines—also contained substantial new Eisner material. Kitchen has since overseen the production of two Eisner portfolios, *The City* and *The Spirit Portfolio*. The Kurtzman association, meanwhile, resulted in a collection of vintage pre-*MAD* strips, *Kurtzman Comix* (1976). An announced reprint of his *Goodman Beaver* (illustrated by Will Elder) has yet to appear.

Today Krupp Comic Works is one of the most prolific comix lines. From regular theme humor books like *Bizarre Sex* and *Dope Comix* to more daring titles like the surrealist *Mondo Snarfo* and Howard Cruse's *Gay Comix* to solo books like Sharon Rudahl's *Crystal Night* and Crumb's *Snoid*, Kitchen's books represent the underground in all its faces. In person, Denis is a soft-spoken, deliberate speaker ("I tend toward Gary Cooper grunts," he warned me when we first discussed doing the interview) who can get quite passionate in his support of artists he particularly admires. As the following interview makes clear, he has also taken on other roles besides those of artist and publisher.

The following interview was conducted by Bill Sherman in Kitchen's Pick-Congress Americana Hotel room during the 1980 Chicago Comicon. Also in attendance were Kim Thompson and Holly Brooks (now Kitchen's wife). The interview was transcribed by Kim Thompson, copyedited by Denis Kitchen, and edited by Thompson.

Bill Sherman: Let's start with some history—that's what my notes say. How did Krupp Comics come about?

Denis Kitchen: I was in college, in Milwaukee. I got drafted right out of college. I'd always had aspirations to be a cartoonist, but I don't think I was terribly serious about it until I was drafted and twenty-two days later became a civilian—but that's a different story—and decided I did want to be a cartoonist after all. I was browsing in a bookstore in Milwaukee and saw a copy of *Bijou* #1, and I remember thinking to myself that that was the sort of thing I would like to create. I bought a copy and took it back to my hovel. My roommate said he would vigorously promote the book if I would draw my own. So we formed a brief partnership, and that's how *Mom's* #1 was created. It was strictly for local consumption and in fact had a lot of Milwaukee jokes. To my astonishment four thousand copies sold very quickly in Milwaukee. In fact, Bill, the roommate, went to San Francisco with a box in his trunk, dropped them off at Gary Arlington's San Francisco Comic Book Store, and within a week the box had sold. Gary wrote me, asking for more. But I was running out of copies. And then the Print Mint, which at the time was the only viable underground publisher, offered to be my publisher, and I was delighted. I was beginning to think that maybe I could actually make my living at this. At this time, of course, there were tens of thousands of "hippies" looking for their "own" literature, and this was a mushrooming phenomenon.

To make the long story short, I was unhappy with the Print Mint for a variety of reasons, and I decided to publish books myself. Based on my brief experience in Milwaukee, I thought I knew "all about" publishing, which was terribly naive. With the help of another friend, I started Kumquat Productions. That didn't last very long at all, publishing only two comics. It reorganized into Krupp Comic Works in September of 1970. I had a certain knack for business even then but was very naive. I was very lucky that there was a great demand for underground comix, that there was a subculture and a network of head shops literally begging for books. Other cartoonists offered me their books. They said, "Here, you print them and distribute them and pay us a royalty," and I said, "Well, okay," and became a publisher by default. I had no intention of ever being a publisher.

BS: The first issue of *Mom's* was all your work.

DK: It's the only solo book I ever did. [*Laughter*]

BS: What happened? Why was the next issue not all Denis Kitchen?

DK: Because already I didn't have time to draw it all myself and I didn't show a great deal of taste in choosing contributors for the second issue. It was put together hastily, and my contributions kept shrinking. To this day I'm probably the least prolific cartoonist I publish, but I still like to draw. I do have a page here and there in various books. But publishing takes at least 90 percent of my time.

BS: How fast are you as an artist?

DK: When I'm just drawing, probably half a page a day at best. I consider that a good rate. But it's hard to find full days. To take two days to draw a page is a real luxury to me now. Usually, the only time I turn out work is when I have a deadline imposed from outside because I don't take my own deadlines seriously. Time after time I have books with myself on the chart and I end up crossing my name out and substituting someone else because I can't produce in time.

BS: Do you think that if you'd had any series characters they could have created a momentum for you?

DK: Possibly it was a mistake not to take a character and stick with it, but you can argue both sides of that coin.

BS: It could seem as if you were making an attempt in the early *Mom's* to create a series character.

DK: I guess none of them were entertaining enough to me. I keep thinking, I'm going to take this Mr. Krupp [Steve Krupp] character who pops up now and again. He's kind of the capitalist alter ego that I see as a foil to the artistic side. I have all kinds of scripts in my idea file which would involve him. He may develop into the closest thing to a regular character that I have. I guess I'm afraid of falling into a trap; you know how it is: The character too often controls the cartoonist. That's a fear that I was aware of years ago when I began, and the last thing I wanted to do was be trapped. Not that I was at that point in my life afraid of becoming too successful by creating a *Blondie* or something, but the tedium of doing the same thing day after day was not a happy prospect. Some of the cartoonists I admire the most have no regular characters—like, say, Art Spiegelman. So you tend to think of Art Spiegelman as an artist first instead of saying, "Yeah, *Beetle Bailey*, who does that?" before you think of Mort Walker. And I think if you're going to be a serious comix artist, you should not be a slave to a paper character.

BS: You never thought of doing scripts that somebody else would illustrate?

Group self-portrait for *Funnyworld* magazine, 1971. Back row (from left): Denis Kitchen, Don Glassford, Jim Mitchell, and Skip Williamson. Front row, Jay Lynch, Bruce Walthers, and Wendel Pugh.

DK: Yeah, but again, it takes time and—really, I have to emphasize that in a small publishing company I'm wearing many hats and I'm not just sitting behind a desk and deciding, "Well, let's publish this book" and then designating different jobs to different assistants. It's a very small operation, really, and I do a lot of the work myself.

BS: How many people do you have in the operation?

DK: There are four of us full time at Krupp, and some part-time people, and of course most of the work is freelanced all over the country. But there are four of us full time.

BS: There was a period where there seemed to be a series of syndicated strips that got reprinted in *Smile* magazine.

DK: Yeah. For a while we were syndicating strips to alternative newspapers and college papers. . . .

BS: It sounds like the Rip Off Syndicate pages.

DK: Yes, it was, as a matter of fact. This was 1971. Actually, it lasted two years, and this was when one of my partners was Jim Mitchell, who did the *Smile* comics. He was in charge of the syndicate, and he wasn't the most organized person in the world, but it still did fairly well. Five of us, Mitchell, Don Glassford, Bruce Walthers, Wendel Pugh, and myself, all did a weekly strip, and we had at one point fifty-some papers and that would have been enough for it to be successful. The problem was not getting them to carry it; the problem was getting them to pay for it [*laughter*]. We had something like a 50 percent collection rate, and that just wasn't enough. We ended up making three dollars a strip after expenses per week, and we just finally had to give up. Also, at that point Jim Mitchell was disenchanted with Krupp and vice versa. He left the organization shortly thereafter and ended up in a Mexican prison for four and a half years. So it was an experiment that could have succeeded if we had persevered, and I think if we'd had a good business manager at the time who knew how to collect and who knew how to get people to sign binding contracts [*laughter*], it could be a syndicate to this day. But now Rip Off is doing something similar, and they seem to be doing it successfully. Of course, they also have the fact that Gilbert Shelton is doing *Wonder Wart-Hog* and so forth for them, and they also have *Griffith's Observatory* and Joel Beck—a really strong lineup. I think Trina's doing strips for them now and some new cartoonists. It does change, but they've had a pretty good lineup of artists, and so as far as I can tell it's succeeding.

We even ran their strips in *The Fox River Patriot*, the local paper that I copublish, and we were able to get away with *Wart-Hog* for quite a while until [*laughter*] it got a little too outrageous and some of the farmers complained [*laughter*]. It's kind of a parochial area, but now we run *Phoebe and the Pidgeon People* and whatever comics we can. I try to inject comix into the community media, and for the most part they're well received. We ran one of Bill Griffith's *Zippy* stories, and Zippy in one of the panels says, "Oh, God!" and we got I think seven letters from old ladies complaining that it was blasphemous. So that's where I live.

BS: What other publishing hats do you have besides undergrounds? I know you do *Yesteryear*. . . .

DK: Right. *Yesteryear* is a monthly antique and collectibles paper for Wisconsin and Northern Illinois, and *The Fox River Patriot* is a twice-monthly feature paper that's circulated in about ten counties in central Wisconsin, and Krupp. Those are the three major things. I'm also involved in a new enterprise called Hollybrook Graphics, which is publishing portfolios. I represent certain cartoonists overseas and this is the vehicle for that representative. [Editor's note: Since this interview was conducted, Kitchen has divested his interests in both *Yesteryear* and *The Fox River Patriot*. He has moved to a new office/warehouse and concentrates solely on Krupp/Kitchen Sink Press.]

Kim Thompson: You're an agent of sorts?

DK: Yeah. I act as an agent for arranging foreign reprints of American cartoonists. That was part of my recent trip to Europe, arranging some of these projects. I also try to use some of the foreign cartoonists over here, because there's a lot of exciting stuff going on over there, as you know.

KT: Can you give us any names?

DK: Well, no. Some of the things are tentative and premature to announce. I met with, for instance, the editors of *Metal Hurlant*. There's a divorce going on between *Heavy Metal* and *Metal Hurlant*, so they are seeking other outlets in the USA, so we may—and I stress "may"—be getting involved in some albums of certain French artists, and it would be premature to discuss it further now.

I also think there's a lot of really impressive material coming out of Holland. I think there are probably more great cartoonists per capita in Holland than in any other place in the world, and the Dutch people have a great craving for comics. I believe there are something like thirteen million people in Holland—New York City would be comparable—and 250,000 *Donald Duck* comic books per week are sold there. No, that was Denmark. Holland was 400,000 *Donald Duck* comics per week. It's just incredible. And also albums. They issue really impressive hardcover collections of some of the weekly magazine strips. They're beautiful and they're expensive and they sell very well. There are something like sixty or seventy comics shops—specialty shops—in Holland alone, and you might not find that many in all of the United States, that simply sold comic books. So in many ways it was inspirational to see what was going on there, and yet they are also interested in what's going on in America, because our culture is very influential, obviously. A lot of European comics, for example, are American westerns. You see all kinds of western themes, and the Dutch artists idolize American culture in ways that are almost embarrassing because they idolize it on one hand and on the other hand, they ask how we can be voting for Carter and Reagan.

BS: Would this be more *Dutch Treat*–type material?

DK: Well, *Dutch Treat* was edited by Evert Geradts. He chose the material. It wasn't a particularly successful book. I don't think I expected it to be a best seller when we did it, but I'd hoped it would do better. As a way of introducing Dutch artists to this country, I think perhaps it could have been done better. It was a potpourri, two pages of him, three pages of him, and perhaps something more substantial by one or two or three artists would have been better. One of the artists there I'm real high on is a fellow named Joost Swarte. There's a book of his called *Modern Art* that he did with [Dutch cartoonist] Willem—it's a marvelous book and I'd love to do that one.

The problem is, it's like being in a candy store as a kid with ten cents and wanting everything, and I wish I had the means and the resources to start a whole series of reprints. Some of the stuff just begs for translation and there must be—this is the optimist in me—there must be enough Americans to appreciate that work to make it possible, but we'll just have to do it very slowly. There are other people besides me who are interested in doing it, so I think slowly but surely there is going to be further cross-pollination. We really see far less of their good work than they see of ours. They import a great deal of American work; in fact, I think about 15 percent of Krupp's business is now overseas, when a few years ago virtually none was sold overseas. So if you ask me what the fastest-growing segment of our market is, I'd have to say the European market, and in fact not just Europe. We sell comics in some of the strangest places now, like Brazil and Australia.

BS: I'd think you'd be tortured for reading a comic in Brazil.

DK: I would think so too. We do have problems—periodically. It is a police state, but they're fairly liberal in what they allow to be imported. Once in a while a shipment is refused but it seems to be kind of arbitrary. I'll tell you, it's much more difficult to get comix into Canada than Brazil. There are ironies in the export business. You'd be amazed.

Another surprise is England. Our British distributor, Titan, had three or four thousand dollars' worth of undergrounds seized and burned without any legal recourse on the part of the distributor. Here, if some agency were to seize books from me and burn them I would sue, I would appeal, I would do something. But over there they just throw up their hands and say, "Well, there's nothing we can do." And it really shocked me because I thought England was different. And it's especially funny because in England you can publish anything you want. It's just a question of what you can import, and they don't want certain foreign material polluting the British culture. Yet they could take the same material they burned and I could sell the rights to an English publisher. They could print it there and it wouldn't be burned. So it's really silly.

BS: They had trouble with *Heavy Metal*, I think.

DK: Yes, and I think Warren's had material impounded.

KT: Believe it or not, French censors have come down like a ton of bricks on French translations of Marvel comics. Right next to them on the newsstands, there'd be French comics with the most outrageous things, and when these American comics were just slightly out of bounds, they'd pounce on them.

DK: Crazy.

BS: I wanted to get to how your involvement in the *Bugle-American* came to be.

DK: Sure. In September 1970 I was foolish enough to be the founder of Krupp Comic Works, Inc., and the very same month be one of the founders of the *Bugle-American*, a new "underground" newspaper. The *Bugle* was headquartered in Madison, Wisconsin, and Krupp was in Milwaukee, so I would spend three days a week in Madison, four days a week in Milwaukee, seventy-five miles away. I did this for months. And I was heavily involved in both and really loved both. It finally became exhausting and both organizations were upset that I would spend half my week with the other, so I finally had to make a choice. My loyalties ultimately were with the comic book company, so after the first six or eight or maybe ten months, I began to limit myself to drawing periodic covers for the *Bugle*. Or once in a while I'd relieve somebody when they were on vacation and come in and art direct an issue or contribute here and there. But it went on eight years in all and was one of the better underground papers in the Midwest if not in the whole country, though it was one of the least political papers and thus it was frequently criticized by the actively political papers as—

BS: [*Laughter*] In Madison, there are about five or six of them!

DK: That's right. Madison, as you know, is the Berkeley of the Midwest. And finally, what happened was, the paper did move to Milwaukee, where there was a much more receptive audience. Milwaukee being a blue-collar town without a real cultural identity of its own, welcomed the *Bugle* with open arms because it had nothing else, except for a paper called *Kaleidoscope*, which was in decline and didn't last much longer. Madison, on the other hand, is a real newspaper city and it had a couple of very conservative papers, a daily student paper, several music newspapers, radical papers like *Take Over* and *Madison Kaleidoscope*—

BS: [*Chuckles*]

DK: Yeah, right, the name alone, *Take Over*, tells you. . . . You come into the town with a paper called the *Bugle-American* and they say, "What is this?" In between the radical and I guess you'd have to say the conservative elements of the staff, it never started out saying, "We are going to be a radical paper." It started basically with a group of journalism students who were excited by underground papers and at the same time wanted to do something journalistically responsible, and so when it came to naming the thing, the choice came between very crazy names—hippie names like *Stash* and things like that—versus really straight names, so finally the compromise was to pick something so straight that no one would take it seriously. And that's how the resulting *Bugle-American* came to be. I always thought it was a stupid name. I finally succeeded in at least dropping the "American" part so it was just the

Bugle. That's all people ever called it anyway; it was such a mouthful. It was always more of a graphic underground paper, used a lot of comix covers. . . . To this day I still get collectors writing me or approaching me at conventions, asking if I have back issues of the *Bugle*. I used to stash away a small pile of each issue with comix covers. But in many cases what I thought was a lifetime supply of copies has dwindled to virtually nothing. Dave Shreiner—who wrote that brilliant Ed Gein story in *Weird Trips* #2—was the editor, though we never used hierarchical titles like "editor."

BS: You did a *Lampoon* parody in one of their issues. . . .

DK: That's right. "The National Lamprune," it was called. And there were guest covers by people like Jay Lynch and Bob Armstrong and, oh, God, whatever cartoonists were passing through town, we'd force them to do a cover. . . . [*General laughter*]

BS: "Be political today."

DK: Right. And then it also was where the Krupp Syndicate was based. The *Bugle* was our deadline on which the syndicate was based so that we could then take that weekly package, reproduce it, and send stats out to all the members. So the *Bugle* had the strips a week or two before any other paper in the country and frequently had comics that we didn't use elsewhere because they were either too local or sometimes we would do six, seven strips a week and we could only fit five on the proof sheets. Someday I might even like to go back and collect the best of those, because only a few were really reprinted in *Smile*, and even *Smile* was not a widely circulated comic. So there's a lot of good stuff languishing in the files.

BS: Yeah, I think I've only seen about four or five of your strips from that period.

DK: Yeah? It was probably my most prolific period ever, because I had to draw something every week. That's one reason I liked it: because somebody forced me to draw. I wish somebody now would make me do a strip every week, but nobody will. [*General laughter*]

Holly Brooks: I know. I do my best.

DK: Holly tries her best, but . . . I don't take her threats seriously.

BS: At one point, some California artists were critical of Krupp—Roger Brand in particular.

DK: Yeah, Roger was probably the most vocal critic—he commented in *Funnyworld* at one point that he thought Krupp was the Charlton of underground comics, which really hurt, but I certainly understand why Roger was saying that. The San Francisco artists were certainly the vanguard of the underground artist movement at that point in time, and the Midwest was an awfully dumb place to be in their view and perhaps even from my own point of view. Everyone was migrating out to San Francisco, with good reason: It was a cultural mecca, it was a beautiful place to live, and why I stayed in Wisconsin was because I was stubborn and had family ties and was dumb [*laughter*]. When I was covered with four feet of snow, I often wondered why I didn't go to San Francisco too. But in Wisconsin I did stay and the distance caused lack of communication and misunderstandings.

I think Roger felt what he and some of the other West Coast cartoonists were doing was much more valid at the time—shall we say, more "underground"—and I think probably it's true. Had I published S. Clay Wilson in the Midwest, I probably would have been tarred and feathered out of Milwaukee, which is a large city but would have tarred and feathered me nevertheless. The San Francisco artists had a much freer situation. I was probably more conservative personally than many of them, and I also, at that time, was certainly geographically isolated from the mainstream of underground cartoonists. It changed as more of them began to travel and pass through the Midwest, and as we met in person, a lot of those misunderstandings began to clear up. I know that, for instance, a comic book like *Smile* at the time, which was mainly a collection of Jim Mitchell's work, was considered horribly cute and juvenile by most of the San Francisco artists, in the same way *Barefootz* was criticized later on.

I think part of it was a general California attitude toward the Midwest, which still prevails, to a large degree. If you're on the East Coast or on the West Coast, you're where things are happening, and Midwest bumpkins can't possibly produce anything valid. As the artists began passing through and Crumb began giving me books, and the *Bijou* books came out of the Midwest, more and more things began being done in Wisconsin, and the idea that the Midwest was a stupid place to be began to slowly disappear. I think when West Coast artists visited and saw how pretty it was and how clean the air was and saw what a nice operation we had and saw how low the rent was and saw how friendly the people were where I lived—a lot of these misconceptions just withered away. I have often second-guessed myself, but in the long run I'm glad I decided to stay in Wisconsin from a number of viewpoints.

Certainly, from a practical viewpoint, it makes sense to have a publishing company in the Midwest, because it's a very easy way to ship to all points of the country. It's a printing center; I'm very near paper supplies. You can ask *The Comics Journal* and others. It's a good place to print and to warehouse and to distribute. From a cultural viewpoint I'm sure it would be much more interesting to live in San Francisco. Leonard Rifas, for example, moved to Wisconsin to work at Krupp for about a year. He constantly bemoaned the fact that the library only had twenty-eight volumes and he had to drive thirty-five miles to see a movie and we had no community theater, we had no Indonesian restaurants [*laughter*], and so on. But you just have to weigh the scales, and I think they weigh in our behalf. No one besides Roger ever—at least in print—was that harsh on us. I think that was blown out of proportion and was in a sense a backlash to an article I had written earlier in *Funnyworld* #12 or #13, where I had lashed out against the Print Mint. The Print Mint in Berkeley was a company that Roger was published by and he was close to the owners, and I'm sure some of Roger's comments were the result of my article. I'd have to say in retrospect that the article I wrote in *Funnyworld* was probably a bit out of line. I said some smart-alecky things about Print Mint that implied that they were crooks where I had no hard evidence to back it up. I should have been much more diplomatic in discussing the Print Mint. I don't believe they were crooks. We had disputes, but I should have said it differently, and I'm sure they were justifiably upset, and Roger indirectly was upset and so calling me the Charlton of underground comics was kind of a of whiplash effect, and all that's really ancient history now; I don't know what else to say about it. Things have now come full circle. The Print Mint no longer publishes underground comix, and I was the publisher of Roger's last comic, *Banzai*. Our relations now are very good.

BS: It just seemed reflective of the cultural attitude.

DK: Absolutely. And that still exists. It's something we're always battling, and let's face it, I live in a very provincial area, very rural, a town of 1,400 people, and—

BS: Do you get along with your neighbors as an underground publisher?

DK: [*Laughter*] Well, when I first moved to Princeton, the farmer next door strolled over. He's a man of few words. He asked me what I did for a living. I said I was a cartoonist, and there was about a fifteen-second pause, and he spat on the ground, and then another fifteen seconds later he said, "Depression comin'." And that was the end of our conversation. He walked away. [*General laughter*]

BS: I guess he was trying to tell you something.

DK: It's a wonderful place. If I park my car in Princeton and I don't put enough money in the meter—which takes pennies, incidentally—the police officer will come into my studio and warn me that my meter has expired and ask me to put another penny in or else he'll have to give me a fifty-cent ticket. This is Princeton, and it's one reason I love it.

BS: You mentioned earlier the European markets you sold to. What are the primary markets for Krupp titles today in the United States? Where do you sell?

DK: Well, I wish I could afford a market survey to say for sure, but one observation is that the head shop market is declining.

BS: Head shops are declining! [*Laughter*]

DK: Yes, but don't scoff: there still are a lot of head shops and a lot of them still carry underground comix. At one point, that was 90 percent of our sales. What seems to be growing is record shops, comics specialty shops, and stores around military bases. We sell a lot of comics to soldiers.

BS: Military bases . . . ?

DK: Yeah. Some of our best outlets are in military towns, and of course college towns. I can't be more specific than that because obviously it costs a lot of money to find out exactly who's buying anything. But those are the tendencies that I'm aware of.

BS: The Krupp catalogs that come out, where do they specifically go?

DK: Well, there are two Krupp catalogs. There is the Krupp Mail Order catalog, which comes out of Boulder, Colorado. I only own a small portion of that organization. The Krupp Mail Order catalog is a slick full-color production. It features covers by artists like Leslie Cabarga, John Pound, Bill Griffith, Justin Green, myself, and others. It offers a full line of underground comix and related merchandise to individuals. This venture has continued to grow and grow. The latest mailing was to 800,000 individuals. Krupp Mail Order is run independently by Tyler Lantzy, but we decided years ago when we set up separate companies to share the name "Krupp" for mutual benefit. The Krupp Wholesale Catalog, which I produce, goes to several thousand shops and distributors throughout the US and some foreign countries, I rely almost entirely on that to solicit sales from existing customers and potential customers. I'd like to rely more and more on regional distributors, but there are many places in the country where there is no distribution and I have to supply the shops direct, and that is why the catalog is designed specifically for dealers.

KT: How has the burgeoning specialty shop situation affected you?

DK: Very favorably, because they tend to attract a more discriminating audience. In comics shops we sell—God, I hate to pick words like this—but there's a greater audience for the more intellectual, the more sophisticated, the more subtle comics. I'm not going to name names of comics. But the soldiers are looking for something to be read in the barracks, and they laugh at them and throw them away, and the comics shops obviously appeal to collectors, some of whom are far more neurotic than the soldiers [*laughter*], but who generally tend to be more discriminating.

BS: A book like *Mondo Snarfo* would have more chances in a specialty shop.

DK: I do not sell *Mondo Snarfo*s on military bases.

KT: How about *Spirits*?

DK: *The Spirit* is generally our most popular book in terms of first-day sales, which is one way of measuring a book. It's my highest first-day-sale book. On the other hand, once the collector audience is saturated, a *Spirit* has pretty much run its course, whereas some of the underground comics will sell month after month after month, year after year after year, and go into many more printings. And over a ten-year period can sell well in excess of one hundred thousand copies in some cases. But by most standards I'd have to say that *The Spirit* is the most successful and the one on which I get the most favorable feedback on and the most mail and the most people who want to hug me at conventions and thank me profusely for bringing it into the world. For the most part the audience that buys *The Spirit* is different from the audience that tends to buy the undergrounds, but there is a good overlap.

BS: You initially did two pre-Warren *Spirit* collections. Did they do well?

DK: They did very well. In fact, they did so well that they, in effect, were a test market that enabled Warren to approach Eisner and offer a better package and national distribution. Eisner couldn't turn that down. But fortunately, it's come full circle again, and I'm delighted to be picking up where Warren left off, making further changes and improvements.

BS: I was wondering, because at one point Warren was selling those two back issues in the merchandise pages in the back of *The Spirit*.

DK: Well, what happened was, after the first *Spirit* underground sold twenty thousand copies in a very short period, and the second *Spirit* was coming off the presses, Warren had already made an offer to Eisner that he couldn't refuse, and Eisner didn't want to hurt me in any way. So one of the conditions he gave Warren was that Warren had to buy all of my excess stock of *Spirits* at a favorable price to me. I had only sold a small portion of *Spirit* #2 because it had literally just come off the press. So Warren immediately bought the balance and had no choice but to mail order them for many months, because he couldn't put them on the newsstands next to his other titles.

KT: When you took over *The Spirit* again from Warren, what editorial changes did you make? What policies of Warren's did you see that you felt you should change, if any?

DK: Well, the package is different in that I run very few ads. There's a few in each issue, but I find the Warren monster mask ads and so forth thoroughly offensive and incompatible with *The Spirit*. We are also giving continuity to the issues, running stories together in a more logical sequence, and plan to run prewar *Spirit* stories, Lou Fine ghost episodes, and obscure material from Eisner's fabled vault.

I also felt the magazine should be on a higher-grade white paper. I have encouraged the wraparound covers and, as you may have observed, more editorial content, both produced by Eisner and the column that Cat Yronwode writes. The magazine is continuing to develop in a direction which I think will be best defined as a personal magazine of Will Eisner's. In fact, one of the changes you'll see will be the logo, "Will Eisner's *Spirit Magazine.*" The name Will Eisner will become more prominent. Partly, this will be dictated by the fact that there are only a finite number of *Spirit* stories to print, and partly our desire to have Eisner create more new material.

BS: Was that always a condition of your taking back *The Spirit*, to kind of push him into doing more original material?

DK: Well, I wouldn't describe it as a condition. I would describe it as a desire on my part, because I think Eisner's most exciting material is the material he's creating now. His undeniable talent, his life experiences, intellect, and the elimination of old business obligations have made it possible for him to create the best material of his life, such things as *A Contract with God* and the new *Life on Another Planet* series, which you haven't had the privilege of seeing in its entirety. He's working on the last chapter, and it's literally picking up steam with every page. It's exciting, has surprises that will catch you off-guard, and the graphics and storytelling techniques are pace-setting, still, at an age when most artists have become hacks or retired. He's reaching new levels, new heights. So I'm very excited to have the privilege of publishing this work and to be able to keep pushing him to do more. I'm delighted with the fact that he himself is still excited. I think there's a tremendous amount of creativity still in that man.

To get back to the European market, the *Life on Another Planet* story will be serialized in Europe in a colored version and then collected in a color album that we'll be bringing out in English back here. I think it's going to hold together even better as a complete package. It's been very frustrating for many readers to have to wait three months between chapters.

BS: And the format change was a little alienating.

DK: Yeah, that was an unfortunate decision, and that will be rectified in the collection too. The first two chapters will be heavily retouched and redrawn by Eisner to be able to stand alongside the later chapters that are so much better.

KT: Which European magazines is it being serialized in?

DK: It will be determined by Eisner's Spanish agent. I'm sure they'll be in magazines like *Pilote*, and others are competing for the rights. There'll only be one magazine in each country that can do it. But there's a lot of demand for it. *The Spirit* right now is being run in at least four or five countries on a regular basis; his work is widely admired over there. His book *A Contract with God* was voted the number one comicsrelated book in Holland in 1979 by a panel of comics critics and fans out of a national competition that included three or four hundred books. His was the first American book to ever be voted number one.

BS: This brings us into a discussion of Krupp's relationship with some of its other artists. Well, the first would be Crumb.

DK: There's another guy it's been a great privilege to work with. I think that the term people always use with certain of these artists is "genius," but I'd say this is another example of its being justifiable. Of course, I also come under a lot of heat from various sources for publishing Crumb's work, which is offensive to some people.

BS: For sexist reasons, or . . . ?

DK: Oh, that's one I hear very often. The latest solo Crumb book we did was *Snoid*, which contained material which some people think is his absolute worst and his absolute best work side by side, so—

BS: Is that on artistic or just thematic reasons?

DK: Well, both, but primarily thematic. The strip "A Short History of America" has been universally praised, [and] while some of the other material hasn't been universally damned, it has been severely criticized. Crumb's a very complex person, of course, and I can't explain him. You'll have to ask him. But I still consider it a privilege to be able to work with him closely. He's much more independent than most cartoonists, and he's probably the least likely to take editorial direction, so as a publisher I am basically faced with the prospect of publishing it as is or not publishing it at all, and I can't imagine myself turning down a Crumb book because I found parts of it potentially unpopular or offensive. It stands as a whole, and ultimately, he bears responsibility for its worth.

BS: At one point it seemed as if his relationship with Krupp was somewhat shaky.

DK: Not really. There was a brief period where we were in deep financial trouble and we were forced to pay him in comic books, of all things, because that's all we had, and he, like everyone else, would rather spend money at the grocery store than comic books. But that was a brief period, when I frankly doubted we would survive at all. This was in 1973, the famed Comics Crash of '73. But we did survive, and every year since we've grown. When year after year I would hear predictions that underground comix were dying, dying, dying, in fact we were grossing more than ever. To some degree it's true that there has been a decline in overall sales, and it's true that the price of the books has gone up, thus the annual gross doesn't reflect sales as much as inflated dollars, but I can safely say that we are more stable as a publishing company than we ever were in the past, even though in 1972 sales were brisker. In 1972, distributors would call and literally beg for new books, and as a younger and more naïve publisher I gave in to their demands by publishing some questionable books that I now am a little ashamed to have my imprint on. But every other publisher made the same mistake, and those decisions partly contributed to that crash of '73, not to mention the Supreme Court decision on obscenity and other factors.

BS: Would you say that your current stability is as much based on your more diversified operations too? You have three publishing companies.

DK: Yes, but I'm talking strictly about Krupp–Kitchen Sink now.

BS: Well, it's interesting to see how the entities survive.

DK: Now, Krupp on its own has diversified too. Certainly, *The Spirit* and *Bizarre Sex* and *Class War Comics* and *Snarf* and all these other things in themselves are divergent and appeal to different audiences. I do strive to keep our output varied and feel a responsibility as an alternate publisher to do things that could not be done by the major publishers, such as, for example, the *Gay Comix* project, the *Class War Comics* series, and a number of upcoming projects that I feel deserve to be published. I feel instinctively that not all of them are destined to be best sellers, but some of our more popular titles subsidize the books that deserve to do better but don't. I believe Bill Gaines explained that in the EC line, his personal favorites were the science fiction titles but they sold the worst, so the horror comics in effect subsidized his favorites. In a way I tend to play the same balance as that on a much smaller scale.

BS: Is there going to be another issue of *Class War*?

DK: Yes, I hope so. Cliff Harper originally planned this to be a six-volume set, but I believe it's going to appear in a more abbreviated two- or three-volume set. And it may be a year before the second one comes out, but he definitely will finish it. That next to *The Spirit* has generated more mail than any other books I've ever published, almost universally encouraging sequels.

BS: Was it a slow builder? It seemed like it didn't have the immediate impact.

DK: No, and let's face it, it had some real deficiencies in storytelling, but Cliff Harper was as aware of those as anyone. I think you'll find the second and third volumes much better. He's aware of the flaws and, politics aside, it represents an artist's personal view of the future which I find fascinating. I encourage other artists to create their personal view of the future . . . and present. That was its greatest appeal. It really didn't generate political letters as much as "Hey, this is great, this is a view of the future that I hadn't considered"—basically, a nontechnological, nonhierarchical future, which is totally the opposite of the *Star Wars* futures that people now take for granted. The politics, as blatant as they were in a sense, also weren't so important to many of the readers. When I published it, I said, "This isn't going to appeal too much to the average comics fan, but a lot of the political bookstores that don't normally carry comics are going to carry this." That premise backfired because most political bookstores have an axe to grind and 99 percent of them didn't like Harper's particular brand of anarchism, and the surprising support was in the standard comics outlets.

BS: How did Howard Cruse's relationship with Krupp start?

DK: He had created *Barefootz* and it had had some limited circulation in some alternative papers, particularly in Birmingham, Alabama, which was his home. But he hadn't had any really wide exposure. I liked his stuff from the start, though I've probably been more criticized for publishing *Barefootz* than anything sexist that Crumb did or something obscene that anybody might have drawn. He's an amazingly controversial cartoonist. I get letters and personal complaints from people saying, "How can you publish this cutesy nonsense? It has no place in underground comics." And other people say, "This is my favorite stuff, this is hilarious, this is great." And it's one of those love-or-hate situations.

Now, the surprising development has been in recent months, particularly since his *Little Lulu* parody appeared in *Snarf* and since *Barefootz* #3. Some of his harshest critics have come to appreciate his work, or at least the direction his work has taken. He's developing a more realistic style—well [*laughter*], "realistic" isn't the right word. He's drifting away from the strict *Barefootz* style, and he's developing a more realistic technique that doesn't seem to bother people so much. *Barefootz* seemed to come from kind of a Gerald McBoingBoing school of art, and his new style is much more palatable to comix fans. His writing has always been clever, but some people couldn't get past the simple art style. I think his newer work is opening a lot of eyes.

BS: There's also an increased emphasis on character instead of just straight gag strips.

DK: That's right. But he is a very good gag cartoonist, and I have no doubt that he could be a very popular syndicated cartoonist if he chose to go that route. But he's much more interested in the complete freedom the underground offers, and that's one of the great things. You can't quite define what an "underground" is, but it sure appeals to a lot of people. And it's that indefinable freedom. He would not have to sacrifice a lot to be nationally syndicated, but he's not willing to sacrifice that little bit. "That little bit" turns out to be a great deal and is invaluable to many artists.

BS: In an early underground paper—it may even have been the *Bugle-American*—you described yourself as being ideologically anticapitalist. How do you reconcile that—[*laughter*]? I assume that at some point of your life you reconciled that with being the head of Krupp.

DK: [*Laughter*] Well, the same time I founded Krupp and was a cofounder of the *Bugle-American*, I became a candidate for lieutenant governor of Wisconsin on the Socialist Labor Party ticket. It was a very busy time in my life, and yes, I'm sure I did describe myself as being anticapitalist, but it's impossible to do anything in this country without using money and using capitalism. I was a little self-conscious at the time because of my socialist ideals, self-conscious about starting a corporation. So one thing I did was decide that if I was going to have a corporation, I would have fun with it. So the idea of Krupp Comic Works, Inc., being named after the giant German conglomerate itself was a joke, and the fact that I chose as its symbol an octopus which in each tentacle embraced a division—largely fictional [*laughter*]—was a way of saying to people, "Hey, this is a capitalistic enterprise, but we don't take it very seriously."

As it grew and more money began to pour into the coffers, it became obvious that I couldn't run it on a communal basis. I had to get serious, or it would fail as an organization. The "system" co-opts things, and in a sense you could say I was co-opted. I certainly don't consider myself a capitalist, nor do I any longer belong to any socialist parties. I still think of a "capitalist" as being an industrialist or a financier with a great deal of wealth who exploits workers. Capitalism is a flawed system. But I am a businessman, and I'm not so rigid in my political views as I was ten years ago. I no longer believe I know the answers to everything, as I did when I ran for lieutenant governor of Wisconsin and wanted to change the world. Between you and me, the lieutenant governor of Wisconsin couldn't change much anyway [*laughter*].

BS: Your Krupp Wholesale Catalog also sells a percentage of drug-oriented material that's not underground; I'm thinking of books more than anything else.

DK: Yes, we do carry drug-related books, and again, it's because as an alternate distributor I feel a responsibility to carry those books which will not be carried by normal distributors. I do not carry the *Whole Drug Manufacturer's Book*, which tells you how to manufacture heroin, and I decline to carry a number of drug-related books, but I do carry a couple dozen books on how to grow marijuana and that sort of thing. They're very popular books. Many of the remaining head shops demand them, and I am a natural distributor for them. It's as simple as that. I don't draw—well, I've drawn certain moral conclusions already by not carrying certain books, but I realize it's an area in which there are differing opinions, even among that subculture that is supposed to be our primary audience. I make it a point in our *Dope Comix* series to encourage artists to talk honestly about their attitudes toward drugs, both pro and con. Many people typecast underground comics as being nothing but dope and sex. They probably have never read a *Dope Comix* or they would realize that perhaps half of it is anti-dope.

BS: Someone like Jay Lynch is very strongly anti-dope [*laughter*].

DK: That's right. There are a number of underground cartoonists who are antidrug. Absolutely.

BS: I was wondering whether you felt that current antiparaphernalia laws might affect future sales of undergrounds and drug-related books.

DK: Well, they already have. There are a number of repressive laws that have already been passed or are being seriously considered in state legislatures all over the country. We cannot sell *High Times* or drug books in the state of Georgia right now, and there have been busts periodically in various parts of the country, primarily the South. The threat of some of these unconstitutional laws is enough to cause some shops to voluntarily refrain from carrying comix or drug-related material, besides of course paraphernalia, which the laws are aimed against. They're terrible laws and they're patently unconstitutional, but their main purpose is to scare people, and that they do. When they're challenged, they're ultimately overthrown, but in many states there aren't organizations capable of overthrowing those laws.

BS: Plus, a lot of small businesses end up going down the drain in the process.

DK: That's right. And the "moral" lawmakers know that full well.

BS: There might come a crash again. Do you see a repeat of that happening?

DK: In my most paranoid moments I do, but to date it hasn't been a serious problem. It's been a spotty problem, and it has been nothing compared to 1973 when literally scores of shops were calling and saying, "We're sending back our comix; we're afraid." That was a scary period. Right now, it's mostly Christian harassment in certain areas of the country.

BS: I guess for my final question, briefly: how would you produce an average Krupp title, like one of your anthology books?

DK: Well, anyone who reads our titles regularly knows that I have certain favorites and certain regulars that I like to use, who I tend to use more than some of my competitors, and they have their own favorites. Still, I try to inject new talent into the anthologies. I try to devote several pages an issue to fresh faces, and on the other hand try to resurrect some of the "older" talents who dropped out of sight for one reason or another, people like Justin Green and Kim Deitch, who are not very active. . . .

BS: The *Banzai* book.

DK: That's right. If it's a theme book like *Dope Comix* or *Bizarre Sex* or *Corporate Crime* or something like that, the basis for starting a book is to ask someone if they're interested in doing a story for this title, and they may say, "No, but I'll do something for *Snarf* because I've got a funny story; I think you'll like it." And so I have a complex set of charts in my office on which I try to keep a running track of titles. Since they're not monthly and I don't have cover dates, I never have to worry about rushing something to press by September 1 or be at the mercy of a "national" distributor.

BS: So gathering enough material for an issue is sort of a cruise?

DK: I wouldn't call it a "cruise." The lack of firm deadlines is simultaneously a strength and a weakness. A single slowpoke artist can hold up a book when other contributors have conscientiously submitted their material on time. This can cause a title to drag on interminably at times. *Death Rattle #4* is five years in the making. Now I do try to put out the titles at least annually. *The Spirit* is the only book I do that has a schedule; the others I put together as quickly as is realistic. Partly I'm limited by our schedule, which by now calls for one and a half or two books a month, and that's determined by, basically, cash flow and circulation reports—and that changes. When the graph is going up, I average two or three titles a month; when the graph is going down, I average one or two books a month—but I digress here. How do I put together an average book? I watch my charts, and if I have twenty-eight pages in *Snarf* and I need thirty-six and it's about due to come out, I might borrow six pages, if appropriate, from *Dope Comix* and put out *Snarf*. The covers are assigned well in advance but the inside pages tend to be put together like a jigsaw puzzle, and if I see a theme developing—as, for example, in the last *Snarf*, when I began getting death-oriented stories—then I might ask somebody who has promised four pages to think about developing this theme. But I generally keep the direction minimal. In a sense I feel that each artist is his or her best editor, but at the same time many artists need direction and need criticism and need to be told how to change this panel or this or that, so I tend to edit according to the artist, and I've encouraged other people to edit certain books for me now, according to special interests, such as Leonard Rifas, who edits the *Corporate Crime* series; Trina Robbins, who edited *Wet Satin*; and Howard Cruse, who's editing *Gay Comics*; and I plan on doing that more and more, and just retain certain favorite titles under my own editorial direction.

BS: A book like *'50s Funnies*, which came from outside?

DK: Right. That was edited by Larry Shell. He had hoped to publish it himself and when he couldn't, he asked me if I would do it. He also offered me another book called *Alien Encounters*, which we may pass on,* and a book on human freaks which—who knows?—we may end up doing. As you know, publishing is getting to be a more and more expensive venture, paper costs are skyrocketing, and the money supply is tight, and I find myself being offered packages that other people have done more than ever before because a lot of would-be self-publishers find that when it comes right down to it, they can't swing it financially. Not that Krupp's a gigantic publisher, but relative to some of these small organizations, we are the next logical step in publishing, developing projects, or distribution.

BS: How much of the line would you say is at present composed of those kinds of books that come to you?

DK: Oh, a pretty small percentage right now, but I'm getting offered more and more, and thus I may accept more and more of them. But the majority of Kitchen Sink titles will be self-generated.

* Kitchen did eventually pass on *Alien Encounters*, which was picked up and published by Fantaco early this year. [Editor's note: Published as *Alien Encounters* #1 by FantaCo Enterprises in 1981.]

SIDEBAR ON ERNIE BUSHMILLER

BS: Is it true that you really love Ernie Bushmiller's work? [*General laughter*]

DK: I admire the crispness of his style, but he described himself best as "the Lawrence Welk of cartoonists."

BS: Okay [*laughter*]. It's just that he's been one of your whipping boys. . . .

DK: I parodied him a number of times. In fact, my only appearance in *Playboy* Magazine was an Ernie Bushmiller parody, and I parodied him in the *Bugle*, I parodied him in *Snarf*. I have two of his originals hanging in my office and people tend to conclude that there's something about Ernie Bushmiller I hate or love. I guess it's a combination of both. Bill Griffith once said that he liked Ernie Bushmiller because he drew the essential rock and the essential tree and the essential milk truck or whatever. . . .

BS: The essential hole in the baseball wall [*laughter*].

DK: Yeah! I remember reading an interview with Ernie Bushmiller one time in which he described how he would come up with a gag, and the people at the syndicate would say, "Dumb it up, Ernie! Dumb it up!" And so he would go back to the drawing board and dumb it up, and that basically sums up his career. It's dumb, but I'm perversely attracted to it. I can't pick up a comics section without reading *Nancy* in spite of myself, but I'd hate to this it was a significant influence on my own work [*laughter*].

KT: Ernie Bushmiller lives right down the street from us.

DK: No kidding. You must do something with him! [*General laughter*] He won the Inkpot Award or something a couple of years ago, from the National Cartoonists' Society. I'd love to see a Bushmiller *Snarf* cover sometime. . . .

KT: Did you see the article on him in the *World Encyclopedia of Comics*?

DK: No . . . not his entry.

KT: It was very unkind—particularly for an encyclopedia.

DK: Oh, that's terrible. Well, that wasn't really an encyclopedia; that was Maurice Horn's Favorite and Least Favorite Comics. That's all it was.

Excerpts from "An Industry Roundtable"

INTERNAL CORRESPONDENCE SPECIAL EDITION / 1992

Panel transcript from *Internal Correspondence Special Edition* (November 12, 1992). Reprinted by permission.

David Scroggy: Topic number three: What was the status of the comics medium and the industry twenty years ago? Where will comics be twenty years from now?

Denis Kitchen: The Kitchen Sink empire has diversified into noble areas like candy bars, neckties, and trading cards, but the focus of our roundtable is to look at the past, present and future of the comics medium. Gary Groth once called me the most optimistic man in comics, but taking off my rose-colored glasses today and looking at comics the medium from my experience, I see a growing and disturbing disparity between the giant publishers and the independents, between the enormous success of the best-selling titles and the declining support for those the same industry bestows its awards upon.

Twenty years ago, before the direct market existed, Kitchen Sink sold comics to several hundred outlets. Titles in those days sold a minimum of ten thousand to often fifty thousand or more. Sometimes we cracked six figures. Backlist was an important part of our sales twenty years ago. Twenty years later, today, the direct market serves several thousand outlets, I'm told. I'm presumably wiser. My titles are arguably better, but my average circulation per title, twenty years later, is half what it was two decades ago.

In a remarkable example of the disparity, a new Todd McFarlane comic can sell 300 times more than a Will Eisner comic. And, twenty years ago, I sold underground comics to an easily identifiable specialty audience. I sold to in those days all loved comics. The consumers I sold to loved comics, and they read comics. I had three competitors, and they were all approximately my size. Today my competitors include several publicly traded companies and about fifty other medium and smaller publishers. Many of the retailers that

I am aware of today are no longer enthusiastic about the medium they sell, and far too many comics are bought as purported investments, not for reading pleasure. And my backlist is more of a liability than an asset. So, looking ahead twenty years, I ran these numbers through Mel's computer, and I see that in two decades from now, I'll have one hundred competitors, no collectors will read, backlist will be an archaic term, and my circulation will be one-fourth of what it was when I began. My comic book division will be burning its awards to keep warm.

In the real book world, publishers send reps on the road. In the real book world, retailers look to publishers as their primary source. For better or worse, in the direct market system we don't do things that way. In lieu of publishers having reps on the road, perhaps it's the distributors who need to do that on our behalf. Only the largest publishers at this moment could even afford to think about that. Marvel sends people out. But I mean people who are out there selling. We're going to specialty stores, and within the retail community we know we already have specialists, people like, for instance, Bill Liebowitz, who I know carries my line very successfully. There are other retailers who don't carry a single one of my titles. I'd like to know that perhaps, if not an independent rep organization, perhaps Capital City could consider getting reps out on the road, talking to the retailers and meeting their needs. If they specialize in independent titles, make sure that they have access to them, including backlist—play to their strengths.

DS: Do all retailers know what their needs are?

DK: By and large they should, unless they are start-ups. They know what their own tastes are, and ultimately that's what it is. It's their community, obviously.

DS: Well, do you think it's their own personal tastes, or do you really think it's reflective of what their customer wants in many cases?

DK: I think somebody with tastes running alongside, let's say, the independents in general would be better suited to open a store in a Berkeley or Boulder than in suburban Chicago. Moondog knows that. The downtown stores have a different audience than the suburban stores. I would like to see somebody out there, and I'm throwing it to Capital City because I'm sure it's not an idea that they haven't heard before, but nobody has done it. That is, get people out on the road. Show the product. My biggest concern, my biggest fear is that the retailers don't even know what's out there for the most part. As Bill pointed out about the Top 100, we all know what's in the Top 100. There is a lot of great stuff in the bottom one hundred. If retailers saw it, even if it was a month old or a year old, they might say "I can sell that." I've got customers that will buy that and they never even see it.

SIDEBAR: PRESENTATION ON BEHALF OF
THE COMIC BOOK LEGAL DEFENSE FUND

DK: The Fund started several years ago in response to the infamous obscenity case involving Friendly Frank's. This year we have had three—in Sarasota, Florida; El Cajon, [California]; and Chino Hills, California—all of which are in litigation right now. We decided to keep the fund going after the Friendly Frank's case, because it seemed inevitable that we'd have conflicts again. We had a couple and then nothing was happening for a while. All of a sudden, several cases erupted, and they are sapping our financial resources. We currently have about $20,000 in the fund. Each case, on average, has taken about $20,000, so at a minimum, we need to triple our nest egg. So any of you who have creative ideas on how to raise money, by all means talk to me. If you're a publisher, perhaps you can donate a part of the profits from a designated issue. If you're a retailer, perhaps you can set up contribution bins. If you're in any way able to help us raise money, we can certainly use it. The industry as a whole will benefit.

I'd like to thank those of you who have agreed to contribute all or part of your honoraria today toward the Legal Defense Fund. I'd also like to give special thanks to Peter David. For the last two years, Peter has been donating all of his checks from his column in the *Comic Buyer's Guide*, an amount which now exceeds, I think, $5,000. And Peter doesn't even write the kinds of comics that are involved in obscenity cases. Special credit goes to him for that.

We have, in fact this weekend, a confrontation in Chino Hills at a store called City Comics, whose manager was charged with selling an adult comic to a minor. The buyer was seventeen years and eleven months old, gave a college ID for identification, and swore he was eighteen. The retailer took the college ID as evidence of that. The retailer was busted and has been picketed ever since by some very aggressive local groups. We're setting up a press conference. Saturday, we're having Attorney Mitch Berger from the Defense Fund, Harold Nelson, Frank Miller, and a few others who are going to confront the group via the press conference or in person. It should be pretty interesting. We'll keep you posted.

Milton Griepp: I would like to present to Denis $4,700, the amounts we collected from the group, and Capital City Distribution will be also donating $3,000 on behalf of the three participants from the company in this event for a total of $7,700.

Interview with Denis Kitchen
Capital's Strategic Alliance Partner

INTERNAL CORRESPONDENCE / 1995

From *Internal Correspondence: The Newsmagazine for Specialty Retailing* (September 1995). Industry News. Reprinted by permission.

Kitchen Sink Press was the first publisher distributed by Capital City Distribution way back in 1980. Along with underground artists like R. Crumb, Art Spiegelman, Skip Williamson, Richard Corben, William Stout, and Jay Lynch (just to name a few), KSP brought back to shelf life the renderings of such great comics innovators as Milton Caniff, Al Capp, Wally Wood, Harvey Kurtzman, Will Elder, and of course, the venerable Will Eisner.

Over the years KSP has continued to attract the finest cutting-edge and classic creators. Kitchen's current stable includes such high-profile artists and writers as Charles Bums, Mark Schultz, Alan Moore, James O'Barr, Scott McCloud, Jeff Nicholson, Larry Welz, and many others.

With all the exclusive deals going on in the ever-changing comics direct market, one publisher had to be the first to act in an independent manner, and it is not surprising that Denis Kitchen, publisher and purveyor of quality comics, was the first to sign an exclusive deal with Capital. It is with great pleasure we present this interview with Denis Kitchen.

Internal Correspondence: With all the developments in the comics industry lately, what made you decide to go exclusive with Capital City?

Denis Kitchen: Because Capital executives play the blues better? [*Laughter*]

IC: Well, obviously. But I mean besides that.

DK: This wasn't a decision that we rushed into. We studied our options for several months. We looked very carefully at what the benefits would be from either of the major distributors. We were already leaning toward Capital based on a better historical track record with Kitchen Sink products and alternatives in general.

We've always been impressed with Capital's marketing skills and organization. As some of the larger superhero publishers made a decision to go with Diamond, it only seemed more obvious to us to go to Capital. My instinct, as always, was to be a maverick from the herd. We'll get much more attention from Capital City. Some people raised an eyebrow, but I've been publishing comics for twenty-six years. I didn't just step off the turnip truck. To me it really was a no-brainer.

IC: The publishers that have aligned themselves with that other company are mainly producers of superhero comics. What is the role in tomorrow's world of superhero versus the alternative?

DK: It seems to me that we're seeing retailers evolve into those that specialize or focus entirely on that superhero genre, and we're seeing many other shops start out or evolve in another direction entirely. For them the focus is on alternative-slash-nonsuperhero comics. We sell a disproportionate number of our products in the latter shops—which are smaller in number but which we see as the real growth in this industry. Most critically, I think it's apparent that the best talent is moving into the nontraditional area, and the smart retailer will always follow the talent's direction. We're happy to see that Capital's emphasis will be on this because long term we think that will be the strongest market for us and for similar publishers.

IC: Who is the potential consumer of Kitchen Sink titles? Is it the superhero graduate or the fan of literature who has not yet discovered comics?

DK: In many cases we see teenagers who have finally gotten bored with the formulaic superheroes and who are looking for something more relevant to their changing lifestyle or intellect. So typically, Kitchen Sink would be one brand line they would graduate to. In many other cases new customers find us among the only nutritious comics in a junk food market. These generally are college-age and older consumers who tend to be better educated and more affluent. Our line reflects higher production values, different editorial content, and a generally higher retail price. But our customers are willing to pay for quality. We never have and never will compete with the cheaper superhero comics.

IC: So once readers mature and grow out of superhero comics they go on to more sophisticated comics?

DK: Absolutely. Speaking for myself, I was addicted to Marvel comics in the 1960s until I discovered *Zap*. It changed my life, and I know I'm not alone. I think that's a process that is ongoing. There are still younger and older readers discovering Crumb at the same time they're discovering a Charles Burns or a Mark Schultz or a Dan Clowes, and they'll probably never go back to their previous reading patterns. All of us hold a special sentimental value for our childhood favorites, the same way there are TV shows we loved as kids which are difficult to sit through now. But we move on. Well, most of us! [*Laughter*]

IC: Could you talk about some of the aspects of the exclusive deal, like product availability?

DK: There are some retailers who have traditionally bought backlist directly from Kitchen Sink. Under the new arrangement, Capital City will have an exclusive on all new titles and products for the first six weeks. After that date, retailers have a choice of continuing to get the backlist from Capital or, if they prefer, from Kitchen Sink. But they will only be available from Capital City or Kitchen Sink after that period of pure exclusivity.

IC: How will Capital and Kitchen work together to help retailers sell KSP product?

DK: We want to expand what is currently on Hyperlink to include absolutely everything initially. We have something like twelve or thirteen hundred backlist items. Now some of those, granted, are old and slow-moving titles, but in part it's because most customers—consumer or wholesale—don't even know they exist. I basically want to broadcast this deep, rich backlist both electronically and in some sort of directory. It may literally be a catalog. But, certainly, electronically absolutely everything will be available. I want to stress that twelve or thirteen hundred figure because I think very few retailers have any idea what choice and scarce items are still available. As far as how we are going to market it, there will be a combination of telemarketing and field reps. And then in our more prominent pages of Capital City's *Advance Comics* there will be a number of featured backlist items every month. We will also be advertising more aggressively to pull customers into stores and developing more point-of-purchase devices. Ultimately, editorial quality is the best customer lure.

IC: Could you talk about what's coming up in '96 from KSP?

DK: Well, I think every retailer knows that last summer [1994] there were basically two products that kept them alive through a very poor season, and those items were *The Crow* and *Magic: The Gathering. The Crow* was far-and-away our best seller ever, and the merchandise accompanying James O'Barr's graphic novel also did exceedingly well. We're happy to say that we've worked with James, and we'll be producing several *Crow* miniseries in 1996, and O'Barr will be creating the covers, plotting the stories, and in some cases writing the stories and being more involved in the art. That will vary from series to series, but all of them will be with his full involvement and creative control while he's also working on some other projects for us. Retailers should be aware that there will be a bigbudget sequel to *The Crow* film in the fall of '96. There will again be a tremendous amount of media attention on the property. We hope it will be as successful the second time around as it was the first time.

In addition to *The Crow*, we're working on new *Spirit* stories with top name writers and artists . . . to be announced in the near future. We'll be doing similar collaborations with *Xenozoic Tales*. In each case, Will Eisner and Mark Schultz will be heavily involved in those new team-ups. The object in the case of *The Spirit* is to fill a long-standing demand for new *Spirit* stories that Will [Eisner] will never personally fulfill because he's committed to creating his nonhero graphic novels. [Eisner does] . . . certainly remain fond of his seminal character and is looking forward to seeing how contemporary talent interprets his character. And top creators are thrilled to be involved with Eisner and *The Spirit*.

Mark Schultz has won many awards and is very popular, but his meticulous style only allows one *Xenozoic* per year. This will allow his Xenozoic world to reach a wider audience with a greater frequency, and it will not in any way affect his own ongoing storyline in *Xenozoic*, which he'll continue to do solo. So those are three already-popular properties that will be expanded and enhanced in the coming year, under the direction of the creators.

IC: Could you talk a little about the rumor of the live-action *Xenozoic* movie, the syndication of the *Cadillacs and Dinosaurs* cartoon, and the video game?

DK: *The Cadillacs and Dinosaurs* animated TV series had the misfortune of being in the time slot opposite something called *Power Rangers* and as a result was not renewed by CBS. However, the property is still actively being sought for development by a number of studios. We are at a high level of discussion with a major producer and a top screenwriter at the moment.

It's premature to reveal more, other than to say the property is hardly dormant. SEGA has already released a *Cadillacs and Dinosaurs* game on their CD-ROM format. They are updating it for their new Super SEGA format, and a book from McGrawOsborne will be released shortly as a guide to that game. Mark's work continues to be popular overseas and as a backlist item, so this remains one of our premier titles.

IC: Did you say the film under discussion was live-action or an animated feature?

DK: The discussions that are going on are for a live-action film. In the wings we have two other entities who are interested in animation, but it is Mark's preference that we first try the live-action format and hold animation in the wings.

IC: What other properties have TV or movie producers shown interest in?

DK: The single most important one is the *From Hell* development with Touchstone Pictures, which is moving along. It's at its script stage. The *Button Man* graphic novel by Arthur Ranson and John Wagner, which will be out shortly, is the subject of a movie deal about to be concluded. We are reasonably certain it will be made. It will be a relatively low budget film, in the eight- to ten-million-dollar range, filmed outside of the States but by a group we're confident will do a good job. We're also scheduling the sequel to the first *Button Man* collection for the first quarter of '96. I think the sequel is even better.

IC: Kitchen Sink has always broken new ground with new and innovative merchandise such as the Devil Girl Chocolate Bars, tin signs, and the like. Do you have anything like that currently in the works?

DK: We've been working with Michael Allred for some time to do a *Madman* metal lunchbox with production values the same as the vintage collectible boxes, and we're getting closer to a release date on that. We've been in negotiation with other top talent to create lunchboxes; I can't be more specific at this moment.

IC: Could you speak about the new imprint you're planning?

DK: We intend to create a new imprint for our adult titles called Lucky Dog for the reason any publisher creates an imprint—to distinguish a line which is marketed separately and with a somewhat different target audience than the bulk of our line, like the Eros imprint that Fantagraphics has or the Vertigo line that DC has.

IC: Will *Cherry* be under this?

DK: Yes, *Cherry* will definitely be included in that imprint along with *Melody*, *Stacia Stories*, and similar upcoming titles.

IC: What is *Carload O' Crumb*?

DK: *Carload O' Crumb*, subtitled *The Creme de la Crumb*, is a long-out-of-print collection that we will be bringing back shortly. It includes a special *Snoid* story that Crumb created specifically for that collection, front and back covers that have never appeared anywhere else, and a bibliography of Crumb backlist that's still available from various sources. This is, in part, our response to the strong demand right now for Crumb titles in general and out-of-print underground backlist. We are working with Robert on a new publication as well as spin-off merchandise he and Aline want to design, and perhaps we'll bring back other out-of-print titles of his.

IC: How about one of the founding fathers of all this? What has Will Eisner got coming out?

DK: Ironically, my oldest artist is also my most prolific artist. Having completed the *Dropsie Avenue* graphic novel, Will is hard at work on a couple of new projects. It's premature to describe them because Will thinks it's bad luck, but while fans are waiting for his next new project, we will be publishing the new *Will Eisner Sketchbook* in December. We also have a new twelve-color serigraph featuring one of his sexier femme fatales called Skinny Bones, and that will be a companion piece to the P'Gell serigraph we issued two or three years ago. We'll then produce a *Spirit* serigraph, so the Spirit will be in the middle and you can frame a triptych with the Spirit surrounded by two of his better-looking adversaries.

Since Eisner is now a member of the board of directors of Kitchen Sink Press, he's taking a more active role in the overall planning and development of the company in addition to his editorial involvement. Given his long and unique background in the comics industry, his insight is incalculable.

IC: How will your publishing vision, or will it, change over the next year or so?

DK: I don't see the new distribution developments affecting our editorial plan at all.

IC: Do the industry changes scare you?

DK: I see a lot of gnashing of teeth in the market at the moment and a lot of people unfortunately struggling, but I honestly believe that after all the dust has settled, we're going to have a much stronger and smarter market. I think that the increasing specialization of stores is only going to benefit Kitchen Sink Press and the entire market. I think the exclusive relationships are also going to prove beneficial to all levels of the industry. Like any change, there will be initial resistance and whining, and there will be some short-term inconveniences for retailers in particular. But when we're talking a year from now, I think that we will see there's actually been a change for the better. I don't buy the doomsayers who say this industry will never be the same again in the worst sense. I believe it will never be the same again in the best sense.

Everything and the Kitchen Sink, Part 2

JIM ZALESKY / 1998

From *V Mag* no. 6 (April 1998). Reprinted by permission.

Denis Kitchen: . . . The larger issue is not "underground versus main-stream" but whether the medium itself is growing and having a broader appeal beyond a small number of fans. And the jury is still out on that. In terms of actual sales the comics industry peaked in 1994 and has been in decline since then.

Jim Zalesky: Are you talking about underground-slash-alternative comics?

DK: I'm talking about the entire industry.

JZ: I read there was double digit growth in the 1990s. What was behind the drive of that growth?

DK: Unfortunately, the dark side of that growth was speculation. You may recall seeing in the newspaper that *Superman* #1 sold at auction for maybe $80,000. The point is people began to think of comic books as collectibles, as investments. While the old legitimately rare comics were selling at auctions for very high sums, contemporary comics were printed in very high quantities, and using the rule of supply and demand, no one should think that the newest issue of *Spider-Man* that maybe had a print run of 250,000 was a smart investment. You might buy that comic and put it away and think that your grandchildren might have a genuine collectible and maybe you would be right. The truth is way too many people started buying them in multiple quantities to save and expected them to turn a profit in a couple of years. People were looking to double, triple, quadruple their investment.

JZ: Were these normal collectors?

DK: They were what we call speculators.

JZ: How many would they buy?

DK: Sometimes cases full. There's about a couple hundred copies in a case. The point is that a lot of people initially did make money because there was a perception among collectors in general that these were investments. I know you might seem skeptical if you are not a collector yourself, but if you bought the premise then you might find yourself very quickly caught up in a buying and selling frenzy in order to complete your collection. If you didn't buy a new comic right away and it sold out, you had to have that missing issue to keep your collection intact. You might be willing within a month of that book's release to pay two or three times its cover price to a dealer, who would encourage the fact that this was just the way it was. It was something that was very frustrating to those of us who saw that it would ultimately taint the industry.

JZ: I remember when Spider-Man's costume turned black. Was that just a gimmick to make that issue a collectible?

DK: Absolutely. Not just to make it a collectible but to get publicity and to make you think that the issue in which the costume changed would be of particular value. So speculators would buy more than normal. If you sold an average of 250,000 of each *Spider-Man* and you announced that next month there would be a costume change, your sales would probably go up by some significant factor. The comic book industry was increasingly driven by marketing people at the publishing houses who were coming up with new gimmicks, and speculators who were trying to turn over their money in a way that had nothing to do with the true rarity of a comic book. You had certain speculators who would try to corner the market in certain books so that they could control that market. It's a crazy, crazy thing. The bubble burst in about 1994. Suddenly, people in the field realized that these were just comic books that were mass produced. They weren't blue chip stocks, they weren't gold, they had no intrinsic value, and to a large degree many collectors had been victimized by this obsession with speculation. So the industry shrank to a more normal level and we got back to selling books to people who wanted to read them. There is nothing wrong with wanting complete sets of books. The primary purpose should be to read and enjoy, not to invest. Its value should be secondary.

JZ: Did speculation affect Kitchen Sink?

DK: Not directly, but to the extent that they disillusioned a lot of young collectors in particular. They drove people out of the market who might normally have stayed and continued to buy comics and then graduated to the kind of comics we produce. I think it drove away a lot of young fans and naive fans, so that its effect can never be fully calculated. It's what l call the paperboy syndrome. If you were a fourteen-year-old paperboy who invested in comics, then, a) you enjoyed the comics but, b) you honestly believed you were making a good investment. The dealer behind the counter was encouraging that these were smart investments. Suddenly you are seventeen and you're ready to go to college but your parents really can't afford to send you. So you decide you are going to sell your comic book collection because it has to be worth three times what you paid for it because you have a price guide that tells you that. And you go back to the same guy who sold them to you, and he laughs at you and tells you he can't even give you ten cents on the dollar. That's when you realize that you have been taken.

JZ: Wow. So there are price guides that would actually say such comics were worth three times their original value?

DK: Absolutely.

JZ: Who puts out these price guides?

DK: The people who make money selling price guides. So it wasn't something that the comics industry can be proud of. On the other hand, you can't control these things and it's not unique to comics. The same thing happened with baseball cards.

JZ: What prompted you to move Kitchen Sink from Wisconsin to Northampton?

DK: Basically, it was an opportunity to merge with Kevin Eastman's Tundra Publishing and the theory was that we would combine our strengths. It was a noble experiment.

JZ: In what year did this happen?

DK: Ninety-three.

JZ: Were both companies faltering?

DK: Actually, not in 1993. That is not to say that the two companies were on top of the world, but we were both part of a general upswing in comics. There were editorial problems at Tundra and Kitchen Sink was never adequately capitalized, and so it looked like a perfect opportunity to combine our editorial strength with their capital.

JZ: What were the editorial problems?

DK: Comic books need editors as much as authors need editors and as magazines need editors. You are going to turn this article in and someone is going to edit it or at least make it fit a certain number of inches in this magazine, whether you like it or not. Editors are just part of the creative process; comics are no different. Tundra was established with the noble thought that creators know what's best. I think after two or three years Kevin Eastman concluded that it was becoming a little to anarchic, that in fact comic books do need editing and direction. Kitchen Sink had been doing that for twenty-five years at that point. We saw that that would be a value we would bring to the situation. That's it at the essence. Kevin also had his hand in a number of things, and he couldn't pay adequate attention to Tundra. It was one of a half of a dozen things that he had started which each required attention. Comic books are my sole attention.

JZ: So you were getting an influx of material and talent, and he was getting an influx of editorial know-how.

DK: In essence, we both brought things to the table. We each had our own core of talent. Kitchen Sink had people like Robert Crumb and Will Eisner, which represented a couple of the most respected artists of their respected generations. We had a title called *Xenozoic Tales* which was being developed for television. At one point it was on Saturday morning as a show called *Cadillacs and Dinosaurs*. And that was one we thought had the potential to takeoff just as the *Teenage Mutant Ninja Turtles* had taken off. The fact that it that got to Saturday morning TV was a major coup. But it had the misfortune of being in a time slot opposite *The Mighty Morphin' Power Rangers*, and as we both know, the Power Rangers blew away everybody in that time slot. Tundra, despite the fact it had little editorial direction, had still attracted some of the top talents like Alan Moore, who created a series called *From Hell*, and Scott McCloud, who created what is now a classic in the field, called *Understanding Comics*. Ultimately, we kept the best from both companies and the name Tundra was retired and Kitchen Sink became the imprint. Other partners came on board. It evolved. Now it's a different ownership, and Kevin is not a part of Kitchen Sink Press at this point.

JZ: After you merged with Tundra, there was a group of buyers who bought you and Kevin out?

DK: Yeah, in 1994 we were both not completely bought out, but the control of the company was taken by a group of investment bankers. It looked like an opportunity to grow. We had expectations that there would be more media adaptation of our comics, and the people who acquired control were alleged experts in adapting properties. They believed the comics that we had were a treasure trove that could be turned into TV shows and movies. Initially I bought the idea that it would happen, and there were some modest successes, but essentially they overestimated that opportunity and very little ended up getting developed to any serious level. The fellow who led the takeover made some major mistakes, and to make a long story short, he ended up committing suicide. The promises were unfulfilled.

JZ: Is there a point where you can go way overboard with merchandising? It's nice to make merchandise for fans—like fans of Crumb might appreciate a refrigerator magnet—but is there a fine line where it gets tacky?

DK: It's a subjective area. What you think is tacky might be different from what I think is tacky. What they had in mind is that there would be more movies and to a lesser degree TV shows made from our properties, the way *Cadillacs and Dinosaurs* made it to TV. They thought there could be more and that all you needed was one big success every other year or so. *The Crow* was one of our graphic novels that was adapted into a very successful movie in 1994. The investment bankers believed that we could hit a home run every couple of years. The truth is it's very difficult to hit a home run, and hitting home runs is rare both in baseball and in this business. They had an unrealistic expectation. They set up an office in Beverley Hills as Kitchen Sink West, and they hired a guy who was frankly kind of a drain on the company. It didn't really produce anything after a great deal of investment and wheel spinning, and it ended up with the chairman killing himself.

JZ: What about quality control of an artist's work?

DK: I told you at the beginning that one of the things that distinguished us is that artists ultimately control their work. If someone wants to make refrigerator magnets out of an artist's property, the artist has the final say. If I want to do it, I need the permission of the artist. But if the artist wants to make refrigerator magnets, then we are going to make the best refrigerator magnets we can.

JZ: So this agreement stood even under the control of the investment bankers?

DK: Yeah. It doesn't matter if I personally like them or whether in retrospect think that it was a smart thing to do. The bottom line is I wouldn't have entered into it unless the underlying premise of the company remained the same, which is that these are creator-controlled properties. The publishing company, it doesn't matter who owns it, who controls it, I still continue to run it. But that ownership had nothing to do with the contracts we had with the artists, and those contracts are guaranteed and the artists own the copyrights, and they have the final say. I've had cartoonists who had opportunities to exploit their work, and they didn't want to. There are some who would die if someone made an animated cartoon out of their properties. You have someone like Robert Crumb who could have been a millionaire by now if he wanted to be, but he generally said no to anyone who wanted to adapt his work.

JZ: A few questions about *The Crow*. What was it before the movie adaptation?

DK: At the very beginning *The Crow* was a series of comic books, which were then collected into a graphic novel. Like most properties, you sell the option and it never gets made. But in this case, it was made.

JZ: How come the second *Crow* movie wasn't as successful as the first?

DK: Well, first of all, it wasn't as good. And I think the key was Brandon Lee. The fact that he was accidentally killed on the set meant there was a tremendous amount of publicity. Even though he wasn't a big star, he had enough of a cult following. A true cult developed around him and this movie, and it's just undeniable that the movie was very profitable for Miramax. For ourselves, the number of the books that we sold had everything to do with the success of the movie. While the graphic novel had been successful for us, it became enormously successful for us after the movie. We sold about a quarter of a million copies of that graphic novel, which makes it our alltime best seller. That shouldn't surprise anyone because anything that is media-driven is bound to find more willing buyers. It's just a fact.

JZ: Were there bigger expectations for the second *Crow* movie?

DK: First of all, there was no Brandon Lee, and there were a lot of hardcore fans who wanted to dislike it no matter what. They felt there shouldn't have been a sequel because Brandon Lee was killed and they thought there should be no more *Crow*. The producer felt that the premise of *The Crow* was that a dead guy comes back to avenge justice. And that doesn't necessarily have to be the same guy. The Crow can be the embodiment of anybody. In the comics there has been a female Crow and a Black Crow. The only thing that is a constant is the premise. The truth is, we had nothing to do with making any of the movies. We made all the merchandise on the second movie, but we were promised it was going to be a great sequel. They spent more money on it, but in the final analysis they just didn't make a very good film, and after a strong opening weekend, it died. It probably deserved to die. Again, it has nothing to do with us.

JZ: Are there any future *Crow* ventures?

DK: The producer has announced there will be a *Crow* television series syndicated this fall.

JZ: Do you have any involvement with it?

DK: No, not all. We are talking to them about doing merchandise and we are continuing to do *Crow* comics, and they will benefit if it is a good TV show. I haven't seen anything yet, and I can only cross my fingers that it will be well done. See, once James O'Barr, the creator of *The Crow*, signed the contract with the movie producers, he ceased to have any meaningful creative control. The graphic novel remains his; it's his copyright. He's the sole beneficiary of all the copies sold in any language. The adaptations of it in film are owned by the producer and the studio, and they can do whatever they want, essentially. They allow James to consult, but they don't have to listen to him. That's just the way Hollywood works. Nobody really gets creative control.

JZ: Is there anything new coming out of Kitchen Sink in the near future?

DK: We just published *The R. Crumb Coffee Table Art Book*. It transcends comics. It's an art book and a coffee table book. It's lavish. It's the kind of thing I would like to do more of.

JZ: Is it selling well?

DK: As far as I can tell, yes. We are still waiting for the numbers, but in the book market you don't get them immediately. It appears initially that the sales are very strong and the reviews have been almost uniformly positive.

JZ: Can you find it at any mall bookstore?

DK: Yeah, it's everywhere.

JZ: I read in *The New York Times* that Crumb didn't like the idea of his black-and-white comics being colorized.

DK: Well, nc, he has nothing against color. He is just very particular about color. The way comics are colored these days are with computers. Crumb's old-fashioned, and there are some things that computers do that he has aesthetic problems with. It's the kind of thing where you have a picky artist. He's in some respects a Luddite. He is not personally into computers, and his intentions have to be interpreted by someone else. There were hundreds of panels and each panel had dozens of details and in a few little cases it wasn't done the way he wanted it done. By and large he's probably the only person in the world critical of it. Everyone else seems to love it. His directions had to be interpreted. If he says light blue, that is subjective; so if it was too dark, he was unhappy. He approved the proofs, that's all I can tell you. So when he talked to that *New York Times* reporter he was in a grumpy mood, that's all. Everything in the book was approved by Crumb.

JZ: You started as an underground comics artist. Do you still draw?

DK: Occasionally but not as often as I like. It's very frustrating. I am a slow artist and it's hard to find enough time. Next year is the thirtieth anniversary of the company, and I intend to do a collection of my own work that will be called *The Oddly Compelling Art of Denis Kitchen*. Most of the work is fifteen, twenty, twenty-five years old, but it is all out of print. Stuff like that, I do a page or two a year. I'll probably do a new cover and something new. We'll see, I've got a year.

JZ: Do you have any favorite cartoons or comics?

DK: I think *Ren and Stimpy* was a great animated cartoon. In newspapers I think there are fewer things that are exciting. Newspaper comics are a dying lot. I find something like *Dilbert* can be amusing. I think the drawing style is very primitive and it's typical of comics today, which is the gag-a-day format and little attention is put into the craftsmanship. The newspaper adventure strips are all but dead. In the comic book world I like the alternative comics. There is little in the mainstream comics that I find appealing. There are always exceptions. I am always eager to look. Robert Crumb is probably my single favorite cartoonist. We have work we publish by Will Eisner, who is still doing great work in his eighties. He is an example of somebody who goes back to the beginning of the comics industry in the 1930s, and he is still doing it as well as anyone. He is not as well-known as he should be. If I gave you a sample or two, I would suspect that you would like it even though you're self-described as being not into comics. But Will is somebody who has the ability to break out. What we have to do as a medium is get out of the comics fan rut and find things that appeal to people who like to read, period. What it requires is for people who read to be willing to give graphic novels a chance, and that seldom happens. The exception in recent years, where a graphic novel has been actually read by people who don't read them, is *Maus* by Art Spiegelman. Probably because he won a Pulitzer Prize and received a lot of attention. It was about the Holocaust, so it was a serious subject. A lot of people who thought it was in bad taste to do a comic book about the Holocaust picked it up and realized that it was serious work. It was sensitively done by someone whose parents were in the concentration camps. He was respectful; at the same time he was a cartoonist, and he used a medium that he personally knows how to tell a story with. That opened the eyes of a lot of people. Unfortunately, a lot of the book-buying public regarded *Maus* as a fluke and not as something that opened the door to an exciting new medium. They pick up the average comic, look at it, and put it back on the shelf, if they even bother to look at all. So graphic novel publishers and comic book publishers and creators are still ghettoized to a large degree. We are restricted to comic book shops. We may have a section in a Virgin Records or even in a Barnes & Noble, but it is not a section that people gravitate to if they are there looking for serious literature. There are a lot of things we are doing that ought to be cross-referenced in other parts of bookstores. Will Eisner does a lot of autobiographical work and it's strong. There is no reason that it couldn't be put with other autobiographical books. So if you were browsing you might pick it up, be intrigued, and buy it. And not worry that it was mostly pictures.

JZ: They seem like a good way to unwind, especially if you don't have the time to read a typical novel.

DK: Absolutely. It's not that it is not happening; it's just happening a lot slower than we expected. Frankly, ten years ago we thought we were on the verge of a major breakthrough and bookstores would start having larger displays of the material. *Publishers Weekly* and *The Library Journal* were paying a lot of attention to what we were doing.

They were urging bookstores to do this; they began reviewing the work more seriously. It is still a situation where there is great resistance by book buyers and book sellers. The status quo is hard to change. The literary world likes to think it's progressive, but in many ways it's rigid to letting us integrate the system. We are still basically given no respect. Partly, it's based on the fact that a lot of the stuff being produced deserves no respect. No one is willing to take the time to sort through and carry the best 10 percent based on reviews of whoever you want to use as a guidepost. If you owned an independent bookstore, you would be dependent on the reviews of *Publishers Weekly* or whatever else. It's impossible to read every book; you need advice. Best sellers tend to be driven by mass advertising campaigns or by the fact that the author is high profile or a celebrity. If you are not into comics, you can't tell what is pretty good from what is very good.

JZ: A section in *The New York Times Book Review* dealing with graphic novels would be helpful.

DK: It would be great, but the fact is it is not going to happen. You said you saw the review of *The R. Crumb Coffee Table Book* in *The New York Times*. That was because the format was innately respectful. It is an art book. The very same material that was in a book this big with staples in the side would not get reviewed because of its format: It is a comic book. It's as simple as that. The format has a lot to do with it, and *The New York Times* in particular has a snobbish attitude toward comics. This is the only major newspaper in America that doesn't carry comics strips. And it specifically makes a point of not carrying comics, which sends a message to everyone else. The message is that comics are not to be taken seriously. If they were, they would be in *The New York Times*. In a way, that's worked towards our advantage because comics have always been and continue to be the art of the masses, and that is nothing to be ashamed of. As Robert Crumb said recently, it's a working-class medium, and if you start taking it too seriously it gets weird.

JZ: Backing up a bit: Is it scary when investors own the majority or your stock? Do you fear being kicked out of the company you founded?

DK: Yes, it is scary. I am the founder of the company, and it is named after me. I don't fear that new investors are going to kick me out because when they are buying the company, I am part of what they are buying. It is still scary for lots of other reasons having to do with personal control, my ability to make employees feel that it doesn't threaten them, my ability to convince artists and writers that it doesn't affect them. I've been in business long enough to know that unless you start independently wealthy, at some point you realize you need more than your own wealth to grow a business. I grew it as far as I could, then I needed partners. You have to find partners that are compatible and have a shared vision. It's a crazy business. It's unconventional, unpredictable. Publishing is dangerous thing because you are producing something before you know how many people will buy it. You are gambling on your own taste. It's completely unscientific. Your best guesswork, your best projections, your years of experience can still allow you to create something that will bomb completely. There is always the sleeper that you thought would be modest and it takes off. That's part of the fun and it's part of what's scary at every level of publishing, not just comics. It's like a roller coaster ride. I'm used to the thrill of going up and down. The ride itself becomes fun, but you have to put up with the scary aspects of it. Sometimes it's the scary part that drives you; otherwise, you wouldn't get on the roller coaster.

JZ: Thanks for your time, Denis.

DK: Thank you, Jim.

Talking Heads: Denis Kitchen

JOHAN de NEEF / 1998

From *Universal Comics Magazine* no. 13 (translated from Dutch) (1998). Reprinted by permission.

Johan de Neef: You have been involved in the comic industry for about thirty years. In all those years, did you ever publish something about which you're sorry now?

Denis Kitchen: Yes, there have certainly been a few comics over the years that I regret publishing. I'd rather not mention them by name. There are also various anthologies I'd love to go back and reedit. But these represent a relatively small percentage of all the things I've published over the years, so the choices of material are not my primary regrets.

JN: In which of all the KSP publications do you take the most pride?

DK: I certainly am very proud to have published all of Will Eisner's graphic novels as well as nearly all of his classic *Spirit* material. I have also long been an admirer of the late Harvey Kurtzman and proud to have been close to him. Much of the work he and his collaborators created was originally printed poorly, so I'm extra pleased to reproduce Kurtzman's work as originally intended. Much more of his is planned. Al Capp's *Li'l Abner* was my favorite newspaper comic strip growing up. To be in the middle (volume 26) of a planned fifty-four-volume library of his complete work provides a very personal satisfaction. I'm also proud of having been connected to R. Crumb for three decades and to have published much of his best work, including the recent definitive collection, *The R. Crumb Coffee Table Art Book*.

All of these artists are recognized geniuses. So perhaps I am most proud of having published *Kings in Disguise*. This was shown to me as an outline by unknown writer James Vance in the late 1980s. It inspired me to become very involved in the project. I put Vance together with unknown artist Dan Burr and convinced "guest" artists Harvey Kurtzman, Steve Rude, Mark Schultz,

Cover of *Universal Comics Magazine* #13, art by Adam Pollina, 1998. Courtesy of Johan de Neef.

and Jack Jackson to do covers. I published six serialized comic books and the collection in the face of a comics industry that showed very little interest in historical fiction or support for anything that differed from popular genres. Ultimately, *Kings in Disguise* won many industry awards and is now regarded as something of a classic.

I'm also proud to have been involved in the "underground comix" movement from the beginning and to have been part of a cultural process that altered and opened the medium in many positive ways, both creative and economic.

JN: On June 28, 1980, you were in Rotterdam with Will Eisner. What memories do you have of that trip, and did you like the Netherlands?

DK: I liked the Netherlands and the Dutch people I met very much. One funny memory contrasts the styles of Dutch and British fans. Will Eisner and I first stopped in London for a signing at Forbidden Planet. The British fans lined up in a long and polite queue. They moved along quietly and orderly, asking Eisner only for autographs on his new "City" portfolio and other works when their tum came. When Will and I subsequently arrived at Fantastic Visions, the Rotterdam comics shop, one of the partners approached Eisner and alerted him that the Dutch fans would insist on drawings.

"I'm sorry, I don't do drawings," Eisner said firmly.

Denis Kitchen and Will Eisner, 1983.

"You don't understand, Mr. Eisner," the manager continued. "They will insist." Sure enough. When the store opened, a mob of Dutch fans descended on Eisner's table. There was no attempt at forming an orderly line. The most aggressive fans reached him first and thrust their *Spirit* comics and sketch-books at Eisner. Not only did they insist on drawings, they told him in a friendly way exactly what to draw, such as, "I want the Spirit standing next to Ebony and smiling!"

To my astonishment, Will complied. He drew all day for the Dutch fans and fulfilled every request. But at the end he quietly said, "Never again!"

Will was put into Rotterdam's finest hotel, but to save money I stayed at the home of Agnes and Peter de Raaf. Peter was a partner in Fantastic Visions and an excellent letterer. I remember that an important European bicycle race was on TV and Peter was glued to his TV set, much like an American would be during our football Superbowl or baseball World Series. I knew nothing of bicycle racing, so I asked if the Dutch team was likely to win.

"No," Peter responded.

"Then who do you hope will win?" I asked.

"Anybody but the Germans," he said gruffly.

At the start of our trip Will Eisner asked his wife Ann what he should bring back as a souvenir from our trip to England, Holland, Denmark and France. Ann thought for a moment and then said, "Bring me some Dutch chocolate."

On our last day in Rotterdam, Will asked Peter and Agnes where he could pick up some good Dutch chocolate for Ann. They looked at each other very puzzled.

"When *we* want good chocolate," they finally said, "we go to Switzerland."

JN: Marvel offered you a job as an editor once, which you didn't accept. If you would have accepted, what would the Marvel comics have been like today?

DK: Though I could easily fantasize otherwise, I don't think I would have had a significant or long-term impact. For one thing, I *did* work for Marvel for a year in 1973–1974. I was able to do things that no one did at Marvel before, such as get original art returned to artists, retain copyrights and trademarks for artists, and push the limits on language, nudity, and other taboos. But while Marvel years later permanently changed its most oppressive policies, the only impact in 1974 was that my experimental magazine *Comix Book* was killed after a few issues. My editorial and economic ideas were far too dangerous to Marvel's corporate interests, and the small successes I did have in favor of artists only caused other Marvel artists to make rebellious noises, which threatened to rock the ship.

Stan Lee *did* ask me to stay on after *Comix Book*, but I declined for various reasons, primarily a desire to return full time to my own company's revival. Also, keep in mind that even when I edited *Comix Book*, I did so from central Wisconsin, about 1,200 miles from Marvel's New York City offices. To have had any real impact on Marvel, I would have had to move to New York City, something I was unwilling to do in 1973 and would still be unwilling to do today. Soon, DC Comics will publish *Superman: The Dailies*, a comic made with the cooperation of KSP.

JN: In the past, you did the same with Batman. Whose idea was it to publish these comics and what is KSP's contribution to them?

DK: DC recognizes that Kitchen Sink Press and I have a special interest in classic newspaper strips and comics. They appreciated our care in doing research and finding the best possible source material for often very rare material. We are responsible, in both series of books, for the complete packaging of the material, including new covers by the much-underappreciated Pete Poplaski, new introductions, design and production oversight. DC is responsible for marketing the copublished books. By the way, the new *Superman* series will also include the earliest Sunday strips in color, along with a series of metal signs with a 1930s look by Poplaski.

JN: What dailies would you like to publish in the future?

DK: I would love to do the complete *Gasoline Alley* by Frank King, though I don't think such an undertaking can be done in a remotely profitable manner. Some comics historians regard *Gasoline Alley* as "the great American novel." I'd also love to publish more volumes of Cliff Sterrett's *Polly and Her Pals*, which is a personal favorite, but the first two-color books were not well received. I do intend to do additional volumes of V. T. Hamlin's *Alley Oop*, the *Secret Agent X-9* strips by Al Williamson and Archie Goodwin, and of course the ongoing *Li'l Abner* series, which may not be appreciated much in Europe because Capp's heavy use of "hillbilly" dialogue is difficult to translate. *Smoky Stover* is another possibility. And I have been urged by many fans to do Chester Gould's *Dick Tracy* correctly.

I also intend to collect all of Harvey Kurtzman's various attempts to do a daily strip in one volume. One of the sad and virtually unknown aspects of his rich career is his ongoing but futile effort to establish a daily comic strip. A good number of failed efforts, with sample strips, and often the syndicate's shortsighted rejection letters, are in his archives.

JN: Charles Burns took his *Black Hole* series to another publisher. Why did this happen and whose decision was it?

DK: Frankly I was devastated by Charles's decision, since I had personally put great deal of care and special effort into all of our Burns projects over the years and I regarded Charles as a personal friend. But Kitchen Sink Press suffered a serious financial crisis in early 1997, which lasted several months. During this period Charles became very nervous about my company's stability and made a strict business decision to take *Black Hole* to an unfriendly competitor who was very aggressively seeking it. There are no hard feelings. KSP retains the world publishing rights to the first four issues of *Black Hole*, as well as several earlier Burns comics, and I fully expect to eventually lure Charles back.

JN: Many of the KSP publications can't be found in *Overstreet Price Guide*. Does this bother you or not?

DK: It doesn't bother me on one hand because the *Overstreet Price Guide* has always been associated with traditional American comic books, primarily those superhero, adventure, and humor comics published by mainstream companies. This editorial policy was only enhanced when Steve Geppi of Diamond Comics acquired Overstreet's publications. Geppi is widely known as the biggest buyer of Golden Age and Silver Age comics, but neither he nor Bob Overstreet have any personal interest in alternative and underground comic books.

On the other hand, many collectors rely on *Overstreet* as a historical guide to which comic books exist, when they were published, and so forth. So it *is* frustrating to see that most of our comic books do not officially "exist."

Jay Kennedy is working on a new definitive "Underground Comix Price Guide," which will update collectors who bought his first edition many years back. This, when published, will fill in the many gaps in the *Overstreet Guide*. I also expect other serious collectors and researchers at some point to create a definitive guide to *all* comix and comics, perhaps on a CD-ROM or a comprehensive Web Site directory.

JN: Some while ago I heard that Steve Geppi bought himself into KSP to save KSP from a financial downfall. How much of this story is true?

DK: When KSP was struggling in early 1997, I approached Steve Geppi to be an investor. Steve is a big fan of Will Eisner and some of the more traditional titles published by KSP. As the sole owner of Diamond, the only surviving comics distributor of any impact, he had the means and the incentive to be a participant. We had serious discussions, but for many complicated reasons, it did not work out. He ultimately never invested a penny in KSP, despite rumors to the contrary. I subsequently found a great investor and partner in Fred Seibert, a producer of animated cartoons.

JN: Not everyone that works for KSP is easy to work with. Robert Crumb, for example, is someone that is impossible to approach for me. How do you deal with that?

DK: Few cartoonists approach rock star status and the demands that can come from such public adulation and out-of-control egos. It's true that many artists are difficult to work with, but in my experience many of the most talented are the easiest to deal with. Will Eisner, Mark Schultz, Dave McKean, Harvey Kurtzman, and Milton Caniff are examples of true gentlemen with quiet confidence who never let their talent go to their heads. I personally find Crumb relatively easy to work with, but I've had the advantage of knowing him since we were both quite young and of having many personal meetings and a long history of correspondence. Quirky but fierce integrity and personal privacy are big issues for Crumb, and both can put off new people who try to do business with him or who try to get to know him.

The most difficult cartoonists for me are the insecure ones. I find that I have less patience with these kinds of artists as the years go by. Thankfully I have editors who deal with the most problematical ones these days.

JN: You were drafted when you were younger. My own experiences during military service were quite good. How did you like it?

DK: My impression of the Dutch army is that it is rather liberal and unconventional. With America acting too often as the world's policeman, we don't have such a luxury. I was adamantly opposed to the Vietnam War, which was at its height when I came of draft age following college graduation in the late 1960s. Ironically, I had entered college in 1964 as an ardent patriot in ROTC, a program which trained young college men to become military officers. But the controversial war in Southeast Asia, as is well documented, created a generation which rebelled against military service. I was among them. Given the choice of running to Canada, going to prison, or accepting the draft, I dutifully chose the latter, but was sent home twenty-two days later. That is a long story best told elsewhere.

JN: Apart from being a publisher, do you have enough time for a private life and what do you do in your spare time?

DK: I don't have as much of a private life as I would like. Running Kitchen Sink takes long hours both at and away from the office. But I have found the time to get remarried. My wife Stacey and I have a one-year-old daughter [Violet] the current light of my life. (My other daughters, Sheena and Scarlet, from an earlier marriage, are in their mid-twenties.)

We live in a relative wilderness in western Massachusetts on the site of a 1750s dam and sawmill (ancient by American standards). I spend many hours on weekends building stone walls, pruning the paths running through our surrounding forest, and tending the creatures in and around our pond and stream.

I'm also a collector of original cartoon art, topical postcards, 78 rpm jukeboxes, tin cars, robots, Shmoos, aliens and flying saucer toys, and *Mona Lisa* kitsch, among many other items. So our home is in many ways a strange popular culture museum, which requires much maintenance and my wife's indulgence. When I really have spare time and the muse strikes, I am still a cartoonist. I don't know if I can last another three years, much less thirty, in such a crazy and erratic business. But if the company survives, I imagine it will evolve into something much different than it is now. I suspect that American comic books, as we now know them, will gradually atrophy and be replaced in two general ways: by more expensive graphic novels and books, and by less expensive electronic versions. Each will have an economic impact on the way artists are published, distributed, and compensated. I also expect the comic book world and the "real" book worlds to increasingly blend. Hopefully all these changes will benefit artists, fans, and the art form alike.

I personally hope that before long I can retire from the business end of comics and return to the drawing board where I can produce the comics that still rattle around in my head, as well as things of a completely different nature, like children's books and paintings.

JN: Which comics that are currently being published by other companies would you like to publish yourself?

DK: I'd love to be publishing anything by Jim Woodring, Dan Clowes, Chris Ware, or the Hernandez Brothers. I'd like to have Joe Matt's *Peepshow* back, as well as Burns's *Black Hole*. I think Evan Dorkin is the funniest man in comics. I lust after Mike Mignola's *Hellboy*. And I'd like to figure out a way to get Joost Swarte's work published in America. There are certainly others as well. I want *all* the good stuff!

JN: How do you feel about the comic industry as it is right now, and how do you expect the market to be in, say, ten years from now?

DK: I'm very concerned about the state of the comics industry right now. I've never seen such a deep and prolonged slump. Will Eisner tried to cheer me by saying that he's "seen the comics industry die four times in his career," implying that it never dies, it only goes through cycles of being sick, recovering and riding high. But it's hard to be optimistic after four or five continuous years of stagnancy and decline, despite much brilliant work being produced. As far as the future goes, I think I answered this in an earlier question. I think we'll be seeing some radical changes in format and distribution, which will allow the top talent to reach an appropriate intellectual audience. The lesser material may die, and deserves to, but will probably find some way to continue to reach the masses.

JN: If you wouldn't have become a publisher or a cartoonist, what profession would you have had?

DK: I had opportunities early on to get into advertising, but I don't think that would have lasted. I may have been attracted to film, as an editor, designer, or director. Or I could see myself being a book editor or an art director. I could easily have been a journalist (my university major), a librarian, an antique or art dealer, an archivist, or a baseball statistician. If I had inherited a lot of money, I could have been a great bum.

JN: If you ever quit your work for KSP in about a hundred years from now, will that mean the end of KSP, or do you hope that others will continue what you started?

DK: I would hope that others in the organization would carry it on. I would simply hope that the name would have a meaning that it would represent or at least aspire to publishing the best comics and artists of the past and the future and not simply evolve into a candy bar empire.

JN: When your box with reference material arrived, my neighbor received it since I was not at home when it was delivered. She saw the name Kitchen Sink and thought the box contained some kitchen utensils. Do people often draw the wrong conclusion when seeing the name Kitchen Sink?

DK: When I was located in a small town in Wisconsin and had my large company logo on the side of the building, people would periodically call or come in thinking that we were plumbers or a plumbing supply company. It didn't happen often enough to be annoying, so I simply laughed these misunderstandings off. It's the price of having an unusual name and then complicating it with a bad pun. On the other hand, having an unusual name is usually good in business—people don't forget it.

JN: In 1986 you founded the Comic Book Legal Defense Fund, of which organization you're the chairman. What does the CBLDF do, and is it still necessary for this organization to exist?

DK: The CBLDF protects the First Amendment (guaranteeing American citizens the freedom of speech and expression) within the comics industry. Unfortunately, it *is* necessary to maintain this organization because comics retailers, artists, and sometimes distributors and publishers several times a year come under attack from overzealous police officers or local district attorneys who are out to "protect" their communities from controversial comic books. The literary and film worlds long ago established their fundamental right in America to produce a wide range of material for all ages, but our industry still suffers from a common perception that we are a juvenile medium. The CBLDF hires and pays for the best legal specialists to defend those who come under attack. We have an excellent record of protecting those who are being prosecuted and in many more instances succeed by preventing small incidents from becoming larger ones.

JN: If I'm correct, you're fifty-one years old now. Do you ever think about retiring from the business?

DK: Every day.

Comix Book—A Marvel Oddity: Denis Kitchen Talks About Stan Lee's Short Strange Trip

JON B. COOKE / 2000

From *Comic Book Artist* no. 7 (February 2000). Conducted by Jon B. Cooke. Transcribed by Jon B. Knutson. Reprinted by permission.

For over twenty-five years Denis Kitchen was the publishing mogul behind Kitchen Sink Press, the lamented comic book company which transcended its underground comics origins to become a premier direct market power in the industry. While KSP has since closed its doors, Denis—a talented cartoonist in his own right—continues to be involved in the industry as a consultant, and he kindly consented to an interview during International Comic-Con: San Diego in August 1999. Denis copyedited the transcript.

Comic Book Artist: When did you first get into comics?

Denis Kitchen: As far back as I can remember. It was one of those childhood "addictions," like all of us in the field.

CBA: Were you into the Dells?

DK: I had a lot of Dells, *Superman*, *Li'l Abner*, the early horror comics—like Atlas, I really dug those—just about everything. I enjoyed *Uncle Scrooge*, *Donald Duck*, *Humbug*, and *MAD* when I could find them; it was a pretty eclectic diet. All the kids in my neighborhood collected and we traded, so all kinds of tastes would get mixed up, because you'd just swap your stack for someone else's. It was great.

CBA: When did you recognize something was happening with Marvel Comics?

DK: Well, I was at the right age, I was about fourteen or fifteen when Stan's Marvel Revolution took place. I was just starting to earn money part time, so I was buying the comics; I was there when the first *Spider-Man* and the first

X-Men hit the stands. I think I discovered *Fantastic Four* with #4. I became very hooked on these things and—I hate to admit it—I was what you would have to call a "Marvel Zombie" as a teenager. They were a genuine phenomenon back then. I continued reading and ardently collecting them through college. The smartest thing I ever did, in the 1960s, was I used to buy five copies each of those earliest Marvels, put four away and keep one to read, long before I was even aware of an active fandom. I ended up selling most—not for nearly what they're going for now, but at many, many times over what I paid for them, and they helped me start my publishing company. So, in an ironic way, Marvel helped capitalize me, and in the 1970s, they subsidized me. So they unintentionally supported underground comix.

CBA: Did you recognize [Jack] Kirby as being special?

DK: I did. I certainly admired Kirby, and [Steve] Ditko I liked a lot. Like everyone, I had some strong tastes, but I most enjoyed the Kirby–Sinnott *Fantastic Four* and the Ditko *Spider-Man*, the flagship titles.

CBA: Did you recognize the editorial voice of Stan Lee being a hip kind of thing?

DK: You know, I did, and when I self-published my first comic, *Mom's Homemade Comics* #1, in 1969, I sent copies to a handful of professionals—not thinking I'd ever get a reply back—and one of them was Stan. Well, he sent a very sweet letter back, encouraging me. That began a correspondence I never anticipated, because he was a pretty busy guy, and I was just some kid in Wisconsin; but I guess he saw a spark, and I appreciated his commentary. (That's not to say we were weekly correspondents, but we sent letters back and forth every few months.) He actually started calling me, offering me jobs, which flattered me, but at that point I was very much into the underground comix scene. I really didn't want to move to New York and work for Marvel; but I was flattered that Stan was periodically calling and writing me.

CBA: Do you remember the initial call?

DK: I can tell you it would've been in the early 1970s, probably 1971 or '72—because our deal finally happened in 1973, so it had to be the year or two preceding that.

CBA: Were you surprised Stan the Man was reaching out to you?

DK: Very surprised, but, you know, there were little things I did that he seemed to appreciate. For example, I used to change stationery all the time, as I enjoyed having a variety of letterheads. Early on, for Krupp's corporate symbol, I created an octopus, and each tentacle held a different division, and each division had its own letterhead. [Krupp was the "umbrella" company that eventually became Kitchen Sink Press.] I'd just get tired of writing letters on the same letterhead. It'd be like, "Okay, it's Tuesday, I'm going to use this one." We had a studio we called "The Cartoon Factory," and there were two artists and myself, and we did a jam drawing at the top. It was a literal cartoon assembly line (which maybe Stan related to), but at the bottom, the address read "Studio at 1530—something North Street, located above the prestigious Polly Prim Dry Cleaners," or something like that; it was very tongue in cheek. [*Laughter*] Stan told me it made him laugh out loud, and he said, "We need clever guys here, come over to Marvel and we'll put you to work." So, on one hand, it was very flattering because he'd been a childhood hero, but I really didn't relish the idea of going to New York. That was a large part of it—I just liked being where I was; and also, I didn't know how I'd fit in at Marvel. I really didn't want to write his kind of comics, I couldn't draw his kind of comics, so he saw me in an editorial role, but I didn't want to edit Marvel comics, even though I had enjoyed reading them during my formative years. The kinds of comics I wanted to do increasingly made Stan's hair stand on end, but then finally a couple of coincidences changed things.

I started Krupp-slash-Kitchen Sink in 1969. The underground comix industry—which had been burgeoning, mushrooming in size—ran into a couple of serious hurdles in 1973. First, the Supreme Court came up with a new definition of obscenity that basically threw the definition back to local communities to define. That sent a chill through all of the head shops that were the base of our distribution. These retailers were already paranoid because they were selling drug paraphernalia, and the authorities were looking for a reason to bust them. So they figured underground comix were where they were the most vulnerable. Overnight, a lot of our head shop accounts literally stopped buying underground comix, and that cut out a good part of our mainstay. (You've got to remember, this is well before the direct market.)

CBA: So it wasn't necessarily tied to declining interest in the books?

DK: Well, actually, when I said there were two things, the other thing was a glut in the underground market. They had been so successful in the late 1960s and early '70s that a lot of what I called "wannabe" publishers and artists jumped in. These were often more amateurish and more derivative guys who would just be copying Crumb, instead of being inspired to do their own work. Just like today, the problem is a lot of retailers weren't paying close attention to the product. They would carry anything and put any comix on the shelf just because they thought everything was selling; and it wasn't. The consumers began to say, "Some of this stuff is shit. and I'm not going to buy it," and it started clogging up the racks. And these retailers—who by and large were not comics fans (remember, they were primarily selling tie-dyed shirts and bongs

Denis Kitchen, "The Birth of Comix Book" from *Comix Book* #1, 1974.

and beads, so they didn't necessarily know a great underground comic from a horrible underground comic) . . . that combination put a lot of us on the ropes. We all stopped in our tracks. About that time, good ol' Stan called—I'd also just married and had at that point an infant daughter and another on the way— and suddenly his offer sounded intriguing! It also sounded like a lifesaver.

CBA: To go to New York and work at Marvel . . .

DK: It was not specific. So basically, I said, "Stan, tell me exactly what you have in mind, because maybe now circumstances are different." So he said, "Fly out here, and let's talk!" So I went out there and met with him in New York. I've even got a terrible picture somewhere with me—hair well past my shoulders—with my arm around Stan or something. Sol Brodsky was there— Sol was his production manager, as I recall. The three of us sat down at Stan's desk and he said, "I really admire the energy that's going on in underground comix, and I'd love for Marvel to capture a piece of that energy. Do you think you can put together some kind of hybrid magazine for us and bring some of that talent to Marvel?" There were a lot of reasons why much of that talent would not want to work for Marvel, but on the other hand I said, "A lot of these artists are very eager to expand their distribution and audience, and you've got distribution clout. Right now, our distribution system is in real disarray. Maybe there's enough each side can give the other and we can make it happen." So we worked up the terms, but it was conditioned on my not moving to New York. I insisted I stay in Wisconsin, and Stan said, "Well, we just don't work that way." They had the bullpen in New York, and everyone worked there, but I said, "Why spend New York rent on me when you can pay Wisconsin rent? I'll send stuff to you promptly; I'll be in constant touch with you or Sol or whoever you designate; I'll meet my deadlines. So does it matter where I am?" It was basically the equivalent of flex time, and surprisingly, he relented. If he hadn't. I would've just nixed it, even though I needed the work—I would've done something else.

CBA: Stan was very anxious to work with you?

DK: Yes, surprisingly. Honestly, I really didn't get it. I still don't completely get it. I guess he was trying to prove that he was hip—or Marvel was hip. Anyway, when he met that condition, I thought, "Wow!" And he offered me a salary of $15,000 a year—gold in 1973 compared with the pittance I was making in underground comix. It was suddenly like . . . I couldn't believe it!

CBA: Yeah, working through the mail . . .

DK: The other nice thing was I didn't have to stop my own publishing company! Basically, I moonlighted for Marvel, and I continued to do what I did before. I just didn't have to draw any money out of my company. So that's how Marvel subsidized Kitchen Sink!

CBA: Were you basically, after living expenses, pouring money back into KSP?

DK: Yeah, absolutely. Especially at that time. Because the margins were even thinner, with fewer shops willing to carry them, we had to basically work harder on our mail order business and to find other kinds of shops and book-stores to carry our books. At that point, there were just a handful of what you could call comics shops. Bud Plant was doing mail order back then, Phil Seuling had his conventions and was doing a bit of distribution—they were our first real alternatives to the head shop system. We couldn't have antici-pated how the direct market would grow and turn into thousands of shops. At the time, it was just a curiosity that a few guys could actually just mostly sell comics. I didn't see it as the next big industry trend. Getting back to Stan, what appealed to me was that Marvel, through Curtis Distribution, could get our magazine to newsstands—that was our dream. Instead of printing maybe 10,000 underground comix, getting them to our reader, through this rickety head shop distribution system, with *Comix Book* we could have a couple hun-dred thousand printed and out in front of a much wider audience. So I signed the bottom line, and we were in business.

CBA: So when did the issue arise of returning original art?

DK: At the very beginning, I tried to explain that I could not, in good faith, invite the artists I knew to work for Marvel if they had to give up the artwork and copyright and freedom they were accustomed to. And Stan kept saying, "Well, this is a hybrid. They've got to learn how to compro-mise, and we'll learn to compromise, and we just have to find a place we can compromise on."

Basically, the point we won the quickest was the original art, because I just said that was nonnegotiable. We simply would not give Marvel the art. If they insisted on it, there would be no deal. So he said, "All right, fine, fine; but we've got to own the copyright." And we just argued and argued about it. So the first compromise was they agreed that any preexisting characters—like Skip Williamson's Snappy Sammy Smoot, or any character like that—the artist would continue to own the trademark, and Marvel couldn't make any claim on any material, ancillary products, foreign or otherwise. Once I won that point, I just kept hammering away on the copyrights, and initially, as I recall, we compromised to the extent that Marvel would own the first pub-lishing rights, and they had certain limited and defined rights. It didn't make either side enthusiastic, but it was a compromise. Then, ultimately, I think I just wore Stan down, to be honest. Since this was not a typical Marvel prop-erty, Stan saw it as an experiment, and he finally in exasperation just said, "All right, fine." As soon as he said that, I immediately sent out a letter to all the artists, because I knew that would make a lot of difference to artists who would never contribute if they had to give up the copyright. So that automat-ically expanded the number of potential contributors.

CBA: Were you frank with Stan about what was happening in the marketplace, or did you just feel it was a distribution problem at that time not worth mentioning?

DK: I think I didn't want to give away too much. I didn't want to say, "Stan, my business is on the verge of collapse." I think what I said was that it was changing and we were adjusting, but distribution was the core of the problem and that they had something we needed, and vice versa, we had something he needed, which was fresh blood, fresh perspective. I think he already saw that during his career he'd seen superheroes flourish and then die and be reborn, and other genres he'd been involved in—like *Patsy Walker* and those kind of teenage comics, romance comics—he'd seen all these genres go; it was cyclical, and here was a new generation, doing these newfangled underground comix, and he wanted a piece of it. Stan wanted to be the guy who brought them in before the competition. I don't think he realized how intrinsically incompatible they were philosophically. To be honest, I don't think he read very many of them; he just spotted a trend. I kept trying to explain to him that guys like Crumb and S. Clay Wilson and so on were going to be doing things that might be shocking, and he said, "No, no, we can't be too shocking, the newsstand distributors won't carry it." He gave guidelines, and we pushed and shoved, and basically, we ended up with typical kinds of compromises; it didn't make either party happy. For example, we were allowed limited nudity—which was another first for Marvel—but we were not allowed frontal nudity (I even made fun of it on my cover); we were allowed swear words, but not the "ultimate" swear words. . . .

CBA: So what were you allowed to say?

DK: I think we could even say "fuck," but you couldn't say "motherucker." Things like that. I just remember Stan was very uncomfortable when we tried to push it too far, but he kept saying it wasn't him, it was the distributors who would never allow that sort of language. Curtis would not allow frontal nudity. We even got around frontal nudity, because in the very first issue, John Pound had a centerfold on the wall with pubic hair, but it was a centerfold, not a character. So we were always trying to figure out ways to break the rules, because part of it was that the whole generation of young cartoonists was part of this antiestablishment, revolutionary fervor, and the last thing we wanted to be told was, "You can't do something." Marvel was paying us very good money—at that time, it was one hundred dollars a page, which was well above the underground rate—and I think there were enough hungry and pragmatic cartoonists, and I was among them, to be willing to do *Comix Book*.

My feeling was the worst that could happen was we'd increase our exposure and get through this tough time in our core market; the best that could happen is it would be very successful, and a much larger audience would find us.

CBA: What was KSP's best-selling book before the crash?

DK: Well, in 1971 I published *Home Grown Funnies*, which was a perennial. We just kept reprinting it. R. Crumb did the whole thing. That cumulatively reached, I think, 180,000, but not by '73. That was just one where every year we'd reprint it once or twice, and it just kept adding up. It was hardly ever out of print.

CBA: What was the typical print run?

DK: Typical was 10,000. We never did anything less than 10,000. It depended on the artist. When Crumb did *XYZ Comics* for us, our initial printing was 50,000, and that wasn't something that came from a purchase order from Diamond. It just came from the gut. For twenty years, I picked numbers from the "gut system."

CBA: Ulcers in that gut! [*Laughter*]

DK: But you know, it was relatively easy to sell ten or twenty thousand copies of any underground comic.

CBA: What was the distributing cut?

DK: Pretty much the same: We sold at 60 percent off, we paid the creators 10 percent of cover royalty, and we lived on what was left after paying the printer and covering overhead.

CBA: Was the average cover price, fifty cents?

DK: In the beginning it was fifty cents, and there was a period when there was rampant inflation, and comics rapidly went to seventy-five cents, a buck, $1.25, etc., until they got where they are today. When we started, it cost only about a nickel to print a comic, so they could usually retail for fifty cents.

CBA: Did you get on the phone to R. Crumb and S. Clay Wilson?

DK: Yeah, Wilson was willing to contribute, but Crumb was not. Crumb had a very strong prejudice against Marvel, and I knew that—I knew he was not going to be on the list.

CBA: Was it because Marvel was the "establishment"?

DK: Exactly. I think he saw it would've been some kind of sellout, and I respected that. I didn't expect him to at least initially do anything. My feeling was if we broke enough rules and we were able to impress him with the content, he would eventually contribute something, but if he didn't that was fine. The truth is, I expected him to do stuff for Kitchen Sink Press, and I didn't count on him for *Comix Book*. To me, using Marvel terms, these were parallel universes, and the overlap was fairly minimal. I knew there were certain artists more appropriate for the Marvel product—with exceptions, the hungry, more pragmatic, less political, and those capable of doing more mainstream work. I also wanted to mix it up editorially. Again, it's hard in retrospect when I look at those magazines; it would've been done a lot differently now, but at the time, I was trying for a real mix, and I thought the feedback we got from the letters column and distributors and so forth would start to help us know what was most successful. The truth is, aside from the hardcore "hippie audience" we were reaching with our Kitchen Sink comics, I wasn't sure who would pick this up off the newsstands, and neither was Stan. That's why we called it an experiment, and a hybrid.

One of Stan's biggest concerns was how closely he'd be associated with it. He was very concerned that we'd embarrass him and Marvel, so he wanted to distance himself from *Comix Book*. At the same time, he desperately wanted to get credit if it were a trendsetter and successful. That quandary lasted right up until the moment the first issue went to press. As I was finetuning the contents page, I had basically everything in place except whether Stan was on the masthead or not, and if so what his title was. He'd already made it clear he didn't want Marvel's name on it. I think the only clue was Curtis was on the cover. So, basically, I remember on the last day, I had to get this thing in Marvel's production all pasted-up. I called him and said, "Stan, you've got to tell me: Are you the publisher, or are you off the masthead altogether?" And he said, "I'll tell you what: Why don't you list me as 'instigator,' because if you guys really embarrass me and get me in trouble, I can just wave my hand and say, 'Look, I just instigated the thing.' But if it's very successful, I can get credit and say, 'Hey, I instigated that!'" That was the ambiguous term he thought would fit both scenarios, so that's how he was listed.

CBA: The "sort of" introduction page you drew featured Stan pretty prominently, looking a lot like J. Jonah Jameson.

DK: Yes, I drew Stan as Jameson. What I wanted to make sure Marvel understood was that they were not going to be immune to satire, and I wanted to set the tone early on by kind of poking fun at Stan! So it was very tongue in cheek; it was basically my way of saying, "We kind of, sort of, sold out . . . but don't worry, we're still feisty and we're still going to be throwing punches, and no one's going to stop us, not even the hand that feeds us. So stick with us."

CBA: How do you think *Comix Book* did? Was it successful?

DK: Measured by sales, it was apparently unsuccessful. That was the official word.

CBA: How privy to sales reports were you?

DK: They did not reveal it to me. I know they printed between 200,000 and 250,000 copies of each issue, and whatever the breakeven was (which I think was somewhere in the 30 percent range), we'd obviously all hoped it would sell half the copies and be profitable based on comments Sol Brodsky made to me. I think it was selling somewhere in the 30 percent range, and it was looking to break even or not quite. So, early on, I remember saying to Stan that I wasn't an expert in the magazine field, but I knew from what I had read that a lot of magazines start out unprofitably, and they require the publisher to have some patience. I used to say to Stan, "Give me some rope on this. It doesn't look to be immediately profitable but let us flex our muscle. Give it a year, at least."

CBA: You had Skip Williamson, Howard Cruse, Kim Deitch, Justin Green, Trina Robbins—just in that first issue. And of course, you had Art Spiegelman's first version of *Maus*.

DK: *Comix Book* gave the first real national exposure to all of them, including *Maus*.

CBA: How long did the magazine last?

DK: Basically, I was working on #5 when Stan pulled the plug on it, and they had published three. My cover was on #3, the last one Marvel did. There were two in the can when he canceled it. And so I negotiated the right to publish them under the Kitchen Sink imprint. So #4 and #5 are the ones we did ourselves.

CBA: So you were just committed to using up the inventory?

DK: Well, sure. It deserved publication. What was happening at that point at Marvel was what I call the "Pandora's Box Effect." When Stan made these concessions—letting us have our art back, letting us keep copyrights and trademarks and pushing the envelope with nudity and all of these things, the other people who worked for Marvel (in the bullpen and the freelancers) all started giving him a lot of shit about it, because they resented that these newcomers had a different deal than they did. I think it was Lee Marrs who told me she was in the office and heard a lot of grousing about "How come the hippies get special considerations; what's the deal?" It seemed that Stan had to either broaden those rights to include the other artists or just stop. And that's why I still don't know exactly if *Comix Book* was killed because of sales alone, or whether the political issues raised were causing so much trouble that he just had to cut it and then say to people, "Well, look, it was just an experiment, one time only, never gonna do it again, stop asking for it, just get out of my face." But I know there were some disgruntled voices—and I'm not surprised. I'm glad, because the truth is, all of us were part of what we thought was a generation that was making change, and the comic book industry certainly, desperately, needed a change. The way artists were treated was just plain wrong. I certainly understand even today that a house-owned property like *Spider-Man*, for example, has to be work for hire, but what we were championing wasn't house-owned properties. We wanted to do creator-owned properties and autobiographies and illustrated histories—all kinds of things that various artists were excited about doing that were not part of mainstream comics. So when I heard inklings of discontent, I thought, "Great, even if the magazine fails, we let a few demons out of the box, and they'll never quite be able to put them back." The truth is, gradually, grudgingly, all these things came to pass in terms of returning original art and treating artists more fairly. Obviously, the big houses still can't give the same broad rights to creators working on company titles, but they are, for example, paying royalties based on reuse, foreign editions, all kinds of things that, when we were started *Comix Book*, were unheard of. You got a flat rate, and that was it—it didn't matter if they sold 100,000 or a million. It didn't matter if there was a German edition or a Brazilian edition; it was like, "Here's your check; go away." So, in a lot of ways, the underground comix forced economic changes in the industry, as well as obviously opening up the kinds of topics comic books tackled. They broke the formula in many ways, positive ways.

CBA: It's also interesting that *Comix Book* seems to be a precursor of some sorts—at least maybe the catalyst—for *Arcade*.

DK: Yeah, in fact, it was—in an interesting way—perceived as a too-cautious and limited experiment to a handful of artists like Spiegelman and Bill Griffith. When it started, I inadvertently forgot to send an invitation to Bill Griffith, and he was pretty miffed by that. He sent me a nasty note. He thought the snub was deliberate—it was not. Spiegelman consented to being in the first two issues, but he was not happy with some of the other contributors. For example, he detested Howard Cruse's work. He detested a squirt gun piece that Mike Baron wrote that Art thought was infantile. Art just went off on what he saw as flaws in the first issue or two, and basically, he and Bill decided they'd go to Print Mint, and they'd do their own magazine as kind of an answer to this. Ultimately, they did a great magazine series in the traditional underground format of no rules, no restrictions. As a result, they were able to get Crumb to do covers and contributions, and it was a marvelous series. In fact, I actually contributed to it myself—I made up with Bill and Art. We always got along personally. What it really boiled down to was I was in position where I, personally and professionally, had to do something pragmatic, and I was willing to do something pragmatic, weighing all the possible consequences. My wife abandoned me with two baby girls. She never came back. I was feeling desperate. I think Art and Bill saw it as some kind of betrayal to what underground comix were all about, in that you couldn't compromise. So they put out *Arcade* as a more "pure" underground comix magazine. The downside with *Arcade*, of course, was that Print Mint could not get the kind of national distribution that Marvel could, and so it ended up being distributed no differently than any other underground comic, except it was a magazine, which made it tougher to sell. Its circulation was relatively modest.

CBA: How was that distributed? To music stores?

DK: They probably tried, but no, I don't think they had much penetration there. I think it was just like the other three or four "major" underground publishers—which were Rip Off Press, Last Gasp, and Kitchen Sink, along with Print Mint—all relied initially on the head shops as the primary outlets, and then it was whatever you could find retailers willing to carrying 'em—the independent bookstores, college bookstores, used record stores . . . and then the Bud Plants, the Phil Seulings. I think they knocked themselves out and did a great magazine, but it was also not commercially successful. So you had two magazines failing for different reasons, and each having—I think—a positive impact on the medium.

CBA: I believe you said, if you could, you'd do some things differently with *Comix Book*?

DK: I think the cover choices and color could've been better. I would've lobbied hard for a color section, and I think when I saw Stan making the concessions that he did, I should've tried to get a firmer commitment for a longer rope. I think we had it yanked out from under us before we really got a feel for it. I thought *Comix Book* was building momentum, growing.

CBA: How long was it? Nine months?

DK: I think it was a little over a year. I actually worked for Marvel. I know it was 1973, '74, but I can't offhand remember the months. I think it was over a year, and even at the end, when he killed it, I think he gave me a few weeks as kind of a bonus so that I wasn't suddenly cut off. Stan was very decent to me on an economic level, and I think he honestly was trying to do a good thing in making the compromises he did. I think he just probably caught political flak from the other people in the organization who . . .

CBA: From below and above . . .

DK: Yes . . . below and above, who found it intolerable that these concessions had far-flung ramifications. Stan must've given it some thought; I think in his mind he could segregate this from Marvel Comics, that the twain would never meet, and he could somehow pull it off. He was politically naive in that regard.

CBA: *Comix Book* is quite the oddity in comics history.

DK: That it is. I'm glad you're doing this, because a lot of people, you know, the younger fans, don't have a clue this existed, that Marvel ever could or would do such a thing. Even Stan, when I occasionally see him at one of these shows, he always jokes about it in a way that gives me the impression he has fond memories of it. I think he likes the fact he gets some credit for experimenting and doing something rather unconventional. He doesn't seem to have any regrets about it, and neither do I.

CBA: Did it really help pull you through that year?

DK: Absolutely.

CBA: Were you able to get back on your feet?

DK: Yes, the timing was just about perfect. About the time Stan said, "Look, we're going to kill this," the industry was rebounding, principally because the glut I described took care of itself, because the newcomers couldn't sustain themselves. They dropped out. They were weeded out. The "Big Four," if I can call them that, were able to survive the scare, and even the Supreme Court decision which sent that chill didn't have the effect people feared it would; cops didn't start busting shops for carrying comics. Basically, the shops just got bolder again, and I think what happened is a lot of the customers missed the comics rack—you've got to remember, it was hard to find these things anywhere, so if you normally found them in the Electric Eyeball on Main Street, and you said, "Hey, where's the comics?" If enough people asked that, the retailer finally would say, "Let's bring back the comics; the cops don't seem to be hassling us about it."

CBA: Did the mail order start to pick up then?

DK: That's about the time we created what we called "Krupp Mail Order." My partner Tyler ultimately spun that off and moved to Boulder, Colorado, and kept it going for a long time. We were in geographically separate areas though still partners, and mail order proved to be integral to our survival and growth. *Comix Book* was an interesting piece of underground comix history and Marvel history. I think the changes we "instigated" would have happened inevitably, but we sped them up. I enjoyed being a saboteur, of sorts, at Marvel.

SIDEBAR: MISSIVES TO STAN THE MAN

Living far afield of Marvel's New York base, Denis Kitchen retained a correspondence with Stan Lee regarding the progress of *Comix Book*. [The article
reprinted these letters on Kitchen's stationary.]

February 13, 1975
Dear Stan—
Send your lovely secretaries out of the room for a while and tell them to hold
your calls . . . this report may take a bit of your time. But I think it's important
to fill you in on the state of the West Coast artists I've visited.

As you are probably aware from many different sources (a proliferation of
scholarly "histories," attention in *Playboy* and other top magazines, product
spin-offs, etc.), the underground cartoonists are an important development
in comics. They are too numerous and influential to ignore. And they are too
independent and irascible to submit to a traditional assembly-line role. *Comix
Book* was the first attempt to bring this talent into a regular newsstand publication. The mail I've been getting is overwhelmingly favorable, and the new
direction we have taken has been applauded by most artists. The mere fact
that we are facing a number of new imitators should prove that a market does
indeed exist, and you can take pride in being the first to crack it.

But let me break down some of the key subjects. I'll try to be succinct. If
you want to discuss any of them further, just give me a call.

DISTRIBUTION. Every artist I talked to said *Comix Book* was difficult to
find in the Bay Area. The few places that carry it sell out quickly, but it is just
not readily available. This is a particular shame because the Bay Area could be
the single best sales area in the country for this publication. It has always been
the backbone of the underground comix industry because an underground
comix publisher could sell tens of thousands of comix in his own backyard,
using the most primitive means of distributions. So by all means have your
road men check out the problems there. Artists and friends in Chicago and
Milwaukee report a similar situation: They cannot find the magazine. I talked
to a distributor in Michigan named Donahoe who said he had sold 100 percent of his shipment of *Comix Book* (some 1700 copies), but he also relayed the
story of another distributor who never even opened his boxes. He allegedly
reported a small sale and returned the rest unopened. I shudder to think
that this is happening on a large scale. It's frustrating to hear these stories,
because there is an obvious demand for the book, but [there are] widespread

reports of bad distribution. I just hope the road men you now have can educate and prod the local jobbers.

COMPETITION. There are basically four competing publications available or in the works.

Funny Papers. This may not be in direct competition because of its tabloid format but it has the advantage of being colorful; it allegedly is being promoted by a series of national radio spots; and it is allowing artists to retain the copyright to their work. The first two issues contain cameo Crumb pieces because Crumb's lawyer is one of the copublishers, and the lawyer owns some of Crumb's stuff. But Crumb himself is not involved in the publication. A couple of *Funny Papers* regulars (Trina and Ted Richards) are also *Comix Book* regulars. The last time I spoke to you, you reported that *Funny Papers* was having difficulty with its distributors . . . that an overwhelming number of the first issue were returned. But, according to the artists I spoke to, the project is still going strong and artists are being paid for work in forthcoming issues.

Comix International. As you are probably aware, Jim Warren fully intends to develop this title along the lines of *Comix Book.* Warren gave Keith Green an expense account and authorized him to put together an underground-format magazine. I can safely predict that this venture will fall flat on its face. Nearly every artist I spoke to had nothing good to say about this project. There are three primary objections to it: 1) Warren (deservedly or not) had a bad reputation among the artists; 2) Keith Green displays a reckless arrogance that offends many artists, and he has a history of being personally unreliable; 3) the artists don't like the idea of sharing a book with dozens of pages of monster type ads, which are essential to Warren's operation. Green apparently gave up hope of getting any new material, so he has begun soliciting permission for reprints, but he is running into considerable resistance here too. So I strongly suspect that Warren will be able to offer no competition to *Comix Book,* certainly not with Keith Green at the helm.

Arcade. This book has yet to appear. Its initial deadlines have already been stretched, but from the information I gathered, it will apparently be strong in content. It's also weak in terms of organization and distribution. The biggest thing going for *Arcade* is that it allows artists to retain their copyright. This has allowed them to obtain the loyalty of certain of the more militant artists, Robert Crumb has designed the front cover but has little inside. Bill Griffith and Art Spiegelman share the role of editor. They also share personality flaws: extreme arrogance and intolerance. This stance has created a cliquish atmosphere around *Arcade.* It is being published by the Print Mint, the largest of the remaining underground publishing houses, in an initial press run of 25,000.

They hope to do well enough on this small run to attract a national distributor through contact with Woody Gelman in New York. Their current rates are only fifty dollars per page, but the copyright policy has attracted some top talent.

Apple Pie. I mention this as a fourth competitor only because it is beginning to solicit work from more and more underground artists. The publisher, Dennis Lopez, is paying one hundred dollars per page, which equals the *Comix Book* rate. But he has begun to promise the artists a compromise on the copyright policy. I did not see this new policy in writing, but according to one artist (Kim Deitch), Lopez is allowing the artist to retain the copyright on his work in return for which Lopez gets exclusive use of the material for something like eighteen months and has a special option for reprints. If this is true, it sets a precedent that will attract many artists.

COPYRIGHT ISSUE. The copyright question is the most volatile issue concerning underground artists. It is, in fact, of grave concern to many older, more experienced artists as well. Like the women's liberation movement, it is a groundswell which shows no signs of abating. The artists generally concede that where house characters are involved and where traditional assembly-line techniques are used, the publisher has a valid claim to copyright. But where an artist is the sole creator (writer, penciler, inker, letterer, etc.) and sees his creation as a work of art, he sees no reason why the copyright should not be retained by him. Authors of novels retain the copyright to their creations. Comic book artists are beginning to feel the self-respect that questions the old practice. Obviously, the publisher has concerns too. As you have pointed out, profits are ultimately made in many cases only by reprinting, selling to overseas markets, etc. But some compromise must be possible. If you examine *National Lampoon*, *Funny Papers*, *Apple Pie*, existing undergrounds, and other publications in this genre, you'll see that each artist retains the copyright. As the list of publications allowing this grows, my ability to recruit top talent becomes more inhibited. I'm not saying that I cannot put together a package under the current arrangement. but Marvel will find itself in an uncompetitive situation if the current trend continues.

If all other factors are equal, I can put together the best damn comix magazine anywhere. I can recruit Crumb, Shelton, Kurtzman, anybody—you name him—if we can resolve this copyright dilemma. But I feel like I have an editorial leg-iron. Do you see the point? Can you think of an arrangement that can protect the interests of Cadence/Marvel and still give the artist ultimate control over his creation? I think some sort of compromise will need to be worked out if we are to attract the top talent. And we need to attract the top talent in order to reach the high circulation figures we both believe are possible.

You personally have a lot of respect from the artists I know. They realize that you have stuck your neck out to publish *Comix Book*. They see you as an innovator. Most grew up on the early pure—Stan Lee Marvels of a decade or so ago . . . and they see *Comix Book* as the beginning of a whole new wave. But you must also know that today's young cartoonists have an acute awareness of comic book history. They know all the stories. They see a Will Eisner who kept the rights to his work and they see a relationship between his being a great artist and his retention of copyrights. They hear about the contemporary French cartoonists who retain rights to their work—and the French publishers still flourish. And there is a whole group of underground artists who own their work and who are reluctant to compromise on this key issue. There are a good number of second-level talents who will opt for the quick money, but the best artists will produce their best work only when the proper incentive is there . . . and that will mean a book, which (if your editor does his job right) will sell better and be even more profitable for the publisher.

If I seem to dwell on this subject, it is because I was bombarded with it during my four-day visit to the coast. Excitement is in the air. New titles. Lots of activity. But I wanted to convey the general mood to you in hopes that we can continue to maintain our vanguard position in what is proving to be a large new market. I'd love to hear your attitudes and ideas along these lines sometime soon.

Best regards, Denis

[As the next Kitchen letter indicates, apparently Denis and Stan have had a phone conversation in the interim, hashing out a revised copyright policy, and Stan made a suggestion for spicier material. The following was edited for pertinence.]

February 28, 1975

Dear Stan: [N]ow that your feelings toward spicier material is clear, I will point artists in that direction more. I think you'll agree that each issue has gotten progressively better. You'll love the cover for the fifth issue, and, as I indicated earner, Richard Corben has left Warren and will be doing the sixth cover for *Comix Book* (probably a combination of the two things he draws best: monsters and women). I also have a promise from Ron Cobb for a cover. Cobb, as you may recall, is an excellent political cartoonist who appears in virtually every underground newspaper.

From the mail I'm getting, and phone calls, I can sense a growing surge in favor of the magazine. The mail I get is 95 percent favorable. I have to work hard to fit in a derogatory letter to balance the letters pages. People like Kurtzman, Eisner, [Michael] O'Donoghue, and other respected professionals have had high praise for the magazine. The recent trip I took to San Francisco indicated support from artists I previously considered unapproachable, like Gilbert Shelton. And the new copyright policy will undoubtedly result in better work from the current staff and new contributions from the top artists around. I just hope you and [then-Marvel president] Al Landau are aware of the unique position of *Comix Book*. You told me over the phone that you expect all your books.to make money right from the start. But in our very first conversations you told me you wanted a magazine with a European flavor; one that commanded respect and one that had a high growth potential . . . one that could ultimately reach the circulation of something like [*National*] *Lampoon*. I firmly believe I can meet those initial goals, but I'm also worried that I have a very short rope around my neck. You apparently are unable (or at least Cadence is unable to) give the magazine too many issues to establish itself in the black. I can understand that from the publisher's viewpoint, but I think there are other factors to consider. Lampoon was allowed to lose money for eight issues, but then it grew into one of the hottest magazines on the market, with sales in the area of 1,000,000 a month. *Comix Book* is probably one of the few books Marvel/Cadence has with the potential to reach that kind of circulation level.

In terms of sheer respect, I think you personally have received and deserve a lot of it for getting *Comix Book* off the ground. I think you will be rewarded financially as well, when the magazine establishes itself.

I realize you have far more experience in marketing magazines than I do, so I am steering future covers in the direction you've indicated: blurbs, sexy girls, and a more blatant "underground" image. I'll also intend to make greater use of text pieces to break up the cartoons and to avoid juxtaposing styles that are too similar.

I have prepared a form letter to send to contributors and potential contributors outlining the new policy on copyrights, based on our recent phone conversation. I explained that Marvel/Cadence will allow artists to retain the copyright to the work, with the clear understanding that Cadence/Marvel can reprint the stories at any future date without further compensation. I'd appreciate it if you'd send me an official note confirming that position.

Best regards. Denis, Your favorite Wisconsin editor.

[Our last missive is the form fetter sent out to *Comix Book* contributors regarding the revised copyright policy.]

March 5, 1975

Dear Artist—

Working for a large publisher like Cadence/Marvel has its advantages, such as large circulation and high page rates (paid promptly). Cadence has also altered some of its traditional policies to the benefit of *Comix Book* contributors. It now returns all original artwork to the artists, and it has ceded trademark rights to characters in *Comix Book* to the artists.

But there has been one area that has continued to disturb most artists . . . copyrights. Cadence/Marvel has been paying contributors to *Comix Book* one hundred dollars per page for new material. For that they have been buying permanent rights to the material (except trademark rights to the characters).

Those of us who have worked for the various underground presses have been accustomed to retaining the rights to our work or have been assured of receiving future residuals from the copyright owner. But large publishers of comic books have traditionally owned copyrights outright. In cases where house characters are produced by a changing lineup of writers, pencilers, inkers, letterers, etc., it is understandable that the publisher owns the material. It has also been the publishers' claim that the only way they can make a profit off their comics is by reprinting them later. But underground artists, in most cases, work on a solo basis, creating their own characters, consider their comix as Art, and feel a basic moral right to own the material.

I am happy to announce a major policy change with regard to future contributions to *Comix Book* (beginning with issue #5). Henceforth each artist will retain the copyright to his/her own work, with the understanding that Cadence/Marvel may reprint the work without further compensation. But the artists are now free to arrange their own reprints in anthologies or elsewhere. This compromise allows each side, I think, to operate with maximum flexibility and protection. It should be remembered that if we want the rates and exposure a large publisher offers, we cannot expect to also retain *total* control over our work, although that should be our ultimate goal.

Sincerely, Denis Kitchen, editor

True Confessions: The Bitter Truth About True Confections and Its Controversial Leader

GEORGE O'BRIAN / 2000

From *BusinessWest* (April 2000). Reprinted by permission.

The slogan for the Amherst-based candy bar maker True Confections is "the truth is sweet," but the truth about the company and its president, or "Grand Wazoo" as he likes to be called, Donald Todrin, is anything but. Found guilty of bank fraud in the Heritage Bank scandal and suspended from practicing law, Todrin used his financial and legal skills to pull comic book publisher Kitchen Sink Press out of the abyss. He then blended his financial "talents" and powers of persuasion to maneuver away the struggling company from its owner and reinvent it as a distributor of candy bars featuring the likenesses of Betty Boop, Scooby Doo, and Lara Croft. How Todrin arrived here is a story that seems right out of a best-selling comic book—complete with heroes and villains— only most who know him predict that story will not have a happy ending.

Donald Todrin's business card at True Confections bears a cartoon image of the president, or "Grand Wazoo" as he's called, in Superman-like garb and pose—arms crossed, red cape flowing—a true superhero, albeit one with a paunch not becoming the Man of Steel.

But superhero is most definitely not the image that comes to mind when most think of the disgraced former attorney, convicted felon, and now strug- gling candy bar distributor.

Instead of a hero, they see a comic book villain—literally, what one for- mer colleague called a "charming scoundrel." Indeed, like the villains in most comic adventures, Todrin possesses large doses of charm, wit, intelligence, and cunning, as well as a distinct lack of remorse. Said one now former employee, "If he wasn't ranting and raving all the time, he would actually be a pretty nice guy."

And villain is certainly the role most observers would say Todrin played in the demise of the Northampton company known as Kitchen Sink Press (KSP), which was started thirty years ago by industry legend Denis Kitchen and hit its peak in 1995 with nearly $5 million in sales.

However, Kitchen doesn't mince words when he says that he sketched his own demise when he hired Todrin—then running a company known as the Workout Group—as a financial consultant to save the company when it was on the brink of collapse, and kept him on, despite being warned several times that he might not want to do business with the likes of Todrin, even after Todrin started coming to work wearing an electronic ankle bracelet that was part of his sentencing to house arrest for bank fraud.

In Northampton, the language you hear often that of Todrin "stole" Kitchen Sink out from under its popular founder. But Todrin told *Business-West* that assessment doesn't jibe with the facts. While many say Todrin got Kitchen fired from the company he started, Todrin, and even Kitchen, admit that it was Kitchen that forced the company's chief investor—brought in by Todrin to provide some much-needed working capital—to choose between the two. And when forced to make a choice, that investor, Fred Seibert, president of MTV Online, chose Todrin.

THE DEMISE OF KITCHEN SINK

To hear Todrin tell the story about KSP, he was the hero in this strange saga, at least to the extent that he gave Kitchen a fresh start with his company when he was only a few days away from declaring bankruptcy—a start Todrin says Kitchen thoroughly wasted, as he's wasted other opportunities, including the well-chronicled collaboration with Teenage Mutant Ninja Turtles cocreator Kevin Eastman (that was a disaster in every sense of the word).

But while even Kitchen will grant Todrin praise for his ability to pull the company back from the brink, he has nothing but disdain for his performance after that. Kitchen and others say Todrin ruled Kitchen Sink like a tyrant—an unqualified tyrant—and, when he couldn't find a way to squeeze out a profit, he changed the name to the present True Confections, changed the product (from comics to candy), and ran and hid from creditors and dozens, perhaps hundreds of struggling artists who were owed money.

Of course, Todrin spins the tale differently, claiming that it was a lovable but bumbling Denis Kitchen, living in the past and unable to cope with the present, that prevented Kitchen Sink from having a future. He lays blame for the failure of the company squarely on Kitchen, whom he called a "dinosaur," an "idiot," and a "fabulous liar." Todrin says he tried to pay vendors and artists, but Kitchen and his brother James bled the company dry and then blamed him.

Assessing the past, as one can see, is a trifle confusing given all the players and changing company names, and also a matter of one's interpretation of the events. But the present is no mystery, say current and former True Confections employees, who say Todrin is running the company he presides over into the ground. Their accounts are replete with tales of bounced checks, unpaid creditors, repossessed copiers, canceled bank accounts, even phony invoices to fool potential investors.

They say the pertinent question now isn't whether, or how, Todrin saved or ruined Kitchen Sink, but whether he can somehow keep True Confections afloat in a sea of debt.

BusinessWest looks this month at this almost comic-like saga and about how it might end. Most observers say it will take a real superhero to save the floundering company, but others wouldn't dream of doubting Todrin's ability to survive.

One source likened him to a "mutant cockroach," adding, "you can step on him, gas him, bash him . . . and somehow he lives on."

SWEET TALKING HIS WAY

Perhaps the greatest irony in this strange tale is that at one time, Don Todrin really was a superhero to Denis Kitchen. And as far as Seibert, the former Hana-Barbera president and one of the founders of the Nickelodeon channel, is concerned, he probably still is.

Out of sheer desperation, and with an admitted lack of knowledge about both Todrin's consulting company and his reputation in the Northhampton business community, Kitchen hired him to save KSP when it was at death's door in 1997. And Todrin did just that, in the process winning himself a permanent job with Kitchen Sink and later True Confections. He did so essentially by selling himself and his abilities to Seibert, who, by all accounts, still has a world of faith in Todrin.

And that would put him in fairly exclusive company. Former employees and other sources we spoke with talked about a man who stepped over just about everyone in his way. People who know Todrin concede he has generous portions of charm and sophistication, but for the most part, they say, he uses and abuses people—and then moves on to the next unsuspecting person like a wolf looking for his next dinner.

"With just about everyone he meets, he comes on strong with the charm at the same time as he's looking for a way to bend them over so he can screw them," said Robert Grover, former sales manager for KSP who left the company in disgust. "He has a very warped sense of what business is all about."

In the final days of Kitchen Sink, Grover and other sources say, Todrin just turned his back on artists and anyone else who was owed money, while taking checks made out to the publishing company and either diverting them to the candy company or, in some cases, to his own pocket.

Todrin, again, paints a different picture. He says Kitchen and his brother James, also an officer in KSP, squandered millions of dollars put up by a succession of investors who were attracted by the romance of the comic book industry.

This is a long story, and perhaps the place to begin is at a lunch at the East Side Grill in Northampton in the spring of 1997. Nearly $2 million in debt and with seemingly no way out except bankruptcy, Denis Kitchen was willing to talk to someone, anyone, who could rescue him and the company he founded in Wisconsin in 1969.

That someone, Kitchen relayed in a lengthy piece on KSP in *Comics Journal*, an industry publication, was Todrin, the disgraced attorney who had started a company called the Workout Group to help businesses and individuals out of fiscal jams like the one Kitchen found himself in. Todrin walked into the East Side Grill wearing shorts and sneakers. Kitchen thought that was a bit odd, but he admitted later that while Todrin's attire didn't impress him, his ability to fathom KSP's problems and recommend a way out certainly did.

When asked for comment on the demise of KSP by *BusinessWest*, Kitchen regretfully declined to comment for attribution, citing a lawsuit he has pending against Todrin, one that includes a clause barring comment to the press on the final days of the company. "I have always cooperated with the press and would gladly have done so in this case; however, in the spirit of the provision in the pending settlement, I can't say anything that isn't already on the record. But I stand by everything that I've said to *Comics Journal* and hope that the facts speak for themselves."

While Kitchen and Todrin didn't meet until 1997, they had actually done some business long before. Back in the 1970s, Todrin was known as the "Rolling Papers King," and Kitchen had ordered product from Todrin's company. As a hippie rebel, Todrin spoke Kitchen's language, in more ways than one. The words he spoke that rang the most clearly with Kitchen that day in 1997 were "I can help you." And Kitchen was in dire need of help. The publishing company that he founded in the 1960s was now on the rocks. The company had experienced innumerable highs and lows, but this time it was on the brink of disaster. How it got that way is a combination of the changing attitudes about comics in America, mounting greed on the part of Kitchen and Eastman, and Kitchen's own business acumen—or lack thereof.

By the spring of 1997, the comic book industry, which had a long history of ups and downs, had hit the wall perhaps harder than ever before. Young people were plugged into video games and other forms of amusements. There was a generation of comic book loyalists still buying products, just not enough of them.

To survive and thrive in such a changing environment, companies had to change with the times and by all accounts, Kitchen was either unable or unwilling to keep up with those changes, said Todrin. Long known as a master of words and images, Kitchen apparently never had a firm grasp of numbers, a weakness that became glaring and life-threatening (as far as his business was concerned) when the bottom fell out of the comic book industry.

Todrin, of course, was all about numbers, and he impressed Kitchen with his ability to quickly assess where Kitchen Sink stood and what it would take to keep it standing. Thus, Kitchen gave Todrin $10,000 of his own money—the first installment of what amounted to a $75,000 contract—and brought him in as a financial consultant. And once in the door, Todrin never left.

DRAWING CONCLUSIONS

Kitchen's fall from the comic heights was a long plunge, one that most observers say began with his dramatic decision to hitch his wagon to Kevin Eastman and his Ninja Turtles back in 1993.

Back then, the comics industry was actually riding high, nearing its 1994 peak of $1 billion in sales, and Kitchen was presented with what seemed like the chance of a lifetime. It turned out to be a disaster.

Eastman, after all the fantastic success of the Turtles, had started his own publishing company, which he named Tundra. The venture was long on ideas but apparently short on the wherewithal to make them happen. Struggling to bring successful projects to market, not to mention profitability, Eastman turned to Kitchen, whose name was still highly respected in the industry, to form a partnership that would make the most of Eastman's ideas and money and Kitchen's ability to bring concepts to print.

Kitchen bit at the apple, moving his company from Wisconsin to offices that Eastman had rented in the Cutlery building in Northampton. In doing so, he relinquished financial control of the company—control he would never regain.

From the start, the Tundra/KSP venture was a colossal failure. Nothing went right. Artists were paid advances for work that was never done; projects were started and never finished; Eastman, by his account, invested millions of dollars in the venture, all of it wasted.

As the losses mounted, and Eastman was unable or unwilling (or both) to put more money into the venture, Eastman introduced Kitchen to some West Coast investors, known collectively as the Ocean Group, who acquired all the shares of what was now known as Kitchen Sink Enterprises for $1 million.

Led by a Hollywood player named Joel Reader, the Ocean Group had big plans to take the characters from the pages of Kitchen Sink creations, put them into movies, TV series, and other Hollywood productions, take the company public, and stand back and count the cash. Among those due to be counting were Eastman and Kitchen.

And while the company did enjoy some success with creations like *The Crow*, other ventures like *Cadillacs and Dinosaurs* eventually flopped. Eastman and Kitchen had movie options for many of their creations, but the deals never materialized.

Things continued to spiral downward. The company needed a cash infusion and got one in the form of a $1 million loan from Sterling National Bank, which was guaranteed by the Ocean Group and Kitchen.

But by early 1997, Kitchen Sink had defaulted on that loan after a continuing series of mishaps, including a *Crow* sequel that bombed miserably.

The company that had shown so much promise to so many investors was drowning in red ink. There were massive layoffs, no money coming in from the Ocean Group, and creditors, lots of them, gathered at the door. Bankruptcy was looming and Kitchen, deeply in debt himself, was desperate for a way out.

NEXT CHAPTER

Which brings us back to that lunch at the East Side Grill.

Kitchen will freely admit that while he located his business in Northampton, he was not a local. He didn't read the local newspapers and didn't know the area's players. Had he looked at the papers or done some checking into Todrin, he would have learned what most others already knew—that in June 1992, Todrin was publicly censured by the state Supreme Judicial Court for negligent and inadvertent use of a $5,000 deposit given him in August 1988 for the purchase of a nursing home. Kitchen would have also learned that Todrin had already pleaded guilty to falsifying applications for $1.4 million in loans to Heritage Bank. Less than a year after Todrin was hired by Kitchen, he was sentenced for his part in the bank scandal and ordered to spend ten months confined to his home, serve three years probation, and perform 240 hours of community service.

People tried to warn Kitchen about Todrin, but he wouldn't listen. Susan Alston, president of the Comic Book Legal Defense Fund, which works to protect artist's First Amendment rights and which was located in the same building as Kitchen Sink, saw Kitchen with Todrin and said to the former, "Do you know who that is? I hope you know what you're doing." She wasn't alone.

By painting himself as the hippie outlaw who stood up to the FBI when asked to rat out his colleagues in the Heritage saga, a role he knew Kitchen would relate to, Todrin managed to retain Kitchen's faith. And the two were rewarded when Todrin engineered a deal that would allow investors such as white knight Fred Seibert, the Kitchens, and others, to acquire the assets of Kitchen Sink in a discounted buyout from the Ocean Group.

The Ocean Group investors were going to take a bath, said Todrin, but he convinced them that the damage would be even worse if the company went into Chapter 7. So they sold their interest. And while most published reports say Seibert gained control of 70 percent of the company and the Kitchens the remaining 30 percent—a point Denis Kitchen stresses—Todrin said Kitchen never had any control of the company.

"He was an employee, it's as simple as that," stressed Todrin. "I don't know what he was smoking to convince himself he owned 30 percent of the company."

The ownership matter aside, what Kitchen had was the fresh start he so desperately needed. He was able to walk away from $2 million in debts and had a team of new investors behind him. It was a happy time, but it didn't last long.

Less than eighteen months later, after a succession of more losses, Todrin, who had now become the company's chief financial officer, and Kitchen would be at each other's throats, each convinced that the other would have to go if the venture was to survive. It was Kitchen who pressed the matter with Seibert in December of 1998. Seibert put the question to a close friend. That friend, according to the *Journal*, advised him to "pick the asshole," meaning Todrin. Thus, Kitchen was essentially fired from the company he started. Was he a victim or the instrument of his own demise? In reality, it was probably both.

What happened after Kitchen's departure is a matter of interpretation. Kitchen, in published reports, and others say Todrin ruled the company with an iron, misguided fist, gaining favor with Seibert while Kitchen was losing it. They say that Todrin eventually broke off the promising candy division of the company into a separate venture while at the same time funneling assets intended for Kitchen Sink and its vendors into his new enterprise.

Todrin, meanwhile, told *BusinessWest* that he agreed to help Kitchen because he considered Kitchen Sink "a national treasure that needed to be preserved for future generations."

The fact that the publishing company won't be around for those generations, he said, is attributable to Kitchen's poor business sense—losing, by Todrin's estimate, another $1.5 million after Kitchen Sink was given its fresh start. Todrin portrays himself as a voice of reason at a company where "no one has any ideas, no one could sell, and no one wanted to work."

Todrin said many in the comics industry, not to mention many of Kitchen's friends and associates in Northampton, have chosen to focus on Kitchen's nice guy image and not his poor business sense. As a result, Todrin says he comes across as the heavy, when all he was trying to do is make the business operate properly.

Todrin told *BusinessWest* that he was kept on by Seibert essentially to keep an eye on his investment and to keep it from being squandered. But while Todrin say it was Kitchen that forced Seibert to choose between the men when both agreed the company wasn't big enough for the two, Todrin told *Comics Journal* that he thought he had to get rid of Kitchen to save the company. "I basically had to shoot him [Kitchen] between the eyes," he told the publication. "I had to kill the Kitchen because the sink was clogged up."

He said his ideas to make the publishing arm profitable—including pleas to print a superhero book—were ignored. Todrin says he broke off the candy division legally (and with the knowledge, if not the direct consent of the Kitchens). "He's an employee—he doesn't have a say."

Todrin contends that the plan was to make the candy operation profitable and funnel that profits back into the publishing arm. The problem was, there were no profits and there still are none. "It's a tough business . . . we're still struggling, but we're going to make it."

A BITTER END

While Todrin paints himself as the voice of reason at the struggling Kitchen Sink, former colleague Grover, for one, depicts him as an abrasive dictator who alienated staff while continuing to put profits ahead of editorial principles. The condensed version of things, through the eyes of Grover and others, is that Todrin continued to alienate the KSP staff while making some bad decisions.

But while the company floundered, Kitchen lost favor and power with Seibert while Todrin accumulated generous sums of both. By Kitchen's account, Todrin became "Teflon Don," a man who successfully averted the many efforts to make the company's problem stick to him.

Grover said that while Todrin did, indeed, beef up the sales force at the company, he did little more than yell at the sales staff to make more phone calls. "He was getting paid $1,000 a week to tell us we were doing a lousy job."

But it was the final days of the publishing company's life that provide the most disagreement. When the handwriting was on the wall, the company designed a shut-down plan that included the liquidation of its assets, including a warehouse full of old Kitchen Sink and Tundra titles. The stated goal behind the liquidation was to pay artists and other vendors who were owed money. It never happened. Todrin said it was because all the money that came in went to pay for the downsizing effort itself. He told *BusinessWest* that it was his intention to pay artists, but there was no money to pay them with.

Kitchen, Grover, and others, however, recall considerable amounts of money coming in at the end—despite Todrin's repeated efforts to give the inventory away for pennies on the dollar. What happened to the money they don't know, but a popular theory is that it went into the newly formed candy company instead of going to the artists.

Grover told *BusinessWest* that it was Todrin's intent to simply ditch the debt and make a fresh start with the candy company, in much the same way that he had orchestrated Kitchen Sink's new start eighteen months earlier. In a letter to creditors, sent out in March of 1999, Todrin wrote, "There will be no further cash distribution to any trade creditors, artists, authors, or creators of any sort for any amount. There are no remaining assets to liquidate; there are only remaining bills that cannot be paid—this will be my last communication to you."

Grover, for one, said the letter was poignant and typical of Todrin's style. For starters, he said, there was still money coming in. What's more, Grover and others said Todrin managed to contrive a phony letterhead for the correspondence that made it appear as through Kitchen Sink Konfections [KSK] was still at its Pleasant Street address when, in fact, the company had moved into Todrin's Workout Group offices on Main Street. "He was just trying to hide," said one former employee, who vividly remembers Todrin frantically trying to piece together letterhead with the former address.

Meanwhile, several sources say, Todrin simply plundered a royalties check intended for one Kitchen Sink artist. When the check came in, two former employees told *BusinessWest*, Todrin loudly proclaimed to Workout Group staffers working for KSK that "we just received bonuses."

Todrin denies any wrongdoing, insisting that he was only what he said he would do—find a way to make the confections company profitable and then funnel the money back to Kitchen Sink.

BAR NONE

The publishing company, the one Kitchen invested thirty years of his life in, died, of course. What survived was its candy bar division—inspired by Kitchen Sink's success with putting its characters on candy bar wrappers—which was first named Kitchen Sink Konfections, and later named True Confections.

Todrin said that the publishing company continued to flounder, he believed that the best way to earn some kind of return on Fred Seibert's investment was to stop selling candy bars in the 2,000 comic book outlets across the country and instead try to sell them in the millions of stores that sell staples like tobacco and newspapers. The company, which has seen some success putting the likenesses of Betty Boop, Lara Croft, and others on its colorful wrappers and is closing in on deals to use Buffy the Vampire Slayer and the WWF [World Wrestling Federation], moved from Todrin's Workout Group offices located on Main Street in Northampton to the former Season's Restaurant building on Belchertown Road in Amherst late last year.

Inside that converted barn, Todrin has created an atmosphere that one former employee said was intended to be Disney World—complete with cute business cards, T-shirts, and other paraphernalia—but instead became Disney's version of hell. Former employees said the company is in complete disarray, and they left not so much because the company was in trouble, but because of the way Todrin was running it.

Indeed, when Tara Baxter left True Confections late last year, she found her stint at the company proved to be a liability when she went to apply for work. For starters, Northampton is a small town, and thus Baxter's tenure as one of the company's sales managers raised eyebrows from would-be employers. People would ask, "Why did you leave the company?" she told *Business-West*. "The reason was because my boss told me to create phony invoices to help him get money from an investor."

That investor turned out to be one Fred Slifka, president of a Boston-area company called Global Petroleum. He declined to talk to *BusinessWest*.

Todrin denies Baxter's allegation, claiming instead that she left the company on her own volition to pursue her dream of being a private investigator.

Baxter says she was compelled to resign because of the way Todrin was managing the company. She says that sometimes she would tell prospective employers the reason she left but soon learned that was a mistake. Because of Todrin's reputation, by merely working for him, she was, in the eyes of some potential employers, guilty by association. "So he didn't just make life miserable for people while they worked for him," she quipped, "he even made it tough for them after they left!"

When asked to describe life behind the scenes at KSP, KSK, and then True Confections, Baxter, Grover, and other former employees painted a picture of utter chaos, with the added anxiety of not knowing how long the doors would be kept open. This was an office where creditors would call every day looking for money; where, several times, managers would announce that people wouldn't get paid because there was no money; where people answering the phone often didn't know which company they were working for; and when there was money coming in, people were advised not to ask where it came from.

This same type of chaos continues at True Confections' new location in the former Season's Restaurant in Amherst. Employees who left the company recently, and even some still working there, say the company, burdened with two mortgages on the property (totaling $750,000 for a building valued at one-third of that amount), and other debts to creditors, is in a fight for its life.

One former employee recalled a trying week recently, when an office copier was repossessed, the company was threatened with being locked out of its warehouse in the Eastworks building in Easthampton, and employees were told they wouldn't be paid on time.

Research at the Hampshire County Registry of Deeds reveals that Todrin, who racked up some $120,000 in state and federal liens at the Workout Group for failure to pay payroll taxes, is already running up a bill with True Confections, with a lien of $4,214. All this from a man who counsels others on how to run a business.

Former employees say the company has had its accounts closed by two area banks and is barely hanging on with a third. Meanwhile, creditors large and small are banging on the door for money while the company struggles to find new vendors willing to do work for them.

While stiffing vendors isn't uncommon, especially with struggling upstart companies, sources who spoke with *BusinessWest* said Todrin made it into a science. More than that, they said, he takes some sort of perverse enjoyment out of running up bills and either not paying them or making vendors chase him to get their money. "He was very matter of fact about it," said Grover.

"If we were doing business with someone, and we owed them a lot of money, Don wouldn't concern himself with paying them. . . . He'd say, 'Eff 'em, who else can we use?'"

IN GOOD COMPANY

As for Hollywood's Fred Seibert, who did not return phone calls from *Business-West*, some wonder if he fully understands who is at the helm of his company. Opinions on Seibert vary from the sarcastic—one cynical source said, "Maybe he has an outreach program for putting convicted felons in management positions"—to the sympathetic. Indeed, another source said that if Denis Kitchen is a victim (and she conceded that this was a big if), then so too is Siebert, having invested so much in the company and having so little to show for it.

The same source, however, said that both Kitchen and Seibert paid a price for putting their faith in Todrin—the former lost his company and the latter is out hundreds of thousands of dollars—and that one can only feel so much sympathy for either.

Asked by *The Comics Journal* if there was a moral to this complicated story, Denis Kitchen, now doing publishing on a much smaller scale with a company called Kitchen and Hansen Agency, pointed the finger at the only person he could—himself. Thinking back to the day Susan Alston asked him if he knew who Don Todrin was, Kitchen has said that he knows now that he should've listened to her and the myriad others who tried to let him know who he was hitching his wagon to.

As for Todrin, he is completely without remorse, on Heritage, and especially about Kitchen Sink. Regarding the former, he told *BusinessWest* it was a case of "being in the wrong place at the wrong time." He said local prosecutors were looking for scapegoats, and he was convenient. "Did I do anything wrong? I pleaded guilty to one charge, so I guess I did," he said. "But does that have to be the one thing that people will know me for? I'm going to do other things with my life."

As for True Confections, while staff, both past and present, said the end is probably near, Todrin remains confident that the company will achieve the profitability he has long predicted. While skeptics abound, no one doubts the survival instincts of the "mutant cockroach."

Indeed, Grover confirmed for *BusinessWest* a quote he gave *Comics Journal*: "Todrin came to me once and said, 'If you're going for my throat, you better make sure you've got a grip on it.'" Sounds like a line from a comic book villain.

Spirited Allies or the Other Man Behind *The Spirit*: Denis Kitchen on Representing Will Eisner

BILL BAKER / 2001

From *Comic Book Marketplace* no. 85 (September 2001). ©2001, 2024 Gemstone Publishing. All rights reserved. Reprinted by permission.

To say that Denis Kitchen and Will Eisner have enjoyed a fairly solid and long-lived relationship is more than a bit of an understatement. For literally a generation, Kitchen served as Eisner's primary publisher and was largely responsible for the continued presence in both comic and book shops of *The Spirit* and many other new and seminal works by the Grand Master. However, when Kitchen Sink Press, the publishing house that Kitchen founded and ran for three decades, closed its doors a few years back, it signaled a change in their professional relationship. Shortly after KSP's demise, Kitchen let slip his publisher guise to assume his current role as Eisner's literary agent. Below, Kitchen talks about his new career and involvement in making sure that Eisner's work will be readily available to the next generation of comic aficionados and even maps out some of the new possibilities for Spiritcentric merchandise that have recently presented themselves.

Comic Book Marketplace: You've known Will Eisner for years and have been publishing or representing him for quite a while now, correct?

Denis Kitchen: Yes. We first met at a Phil Seuling convention in, I believe, 1971. So it's a thirty-year relationship, and during nearly all of that time I served as his primary publisher. For the last couple of years, I've been his literary agent and art agent.

CBM: I suspect that, in that capacity, you probably played a rather large role in helping set up the deal with DC for the *Will Eisner Library* and *The Spirit Archives* series.

DK: Yes. *The Spirit Archives* is a realization of one of the things I had dreamt of doing [in the past], but the investment in a project of that scope, and [printing it] in full color, was something I could never quite pull off at Kitchen Sink Press. So I'm delighted that DC is doing it, and doing it with such taste and attention to detail.

When Kitchen Sink Press collapsed, one of my first responsibilities was to find the right new home for Will. DC, I think, was an ideal fit for Will's graphic novels. Even the fact that they're a New York company, and nearly all of his work is New York based, seems fitting. At the same time, Will has always prided himself on being an independent, and he really wasn't seeking an exclusive relationship with a single company. I made it a point to place certain elements of his work at Dark Horse and at NBM, who also have a place for Will Eisner in their library. But, obviously, as his agent I have to weigh a lot of factors in making recommendations. The financial bottom line is a factor, but it's not the sole one.

CBM: How do you feel about the success of DC's *Spirit Archives*?

DK: I'm thrilled. I think even Paul Levitz and other executives at DC were somewhat surprised that it did as well as it did [out of the gate]. Because I think most of them are Will Eisner fans, and they wanted to do the books for sentimental reasons, and everyone hoped it would do well. But the fact that the series has done so well was a very pleasant surprise. As I understand it, it has actually been outselling the Batman and Superman counterparts. [*Laughter*] So that's very gratifying.

CBM: What were some of the considerations and concerns you had when you were entering and in the midst of the negotiations with DC and the other companies Will works with now?

DK: Well, some of them involved the expectations that Will has of retaining adequate control [over his work]. Working out of a small house like Kitchen Sink Press, it was very easy to accommodate Will in almost every way. A house like DC, which is part of such a large media empire, operates under very different rules. And even a well-intentioned executive, like Paul, can't always do what he'd like. He has to play by certain corporate rules. So my primary concern, and Will's concern, was that it might be difficult for Will's properties to fit into that kind of environment. But I'm happy to say that DC was able to bend and stretch some of its own rules to accommodate Will in their library, and I think everybody has been very happy with the results.

CBM: What were some of the factors that made the books you've placed with Dark Horse and NBM particularly good fits for those publishing houses?

DK: In NBM's case, they had already gotten a toehold with Will on his adaptations of literary classics. Will had agreed to place *The Last Knight*, which is his retelling of the *Don Quixote* story, with NBM just prior to my becoming his literary agent. But it seemed to me a logical fit in NBM's line. They subsequently are doing *The White Whale*, which is the *Moby Dick* adaptation, and will continue to have the inside track on similar adaptations of that type.

Dark Horse has done *Last Day in Vietnam* and done an excellent job of promoting and selling it. Michael Martens, their marketing guru, even used actual army dog tags to promote this book. It's hard to articulate, without getting into proprietary areas, why their particular offer was better, but suffice it to say that everyone's happy with Dark Horse's handling here as well. And sales have been very strong. Likewise, we thought they were best for the compilation of *Shop Talk* interviews that Will did years ago in the old *Spirit Magazine* and *Will Eisner Quarterly*. Diana Schutz at Dark Horse has just finished reediting and, with her staff, redesigning a dozen or so of these interviews that Will had with leading comics creators, and we're delighted with the collection. As a result, Dark Horse will be tackling a similar project, called *One-on-One*. I'll leave it to Dark Horse to reveal the surprise collaborator. But suffice to say there will be an ongoing relationship with all three of these companies. There is also possibly a project involving Jon Cooke at TwoMorrows. I think it's in the best interest of Will Eisner and the industry to spread the work out a bit.

CBM: Are there any other benefits, aside from the obvious one of making sure that his work is available to the reading public, to the new relationships that you've helped Will develop with these companies?

DK: For the first time there's been a greater emphasis on merchandising. For example, in the first sixty years of the Spirit's existence, there were no three-dimensional representations [of the character]. Suddenly, in the course of one year, there's a Spirit statue from DC, a Spirit action figure from Graffiti, and soon there'll be a Spirit statue in Dark Horse's Famous [Cartoon] Characters series. So that's a direct offshoot of paying attention to merchandising. There's also a Spirit lunchbox, T-shirts and other objects in the works. Hopefully, [these are] just the tip of the iceberg.

CBM: I suspect I know the answer, but what's the best thing about your job of representing Will?

DK: [*General laughter*] Lots of long conversations. One of the benefits of being a publisher in general, if you do it right, is you get to develop relationships with people you respect and, more often than not, people you like. And to have spent thirty years talking with Will and working with Will, certainly

[has] been a special perk that comes with the job. I wouldn't want to trade that for anything. You can't assign any monetary value to something like that. It's one of those wonderful intangibles of being a publisher or an agent. It's, in fact, too easy to take for granted, sometimes. But I'm constantly hearing anecdotes or getting insights that I wish other people had a chance to share. I'm kicking myself for not having taken more careful notes over the years, because I can't remember everything. Only now am I starting to really record these things in detail, because I don't want to forget any of them.

Five Minutes with Denis Kitchen

BILL BAKER / 2001

From *Wizardworld.com* (August 10, 2001). Reprinted by permission.

WizardWorld.com: You're starting up publishing again. Why?

Denis Kitchen: [*Laughter*] Well, I guess it's very difficult to keep a foot totally out of the tar baby, Bill. I should say at the beginning, Bill, that I do not intend in any way to get back on the level of a Kitchen Sink Press. This is going to be a relatively modest effort, maybe two, three, four books a year. Unless I get another foot in the tar baby, I intend to create other books in conjunction with other publishers, and there are negotiations going on with a couple of companies now which may lead to an ongoing imprint or copublishing arrangement. But in the meantime, *The Grasshopper and the Ant* represents the first post–Kitchen Sink book I'm doing, and hopefully there will be similar books focusing on what I like to call classic comics, or comics that are deserving of revival.

WW: So is that an indication of what the goals of the new company are, both in the short and long term?

DK: In the post-Kitchen Sink era here, I've really had to reinvent myself, and think about what I really want to do. And publishing's in the blood after thirty years. And I now understand what Will Eisner did when he insisted on publishing two books himself. Even when Kitchen Sink Press did virtually every one of his books, he continued—under his own imprint, Poorhouse Press—to do *Comics and Sequential Art* and *Graphic Storytelling*. And I used to have these mock arguments with him where I'd say, "Come on, Will! Quit holding out, give me those last books!" And he'd say, "No, no. I need to do something myself, just to keep a foot in publishing." And I'd go, "I don't get it, Will, why do you even want to bother with it?" But now I do get it. [*Laughter*] Call it a sickness or whatever you will, but if you do it, you never quite want to give it up. At the same time, I'm not eager to get back to a situation

Denis Kitchen, 2002. Kitchen celebrates his reinvention after the end of KSP with a self-portrait depicting the four foci of his new businesses.

where I have thirty-five employees and the kind of headaches that come with having a company of some size. Not that Kitchen Sink was ever a large company, but it was just large enough to have headaches that went along with the pleasures. What I'm trying to do now is to be smart enough to retain the pleasures and eliminate most of the headaches. [*General laughter*]

WW: Will you be adding new artists to your list, or will you be basically sticking with those people who are your current clients?

DK: The first two books will be by Harvey Kurtzman, starting with *The Grasshopper and the Ant*. The follow-up is tentatively called *The Unsyndicated Kurtzman*. It details and illustrates Harvey's futile efforts over several decades to sell a daily strip to the various newspaper syndicates. Genius or not, he was rejected everywhere! Beyond that it's hard to predict. I have the luxury of having access to all of Harvey's archives, and there are so many wonderful things in there that I'm afraid will never see the light of day. I cannot in good conscience go to a commercial publisher and say, "Gosh, this really deserves to be done, but I can't assure you [that] you'll make a profit on it." The way the market is today, as I'm sure you and most of your readers are aware, it's not an easy place to make money at all, and so most publishers can't afford to indulge themselves in books that are at best are gonna . . . break even [sales-wise]. By doing it myself, with a very low overhead situation, I may be able to make these books modestly profitable. But the point is to just get them out there, because I think there may be a few thousand people who would love to see them, but they're not gonna be obvious best sellers. Maybe we'll be fooled, and maybe *The Grasshopper and the Ant* or one of these other books will have a certain kind of a breakout if it gets some review attention in national publications. I don't rule that out. The material is certainly deserving [of that kind of attention]. I think *Grasshopper* is an exquisite little story that ought to be appreciated by many, many thousands of people outside of the comics field. In fact, to be perfectly honest with you, there may not be that many people in the comic world who embrace it. It may be that it does better in independent bookstores. But the only way to find out is to get it out there.

If I'm approached by other people creators who have work they want to do, a modest little chapbook or something that maybe their regular publisher turned down and they think I [may be] interested, who knows where it will lead? I don't want to describe define any boundaries. There are easily two or three dozen artists that I've gotten close with over the years and respect greatly who may have appropriate projects. And I may inevitably have to take on a staffer or two. We'll see. At the moment, I'm hoping that everything can be done by outsourcing. Beyond that, it's hard to predict, Bill, because I'm sincere when I say I don't want to become a full-time publisher again. But it's simply one hat I want to continue wearing. Just as, for example, I came out of retirement and did a comic story for Dark Horse a couple months back that will be appearing this summer, called "My Five Minutes with God" (for the *Dark Horse Maverick 2001* anthology). I enjoy wearing that cartoonist hat. I have the luxury now of kind of doing whatever I want, and it's kind of refreshing.

WW: Is that comic story a sign of new things to come? Is there a chance that we'll be seeing some more comics from you in the future?

DK: Well, I hope so. I'm afraid I'm a very slow cartoonist. I realized after I did the *Maverick* story for Diana Schutz that if I divided the hours [I worked on it] into the page rate that I probably wasn't making minimum wage. [*General laughter*] But that wasn't the point of doing it. I think I'd like to periodically do stories, and covers, and short things for the same reason I guess I'm doing *The Grasshopper and the Ant*—which is the love of doing it—and If I'm going to be taking that skill into the commercial arena, it will probably be the children's book field, and very few comics fans will probably be paying attention. Because the comic book field, as you probably know, rewards people who are prolific, and it's very difficult to make a living in the comic book world if you're slow. It's a simple economic fact. Even someone as marvelous as Mark Schultz has not been able to resurrect *Xenozoic Tales* because no publisher at this point in time wants to do an annual comic book. The numbers just don't work for anybody. [*Laughter*] Not to really compare myself to Mark Schultz here. I'm just saying it's not a practical matter for me to really pretend to be a cartoonist who regularly contributes to anything. But I hope I'll have a guest story here and there in the coming years.

WW: Well, you've also launched a website—www.deniskitchen.com—of your own. Is this an indication of where you'll be putting some of your efforts in times to come, and how do you expect to use the web in the future?

DK: Well, this is yet another hat. The website fulfills several functions. One is to promote my agency, and even the agency is divided into two parts. I represent certain clients as a literary agent, and I also represent certain clients for the sale of original artwork, such as Will Eisner and the Kurtzman estate and others. So the site is a virtual gallery for seeing what is available, and if you're interested in licensing work from any of the clients, then the website is also a natural conduit.

But the site also has a section which I call "Steve Krupp's Curio Shoppe," which is essentially a retail store. And, in part, it stems from the successful lawsuit I had against my former corporation, Kitchen Sink Press (Disappearing, Inc.). I won several pallets of merchandise in lieu of cash, and so in part this is a way of selling that material, as well as various other esoteric objects and items that have accumulated in the attic for years. My wife, Stacey, who designed the site, is essentially the retailer here, and it's more one of her hats than mine. It's also a chance to revive Steve Krupp, who is the closest thing I had to a regular character over the years. He was kind of my capitalist alter ego. And since, ironically, I don't own the name Kitchen Sink Press anymore, at least Steve Krupp is a character I can continue to exploit. I've always been kind of fond of the guy, so this gives him something to do as well.

WW: Any last thoughts on what you'll be doing in the future and the comics industry's future in general?

DK: Well, given the crazy state of the comics industry right now, I don't have a clue other than I still love the medium, and I hope that—to some degree—I'll continue to be connected to it. I suspect that I'll be going in directions that will take me away from the comics field, but as Al Pacino would say, "It keeps pulling me back in." [*Laughter*] And that's fine. I just can't predict to what degree I will be involved. I'd love to have an imprint at a good publishing house and focus on the creative side of publishing without being caught up totally in the business side of it. And if I can keep drawing and editing and freelancing enough to satisfy that desire, that would be ideal. But I suspect that less than half my time will be involved in the comics field. Beyond that, I think it's dangerous to predict. [*Laughter*] As for predicting the future of the medium, that's a fool's game. But I'm certainly encouraged by the continuing inroads of graphic novels into mainstream bookstores.

The Compelling Milwaukee Art of Denis Kitchen

TEA KRULOS / 2003

From *River Würst Comics* no. 2 (2003). Reprinted by permission.

People may be surprised to know that one of underground publishing's most important figures started here in Milwaukee in the late 1960s. To try and chronicle all of Denis Kitchen's work is an exhausting task. Kitchen ran an empire called Krupp Comic Works, Inc. The most significant factor was Kitchen Sink Press, which published a variety of underground and classic artists for thirty years. He started with his own comic, *Mom's Homemade Comics*, as well as comics by R. Crumb, Art Spiegelman, Jay Lynch, Charles Bums, and other underground legends, as well as collections of classic strips such as Al Capp (*Li'l Abner*), George Herriman (*Krazy Kat*), Bob Kane (*Batman*), and others too numerous to mention. Kitchen Sink won so many Eisner and Harvey awards, it's not even funny. Kitchen helped create the *Bugle American*, later simply known as the *Bugle*, a Wisconsin alternative newspaper that ran for seven years.

As an artist Kitchen's comics and illustrations have appeared in such titles as *Blab, Bijou Funnies, Consumer Comix, Dope Comix, Nard n' Pat*, and the *Milwaukee Journal*'s "Insight" magazine, and many more. He also founded and serves as president of the Comic Book Legal Defense Fund, a nonprofit corporation dedicated to defending the industry's First Amendment rights. Since 2000 he has also chaired the Harvey Awards Committee, which oversees the annual industry awards program. In 2002 he became a member of the board of advisers of MoCCA (Museum of Comic and Cartoon Art) in New York City.

More recently Kitchen now runs Denis Kitchen Publishing, which prints a smaller amount of books, including recent titles by Harvey Kurtzman and R. Crumb. More information and art can be seen at www.deniskitchen.com. I recently interviewed Denis Kitchen about his early days in Milwaukee, and he sent some art from this era to be reprinted in *River Würst Comics* . . . (interview by Tea Krulos).

Cover of *River Würst Comics* #2, art by Chris Millar. Courtesy of Tea Krulos.

Tea Krulos: I'm interested to hear about the early days of Krupp Comic Works, Inc., and Kitchen Sink Press. What was the scene like then?

Denis Kitchen: If you mean the "hip" scene, everyone knows that San Francisco was Mecca. But with regard to the underground comix subculture, there were actually two centers: San Francisco and Milwaukee. That will surprise a lot of people. But I was able to find quite a few really good cartoonists in Milwaukee, and they became a part of Krupp-slash-Kitchen Sink's core. Krupp was the "umbrella" organization (the corporation). Kitchen Sink Press was the imprint and eventually the sole entity. But for a while Krupp had a head shop (Strickly Uppa Crust), a Krupp mail order catalog, a national distribution arm, a commercial art studio (the Cartoon Factory), and, of course, the comic book company, which was always at the heart. As a joke on our own capitalistic tendencies, I created an octopus as the corporate symbol, with a division in each tentacle. At the very same time I founded Krupp, I cofounded the *Bugle* (originally the *Bugle-American*) with several fellow UWM journalism graduates. That ended up being kind of a conflict. I was torn between two different organizations, devoting most of every waking moment to one or the other for the first year or two. But it was an exciting time. There was a palpable sense of revolution in the air. Nobody was making any money, but we were intensely creative and felt integrally part of a larger cultural movement. It seems fairly idealistic in retrospect, but it was, for a while anyway, an amazing period. A quick example: For the first two years of Kitchen Sink, we sent packages all over the country to distributors and head shops on "open terms." We never asked for credit references. If you called and said you were "the Electric Eyeball" in Minneapolis, we shipped the order on thirty-day terms. Yet no one ripped us off for the first two years. It would be unimaginable now to conduct business that way. But in the early 1970s it worked.

TK: What sort of contributors did you have? Were they local artists?

DK: I discovered several great cartoonists right in the city: Jim Mitchell, Don Glassford, Bruce Walthers, Wendel Pugh, and I each initially got together every week to do a strip for the *Bugle*, which the Krupp Syndicate (another tentacle) sent to newspapers. All five also did *Bugle* covers, though I think I did the most over its seven-year run. A bit later Peter Loft, another Milwaukeean, joined the group. Pete Poplaski moved to the city from Green Bay, and Dan Burr became part of the scene. Eight really good alternative cartoonists in one city is amazing. There were only two or three in Chicago, for example, and anyone good in New York City had migrated to the Bay Area, so Milwaukee really was an unusual comix oasis. On top of that local core, artists from all over contributed. Robert Crumb regularly visited Milwaukee and gave us a high percentage of his work over the years. I knew we were doing something right when several San Francisco cartoonists began sending their work to us!

TK: What was your first publication?

DK: *Mom's Homemade Comics* #1, subtitled "Straight from the Kitchen to You." It was done entirely by me—the last time I was able to do a solo book. It retailed for forty-nine cents, with "prices slightly higher in foreign countries and South Milwaukee." It came out on July 4, 1969. I remember hawking them at the Great Schlitz Circus Parade with my brother Jim and another friend or two. Cops stopped us and said, "Where's your seller's permit?" I said, "The press is free, man," and they surprisingly walked away. I subsequently went to every head shop and bookstore on the east side or downtown and placed copies on consignment. That was the primitive genesis of what became Krupp Distribution.

TK: How well did underground comics go in Milwaukee?

DK: Amazingly well. I sold 3,000 copies of *Mom's* #1 in Milwaukee alone. A lot of underground comix sold 10,000 copies in the entire country.

TK: What was the exact address of Strickly Uppa Crust?

DK: Strickly Uppa Crust, our head shop, was at 1234 East Brady Street It had the usual head shop fare but also boasted the "largest selection of comics in the state." There was an entire wall of underground comix, both Kitchen Sink's and all the West Coast titles. We also had a couple token spin racks of "mainstream" Marvel and DC comics. Kareem Abdul Jabbar was a regular customer, and various celebrities visiting the city would drop in. John Mayall, the British bluesman, was the first that I recall. After that the clerks became a bit jaded.

TK: What area of Milwaukee did you operate out of, and what was it like at the time?

DK: I started out of a second-floor apartment on the corner of Frederick and Webster on the east side. For the first year or so I had to pick up comix from our Port Washington printer in my 1954 Cadillac hearse, park in front of the apartment, then carry each box of comix to the back door, walk up two flights of steps to my attic, and start over again. Hard to believe in retrospect. The apartment served as the warehouse, shipping department, and editorial headquarters. Jim Mitchell and Don Glassford used to meet with me for a day each week to pack orders and then shlep the boxes down the steps and to the post office. It was a prayer answered when we finally got a real combination office and warehouse on North Avenue, a couple blocks from Farwell. I think there's a McDonald's there now. One night, working late, Poplaski, Loft and I took a break at the late, great Oriental Drugstore, returning to the Krupp office around midnight. I must have been fumbling with the lock when two of Milwaukee's finest descended and assumed three hippies were breaking into the place. I had to show them my business card with the address. They seemed genuinely astonished that longhairs actually held jobs and worked long hours.

TK: Was there a lot of collaboration with the music scene?

DK: I knew some of the local bands pretty well and frequently did posters and flyers for them. The early ones I recall most fondly were the Velvet Whip, Furry Quim Slash, and the Baroques. The Shags were also big then. Sigmund Snopek III was a friend, as was Paul Cebar. I did the psychedelic album cover for Jim Spencer's *Major Arcana* album, which Japanese and European collectors now pay $200 and $300 a pop for. I was invited to do a Violent Femmes album cover, but that one somehow fell through. Early on I participated in some concerts, sharing poster billing, as a body painter. I'd paint butterflies and various things on girls' foreheads, arms, and thighs (those were miniskirt days) in Day-Glo tempera paint, then they'd gyrate under the black lights while the bands droned on. I sure miss those days.

TK: Did you work with a lot of flyer artists? Was there an exciting Milwaukee music scene at that time?

DK: I created a lot of original flyers, but in those days no one called themselves "flyer artists." I was pretty versatile in that I'd do flyers and posters for acid bands and hard rock bands while at the same time I'd be doing illustrations for *The Milwaukee Journal Sunday Magazine* or posters for Schlitz. The latter paid the bills. But doing underground comic books was always the central focus. I was far too busy to have the luxury of hanging out with musicians all that much. I think they'd say the same thing. We'd see each other at bars or parties, but I wasn't attending a lot of concerts. Kitchen Sink would often hire live music for its parties. It seemed to me that it was an exciting music scene, but I didn't have the music perspective that I had in the comics field.

TK: Why did you leave Milwaukee?

DK: In late 1972 my first wife Irene was in the hospital and begged me to leave the city. She longed to be part of the back-to-the-land movement. I was quite content in Milwaukee. As a matter of fact, I very much loved Milwaukee. But while she was ill, I promised her we'd find a place in the country. We ended up in early 1973 in Princeton, Wisconsin, where two fellow cofounders of the *Bugle*, Mike and Judy Jacobi, already had a farmhouse. The sublime irony is that one year after the move to the country, Irene abandoned me and our two infant daughters, and she went back to Milwaukee. I ended up being the back-to-the-lander! But it turned out to be a good practical move for the business. I was eventually able to convert a large barn into an office complex, kept overhead minimal, built a warehouse, and was able to focus on the comics business without the distractions of the city. The truth is, I hosted and attended a lot of parties in Milwaukee in the early 1970s. Great memories, but it was not the most productive situation.

TK: Why did you leave Wisconsin? Was it because of the crappy weather?

DK: Ha! New England winters aren't much better! Actually, I decided in 1993 to merge Kitchen Sink Press with Tundra Publishing in Northampton, Massachusetts. The new company could just as easily have been in Wisconsin, but I had divorced a second time and could not meet anyone in Princeton, a tiny town one hundred miles north of Milwaukee, and I realized I was culturally starved. Northampton is a smaller version of Madison, which I was quite enchanted with. So I decided to do something radical and uproot. It was the right time. Prior to that I could have been on Wisconsin's tourist board, I was so loyal to the state. But I needed a change at that point and don't regret it.

Poster for a 1976 University of Wisconsin–Oshkosh exhibit of Kitchen's art and collection that included a concert of Crumb's music, a film festival, and a panel with Kitchen, Kurtzman, Messick, and Sanders.

I met my third and last wife Stacey after the move, and we have a delightful five-year-old daughter who is, I might add, as astonishing little cartoonist.

TK: This question is about the Comic Book Legal Defense Fund. What sort of cases have you dealt with? Any notorious ones?

DK: I founded the CBLDF In 1986 after one of Kitchen Sink's comics, *Omaha the Cat Dancer*, was part of a bust in a suburban Chicago comics shop. A self-admitted religious cop found fourteen or so comics offensive, including *Heavy Metal* and a "Satanic" Wonder Woman poster, and arrested the manager, who was later convicted of selling obscenity. I was genuinely upset by the incident and rallied artists to create a fundraising portfolio for a defense fund. About $20,000 was raised, and we were able to reverse the conviction. At that point I made the CBLDF a permanent nonprofit organization. It now raises about $200,000 annually to protect cartoonists' and retailers' First Amendment rights. Our most notorious case so far? It's probably Mike Diana. His is also one of the very few we've lost. Diana was convicted of drawing obscene and blasphemous fanzine comics, which he sold in tiny quantities only to other consenting adults by mail. He was unfortunately living In Gainesville, Florida, when there was a serial killer at large, and he came under suspicion. He was innocent of any connection to the murder spree, but police discovered his crude comics, and he was arrested and convicted of producing obscenity. Part of the judge's unprecedented sentence required that Diana not draw any comics, even in the privacy of his own home! Police were allowed to spot check his apartment for compliance. Astonishingly, the US Supreme Court declined to review this case, the only one to my knowledge in which an artist was forbidden to draw.

TK: Did you run into any censorship issues in Milwaukee? We're sort of famous for that (such as George Carlin being arrested at Summerfest).

DK: I remember the Carlin Incident well. But no, I never had any legal problems whatsoever in Milwaukee.

TK: Do you think computer technology has helped or hurt the comic industry, in particular underground comics?

DK: I believe the best comics are art and, to me, the original inked drawing has an inherent value aside from its communicative value. No computer will ever be able to replace a sable brush on illustration board, nor can any screen provide the aesthetic satisfaction of creating or seeing a hand-drawn original. That said, I certainly believe computers and the internet are an indisputable boon to the medium in that distribution to an audience is much easier, much cheaper, and more international. The problem remains how to make any kind of living doing digital comics. No one yet has solved that challenge, but I suspect it's not far away.

TK: Do you still visit Milwaukee? When was the last time you were here, and what were your impressions?

DK: My mother, a couple siblings, and some close friends live in Milwaukee, so I get back at least a couple times a year, last around Thanksgiving. What I miss most is walking into east side bars and recognizing faces. Every time I come back, I see changes for both better and worse. The closing of the Oriental Drugstore was criminal. I was surprised to see Ma Fisher's on Farwell go from a hole in the wall to a large restaurant a year or two back. I was impressed with the dramatic architectural addition to the art museum. As an old Braves and Brewers fan, I was pleased that the city built a domed stadium, even if a leaky one. But it's no fun reading the box scores out east and not seeing a winning team in the entire decade I've been gone. Truth is, I've lost interest in baseball, like many. I still like Milwaukee, but it's like seeing an old girlfriend. The original spark is no longer there.

TK: A collection of your art is in the design stage. When will it be released? Looking back at years of comics and illustrations, does anything really stick out in your mind as a definitive Denis Kitchen piece?

DK: It's called *The Oddly Compelling Art of Denis Kitchen*. It was announced in 1989 for Kitchen Sink's twentieth anniversary, but I withdrew it when other artists' projects at the time seemed more important. In early 1998 my employees convinced me to publish the book for Kitchen Sink's thirtieth anniversary. I scheduled it, and then in January 1999 the company folded! I finally decided to do it under my new imprint (Denis Kitchen Publishing Co.), though I just received a call from Dark Horse Comics, located, ironically enough, in the other Milwaukie (Oregon), and it looks like they might publish it. In either case, late 2004 is the earliest target. I'm currently editing the material. It will include a lot of *Bugle* covers and other art deeply rooted in Milwaukee. In an ideal world, I'd like to arrange an exhibit somewhere in the city to coincide with publication. It might draw some old Wisconsin hippies out of the woodwork, as well as some younger fans who still seem to be out there. As far as a definitive piece, I'd pick "The Square Publisher," an autobiographical yet surreal piece which ran in *Blab* #8 and will be in the upcoming collection.

TK: To close, any great or wild Milwaukee-related stories?

DK: A wild Milwaukee story? Okay. I regarded myself as a politically progressive guy in the late 1960s. I was the socialist candidate for lieutenant governor. In 1970, I marched with Father Groppi, opposed the draft, and thought my credentials were in order. America was boiling over with burning political issues. The Vietnam War was raging. The civil rights movement was intense. Legalizing pot was a big issue, as were gay politics. The feminist movement was also quickly emerging and was one I was particularly curious about. The counterculture, of course, had its own political divisions. The

local underground newspaper that I was part of, the *Bugle*, was in direct competition with *Kaleidoscope*, a more radical underground. They probably seriously thought the CIA funded the *Bugle*. Nonetheless, in mid-1971 I naively
approached the "feminist collective" that, at the time, controlled *Kaleidoscope*.
I wanted to hear their views. They invited me to their Brady Street office. It
was a hot summer day. They said, "Let's go on the roof. It's cooler up there."
So we went up to the third- or fourth-floor roof with folding chairs. There was
no railing of any kind. I quickly found myself on the edge of the roof with six
angry women surrounding me in a semi-circle. They weren't interested in an
intellectual exchange. They began by thrusting copies of comic books drawn
by R. Crumb and S. Clay Wilson. I protested that I hadn't published those
particular comic books. Unacceptable answer. I was told, as they inched their
chairs toward me, that I needed to stop distributing misogynist comix. The
Brady Street traffic was all too visible over my shoulder as they leaned in on
me. I assured them I would talk to my wayward brothers. "Why don't you
publish comics by women?" they said sternly. "There aren't very many good
women cartoonists," I stupidly responded. They inched their chairs toward
me again. "I'll look harder!" I promised. The intimidation continued. Finally,
one of them, I believe it was Jennie Orvino Sorcic (a local poet with prominent breasts), produced a copy of *Mom's Homemade Comics*. "Why do you
draw women with large breasts?" she demanded. I wanted to say with a smirk,
"I draw what I see," but was scared shitless and instead apologized for the
error of my ways. With that the "meeting" ended. The Brady Street pavement
looked good enough to kiss on my way out. True story.

Not-So-Secret Agent: The Denis Kitchen Interview

DANNY FINGEROTH / 2009

From *Danny Fingeroth's Write Now Magazine* no. 20 (Spring 2009). Reprinted by permission. © Danny Fingeroth.

Denis Kitchen began his career in 1968 as a self-published underground cartoonist, leading to the formation of his pioneer publishing company, Kitchen Sink Press. For thirty years he published creators such as R. Crumb, Will Eisner, Harvey Kurtzman, Milton Caniff, Al Capp, Scott McCloud, Dave McKean, Mark Schultz, Howard Cruse, Justin Green, Alan Moore, Art Spiegelman, and Charles Burns. During these years Kitchen Sink won industry awards far disproportionate to its market share, and sometimes more than any other publisher. In 1986 he founded and for eighteen years served as president of the Comic Book Legal Defense Fund, a 501(c)(3) nonprofit organization dedicated to defending the industry's First Amendment rights. Since the demise of Kitchen Sink in 1999, he has diversified his activities. He is a partner with designer John Lind in Kitchen, Lind & Associates and with Judith Hansen in Kitchen & Hansen Agency, literary agencies representing prominent comic artists and writers. He has expanded Denis Kitchen Art Agency (founded in 1990) into an entity exclusively offering original work by Eisner, Kurtzman, Capp, and other clients.

Here, Denis takes some time to answer my questions about his unique relationship with Will Eisner.

—DF

Danny Fingeroth: When did you first become aware of Will's work, Denis?

Denis Kitchen: I was too young to have seen the original *Spirit* newspaper inserts. I first became aware of Will's work when Harvey Kurtzman featured "Bring Back Sand Saref" in his *Help!* magazine #13 in late 1961. I was fifteen and pretty damn impressed. I don't think I saw anything else until

Denis Kitchen, 2005. Kitchen's cartoon recalls his first
meeting with Will Eisner.

Harvey Comics published a two-issue *Spirit* experiment in 1966. By then I
certainly wanted to see more, but there was no organized fandom, no reprint
programs, no way to even figure out how many Spirits there were. It was
a complete vacuum except for a handful of fans doing mimeo zines, and I
wasn't in that tiny loop.

DF: How did you first meet Will?

DK: I started drawing my first underground, *Mom's Homemade Comics*, in
1968, and successfully selfpublished. Then I started publishing others, the
beginning of Krupp Comic Works (later Kitchen Sink Press). Phil Seuling, the
impresario of the earliest comic book conventions, became aware of my small
Midwest operation around 1970. Phil began distributing Krupp's titles and
also hired me to do custom cartoons for his catalogs and flyers. He invited
me to be a guest at his summer 1971 convention in New York City. It was my
first and, it turns out, Will Eisner's first convention as well. I was rummag-
ing through back issue boxes like any other fan when Maurice Horn, a French
comics historian, saw my name tag and said Will Eisner was looking for me. I
assured him he was mistaken, but he insisted on taking me to meet Will. We
met in a private suite and, after quick formalities, Will expressed intense curiosity about underground comix: their distribution, the freedom, the royalty
system, etc. I explained what we were doing at all levels, and he said these
were all the things he wished he had had when he started. I tried talking about
the "old days" of comics, a subject I was intensely curious about, but he'd drop
a tidbit or two and kept corning back to undergrounds. It was a pretty heady
experience. Will's interest was purely academic because he hadn't actually seen

any undergrounds, so we walked down to the dealer's room where Phil had several tables covered with the latest. Will grabbed one at random, flipped through it, and stopped at a particularly explicit and disturbing S. Clay Wilson page. Will blanched. He had no idea just how outrageous some comix were. I normally took glee in seeing undergrounds shock an older generation, but I was suddenly aghast that I was "losing" Will, the new convert. As we debated the merits of complete artistic freedom, a young artist named Art Spiegelman, standing nearby, joined the fray along with fans, and soon Will, clearly uncomfortable, excused himself. I didn't see him again the rest of the weekend and figured it was the last time I'd ever talk to him.

DF: When did you first work with him?

DK: I followed up the convention with a letter and samples of other comix. I suggested he might find them more palatable, which he did. Then I wasted no time. I proposed reviving *The Spirit*. He was skeptical that my hippie market would be responsive, especially after the Harvey newsstand experiment had failed just a few years earlier, but he agreed to let me give it a try.

DF: What do you think there is about the Spirit that could make the character appeal to a wide audience?

DK: Well, to start, Will's art is so wonderful that it just pulls you in, especially the classic splash pages, the distinctive feathering, the luscious women, the masterful layouts. No offense to *Write Now!*, but art is the initial attraction for all comics. Then with *The Spirit* you also have the skillful writing, likable characters, memorable villains, concise plots packed generally into just seven pages. You've got romance, action, mystery—the whole package. And, as we've seen, it's timeless. *The Spirit* has been entertaining generations for almost seventy years.

DF: Have you been involved in the previous attempts to make a *Spirit* movie?

DK: Not really. At Kitchen Sink I optioned Alan Moore's *From Hell*, was heavily involved with *The Crow*, and got Mark Schultz's *Cadillacs and Dinosaurs* on CBS, but Will regularly optioned *The Spirit* on his own during the nearly thirty years that I was his publisher. That included the made-for-TV movie. When Mike Uslan's group exercised their option a dozen or so years back, they tied it up until the movie by Frank Miller was made. So when Kitchen Sink went under in 1999 and my role changed to being Will's art and literary agent, the die was already cast in terms of *The Spirit* in Hollywood. However, my partner Judy Hansen and I are working to develop certain of Will's graphic novels.

DF: What was your involvement with the current *Spirit* movie?

DK: Hands off. I've met with the producers and Frank and saw his script drafts, but I'm not in the movie business. Will understood that Hollywood would make the *Spirit* movie it wanted to make. He had no illusions about influencing the process and, frankly, no interest in meddling in another medium. Other than helping assemble the image bible for merchandise, quality control, and participating in the DVD extra, I've kept a distance. I didn't even visit the set because I was literally too busy during the shooting. I'll have to meet Scarlett Johansson another time . . .

DF: How did his style evolve over the years on *The Spirit* and on his later work?

DK: The short seven-page *Spirit* weekly format forced Will to work economically to establish the premise and get to the resolution quite quickly. There wasn't time or space to ruminate or stray. Despite those apparent limitations, he created some real gems. He played with various genres; balanced the fight scenes, the smooching, the tension, and the humor; and then jumped right into the next story with no time off. The discipline was good, but the pace tough to sustain. He also had to write for a newspaper audience, a family audience, ranging from little kids to octogenarians. It was different with his graphic novels that came later. There, the stories he wanted to tell determined the length, a luxury he didn't have with *The Spirit*. And he was able to write for a peer audience. He was proud of what he did with *The Spirit* but much prouder of his later work. From an artistic point of view, his art also evolved. The prime *Spirit* art is gorgeous and tight and the folds in the clothing and the brushwork is a wonder to behold. In later years, Will's artistry didn't diminish, but he learned to tell the stories with a more economical line and fewer details but no less masterfully.

DF: Will once told me he wasn't a writer or artist but a cartoonist. Do you agree, or do you think an objective observer can separate the writer in Will from the artist?

DK: I understand what he meant because a cartoonist has those combined skills. Some people can write great and some can draw great; those are rare enough talents. But the combination is especially valuable in comics, where you can be an auteur. A cartoonist doesn't have to fight with a writer over a script or fight with an artist over interpretation or layout; with a singular vision he can theoretically move seamlessly, or at least more efficiently, through the process. It's hard to separate the writer from the artist in Will, but I certainly know which aspect he was most proud of. At conventions he'd often sit at the Kitchen Sink booth signing for a line of fans, and during the minute or so he and a fan were one on one, the most frequent comment was, "Mr. Eisner, I love your art," or "Mr. Eisner, your art is just amazing." And he'd nod and thank each person graciously. But every once in a while, a fan would say, "Mr. Eisner, I love your writing:" In those instances his face would glow; he'd look up and genuinely be grateful for the compliment. Though I'd disagree with him, Will thought drawing was a relatively easy mechanical process. For him it was seemingly effortless. But he thought writing comics was a much more intellectual process, one which called upon a greater talent and insight.

DF: Are there other Eisner-related projects you're involved with?

DK: I was recently involved, along with Peter Poplaski, in finishing *Expressive Anatomy* for W. W. Norton, the final part of Will's instructional trilogy [along with *Comics and Sequential Art* and *Graphic Storytelling*]. It was largely written and penciled when Will died. I helped with Insight's *Spirit Pop-Up Book*, adapting the same Sand Saref story I first discovered in 1961. I work closely with DC on their long-running *Spirit Archives* series, just about to wrap up, and with Dark Horse on their upcoming collection of *The Spirit: The New Adventures*. Handling the sales of Will's artwork is another responsibility, and there are serious buyers for his work well outside of comic fandom, including fine art collectors willing to pay serious money for prime stories, covers, and pages. We're seeing a major trend for blue chip comic art: Geniuses like Eisner, Kurtzman and Crumb are increasingly being treated like museum artists. Probably my most satisfying involvement is curating or providing original Eisner art for exhibitions—there have been roughly twenty since Will died. Sometimes his work has simultaneously been in three or four exhibitions, often overseas—recently Paris, Amsterdam, Frankfurt, and Athens. Next year his art will be in Brussels and Poland, among others. It's a shame that Will didn't live to be the centenarian most of us expected; virtually all of his work is in print, the Eisner Awards are going strong, there's *The Spirit* movie and merchandise in the works, and art traveling around the world. He'd be pleased that interest in his life's work continues to grow.

DF: Anything else you'd like to say about upcoming Kitchen projects?

DK: Well, despite so much happening with Will's legacy, I actually am involved in other things! I recently coauthored a book with Paul Buhle, *The Art of Harvey Kurtzman*, for Harry N. Abrams's new ComicArt imprint this spring. It includes a ton of images that have never before been seen. Harvey, like Will, was a great friend and mentor, so doing a book about his career was intensely satisfying. It was sad, though, in reviewing his career to see how Kurtzman never quite achieved the success his talent and influence would imply. I also just coauthored *Underground Classics* with James Danky, another book on Abrams's spring 2009 list, connected with a traveling exhibition Jim and I cocurated, consisting of fifty-some underground cartoonists. It debuts at the Chazen Museum in Madison in May. On a personal artistic level, coming

Cover of exhibit catalog for *Underground Classics: The Transformation of Comics into Comix* (2009), curated by Kitchen and James Danky for the Chazen Museum of Art, Madison, WI, featuring R. Crumb's art from *Snarf* #6 (1975).

Kitchen points out *Mom's* #1 to Chazen visitors Michael Martens and Jo Ann Jensen, 2009.

full circle, I have a sketchbook in the works and in late 2009 or early 2010. Dark Horse is publishing *The Oddly Compelling Art of Denis Kitchen,* a career overview. My partner John Lind designed or was involved in the design of all the books I'm mentioning here. And then there's my eleven-year-old daughter [Violet], whose third book, *GrownUps are Dumb! (No Offense)* will be published by Disney/Hyperion this summer. With those projects, representing a couple dozen clients and estates with two different partners, and packaging other books, there's not much time for loafing.

DF: Thanks, Denis!

DK: My pleasure, Danny.

Denis Kitchen Q&A

PETER BEBERGAL / 2011

From *HiLobrow.com* (March 13, 2011). Reprinted by permission.

In the 1960s, some rebels marched, some performed radical theater, a few made bombs. Folks like Denis Kitchen drew and self-published comics—in an effort to claim both art and ideas as property of the artists. Though his publishing house, Kitchen Sink Press, closed in 1999, the list of people published, distributed, or represented by Denis and Kitchen Sink, both now and in the past, includes R. Crumb, Charles Burns, Art Spiegleman, Trina Robbins, and other famous names. I spoke with Denis in 2010 about how his childhood love of comics like Al Capp's *Li'l Abner* influenced his own underground publishing exploits and how he and his colleagues changed comics forever.

Peter Bebergal: I imagine comics were the first language you spoke.

Denis Kitchen: I was born in 1946, and growing up in the 1950s there wasn't any kind of comics fandom. Comics were strictly kid entertainment, and if an adult were caught reading a comic it would've been considered an embarrassment. It was the era where Dr. Frederic Wertham was leading a crusade against them, so teachers and parents were anticomics without any real familiarity with them. And let's face it, some of the comics at that time were pretty twisted, and the horror comics in particular were trips in themselves. I still have good memories of being in a closet reading them and thinking, "Whoa, this is weird." I liked to read and go to movies, and I wasn't living in a vacuum, but comics to me were the most satisfying sort of entertainment. I certainly was also addicted to the Sunday newspaper comics and certain ones left an indelible impression on me too, in particular Al Capp's *Li'l Abner*, not only just because he drew the sexiest women in comics but really grotesque looking men.

PB: There was always a hair growing out of a wart.

DK: Yes. He had an amazing imagination, and even as a kid I understood some of his satire and political references. And then early on I developed a love–hate relationship with Ernie Bushmiller's *Nancy*. I found when I was swapping with other neighborhood kids it seemed I had more diverse tastes. The other young boys seemed to be focused on the superhero stuff, but I liked *Little Lulu* and *Uncle $crooge*.

PB: *Little Lulu* and *Uncle $crooge* were pretty mainstream. How did you go from those to seeing comics as something subversive?

DK: Actually, *Little Lulu* and *Uncle $crooge* comics were more subversive than you might think. Lulu was a serious feminist who constantly found ways to infiltrate the boys' private clubhouse or to outsmart their plans. Growing up I don't think I saw the gender politics that are obvious now as much as I identified with Lulu in her struggles against power structure, cliques, and other oppressive situations disguised as a kid's comic. John Stanley, who wrote and drew many of these, was brilliant, though uncredited at the time.

Uncle $crooge was an irascible old coot who lived to hoard and protect his piles of money. He'd dive in deep vaults of coins as if they were swimming pools. Very surreal stuff. The nephews Huey, Dewey, and Louie were the real heroes. What entranced me was the wonderful art and storytelling of Carl Barks, also uncredited. His characters would often end up in exotic locations like the Land Below the Ground or the Seven Cities of Cibola. As an entranced kid, I'd get lost in the psychedelic-like visuals.

PB: How did you ultimately decide that comics would be the vehicle for your growing rebellious spirit?

DK: I don't know that it was ever a conscious decision. I grew up avidly hooked on the comic books of my era, which were blissfully cheap and plentiful and often quite strange. I showed signs of cartooning talent early on and developed it through school publications and self-publishing into college. When the hippie revolution kicked in, in the late 1960s, I was in my early twenties, going to college and influenced by all those things going on: feminism, the civil rights movement, the earliest gay movement, the legalize pot movement and just the general antiestablishment. It was a crazy time to be a young adult facing the possibility of getting drafted and shipped overseas to a war we all thought made no sense. Then in the midst of all that was the proliferation of drugs of all kinds and experimentation, which some delved into more enthusiastically than others. I regard myself as a somewhat—what's the word—cautious hippie in that I didn't swallow any pill handed to me. At that point I expressed myself the best way I could, via comic strips and what quickly became known as underground comix. We lived for the moment, but we also knew we were caught up in something large and culturally meaningful. Being a cartoonist was a longtime dream, but my career would have likely taken a much more conventional route if I hadn't been caught up in the political upheaval and antiwar fervor of my generation and the music, artistic experimentation and the pot and LSD that were part of the times.

PB: Did any of those experiences shape the way you thought about art or thought about what you wanted to do with comics?

DK: It's so hard to sum it up because each trip was unique, generally in a good way. My favorite one was vividly hallucinogenic in a way I can only describe as cartoons come to life. I felt like the room I was in was filled with a maze of little freeways and roads surrounding me and little funny animals like elephants and other goofy things that came out of old Fleischer cartoons would be sauntering around. I'm thinking, "This is the coolest trip I ever took, and I want to come back to this place." But I never did. I feel nostalgic about that trip.

PB: Did acid trips make it into your actual comics?

DK: They certainly did. One of the things that sometimes unnerved the people I was with is that I had a small notebook and a pen in my shirt pocket and periodically I would grab it and write it down. I think my friends thought I was spying on them or writing down their dialogue in a way that was intrusive but I always said, "No, I just got a idea and I don't want to forget it." The cliché is that you have some great revelation or you solved some wonderful mystery of the universe and then of course you forget it later. I did at least one or two cartoons where I said to myself, "I have to write this down, it's the greatest idea ever." Occasionally those would turn into drawings and strips.

PB: Is that how you came up with the infamous cover of *Bizarre Sex* #1 that shows a giant penis breaking through the sidewalk attacking the denizens of a city?

DK: That was an acid flashback. It just came to me, and I jotted it down. Would it have come to me anyway? [Robert] Crumb famously came up with *Mr. Natural* and all kinds of things on what he called very bad acid. God knows what it was. What perhaps grounded me more than some was taking on the publishing side of comix and overseeing the creation and distribution and financial obligations associated with many other comix artists. You couldn't do that if marching and tripping twenty-four seven.

Ad promoting *Oddly Compelling* at the Miami Book Fair, 2010. Courtesy of John Lind.

PB: It seems that the underground artists had something much more playful going on than the antiwar activists or even those hoping for a spiritual revolution, but in some ways it is much more deeply subversive. And it must have been even more rebellious doing this in Midwest than in San Francisco.

DK: I chose to stay in the Midwest for a variety of reasons, partly once described as a perverse pride to be able to have this hip subculture and comics and feel like a full-blown hippie without having to go to San Francisco because it just became to me a kind of a cliché and I went out there. But I loved San Francisco.

Denis Kitchen, 1972. "The Giant Penis That Invaded New York," original cover drawing for *Bizarre Sex* #1.

PB: But were you any more impressed with their comics than anywhere else?

DK: There was something unique that first fully flowered in the Bay Area, and certainly those guys are the obvious pioneers. But in a true sense there was a movement that seemed to be simultaneously bursting forth from everywhere, even in small towns and places where maybe it's less recorded. But certainly, there had to be enough supporters to both put them out and to buy them as there were hundreds of underground comix and newspapers scattered across North America.

PB: It's like the drug dealer who is also a user. You deal just enough so you can keep doing it.

DK: I think that was it. And I think that's an important point too because you can't trade in anything without economics intruding in some way. Speaking for myself and most of the freaks that I knew, there wasn't a terrible motivation to make money. We just wanted to be able to continue doing what we were doing and have fun. Nobody was looking ahead.

PB: Did you want to change the world with comics?

DK: It sounds so dopey to say that, but I think yes. I was already a serious socialist—in fact, a card-carrying socialist—when I was also becoming a hippie, so I had already certain Marxist thoughts about how people ought to best organize and share the means of production. It's a little simplistic looking back, but at the time I was a true believer and it melded fairly easy with the hippie stuff. But aside from the politics, which I wasn't in terribly long, I shared the almost universal feeling among my freak peers that we could bring peace and love and even end the war.

PB: So how did drawing a giant penis terrorizing a city help this cause? Because to be honest, that was so much of what underground comix were at the time.

DK: In a word, liberating. I grew up at a time when comics were under the Comics Code authority. The publishers pledged to not include a long list of things in the comics, and so I saw the comics get less interesting. My generation of cartoonists was taking glee in breaking all those restrictive rules. My contemporaries and I knew enough about the comics business to know it was a pretty shitty set up economically and structurally. You didn't own your own work when you worked for Marvel or DC Comics.

PB: But weren't you secretly reading *Silver Surfer* comics?

DK: Actually not secretly. When Stan Lee started the Marvel Comics generation around 1961 it was really before the hippie movement, so I was hooked on Marvel comics in high school and even into college. Those comics predated any experimentation with drugs and lifestyle so some of the hippies who had already been into them would see them, whether it was Silver Surfer or Dr. Strange, in psychedelic terms. Stan Lee was kind of unwittingly one of the heroes of the youth movement even though he was straight as an arrow himself.

PB: Nevertheless, working for a company like Marvel or DC was all work for hire.

DK: It was all work for hire. It was tedious. They handed you a script. You did what they told you. It didn't matter if they printed 100,000 or a million. It didn't matter if they sold the rights in Germany or Japan, you got the same amount. It was the cartoon equivalent of a factory job, where you were on an assembly line. You did your part, and maybe you got a pat on the back and not much more. It was a dreary prospect. So even those of us who liked Marvel comics and the fewer who liked DC comics, we didn't see working for them as really a prospect.

PB: That wouldn't have been making it in an authentic way?

DK: No, not at all. And yet we loved comics. What was the alternative? Well, maybe I'll do a newspaper strip but then the syndicates were tough. You knew the audience there ranged from kids just learning to read to really old people, so it had to be kind of vanilla so to appeal to everyone and obviously a lot of topics were verboten. You could get richer there; you could not quite own the strip, but you co-owned it with the syndicate, so it was somewhat appealing. Middle class was the word we would've used. So the only way we could make comics was to make them ourselves and figure out a way to sell them ourselves.

You have to understand I first drew my own comics in a vacuum. I'd heard there was a *Zap Comix* but it took me forever to find one and so I just figured out a way to print mine locally; as many as I could afford. There was certainly no distributor who would handle it. I literally went around the Eastside of Milwaukee myself, which was the college area where most of the hippies resided. I would put them on consignment at records stores and head shops. I kept track of everything, and I went back and I would collect the money, give them more. I was methodical about it.

PB: And people bought them?

DK: Yes. Absolutely. They were flying off the shelves, and that was when people would print their own book of poetry and it'd sit there for a year. There was something about comics and the fact that we were tackling social issues and enough of it was either blatantly or subtly part of the culture. The titles and subject matters spoke clearly to a hippie audience. It became self-evident that these were alternative readings, and word quickly spread that if you read them when you were high, it was a trip unto itself. You could get high, and you could watch TV or go to a movie, but with rare exceptions they weren't intended for you to be in an altered state. With the comics you had a sense that the guys who did them might've been in an altered state also. And things would be funnier when you were high.

PB: Whether they actually were or not.

DK: It varied from person to person, and humor is such an amorphous thing anyway. The cover of *Bizarre Sex* #1 just struck me as being a funny thing. Either you laugh at it or you don't get it at all. I don't think anyone ever thought it was pornographic in the sense that wasn't anatomically correct. It was clearly a cartoony, stylized, phallic creature.

PB: Very different from the way, say, Crumb would've drawn it.

DK: Crumb's would have looked more like a real phallus. You're touching on something too, that was kind of an unstated rule. If you were a cartoonist and you were going to work for Marvel or DC, they clearly had a house style. What the underground comics encouraged were total idiosyncratic styles, including lettering. Some artists lettered really neat and some in a way that was harder to read but it was a distinctive signature. You could tell one guy did it. At mainstream publishers the comic was passed from a letterer, to a penciler, to an inker, to a writer. In a sense . . . the French term the *auteur* applied to comics [artists] almost better than a filmmaker because the film-making process is virtually impossible to do singlehandedly, unless you're doing a very small film. Comic books represent the one form of graphic story telling where it really can be a singular vision

PB: Were you worried that being a publisher you would become the enemy?

DK: When I found myself kind of by default evolving from primarily a cartoonist to primarily a publisher, I had these idealistic ethical rules that I insisted on applying. Having been a cartoonist, I had a bad experience with an outfit called the Print Mint, and that just to me made it even more important for me to treat other cartoonists well. I can't even say with 100 percent certainty they were screwing with me. But they wouldn't give me even the most basic accounting.

PB: Did they think you were just a dumb stoned hippie?

DK: I think there were a lot of business people who took advantage of the fact that hippies weren't paying attention to details. But just because I was a hippie, it didn't mean I was stupid or didn't mean I didn't have any business sense. I found out when I evolved into being a publisher that most artists very much appreciated getting an honest accounting, getting checks regularly, being told how many were printed, and getting told when a comic was being reprinted. All those things that just sound basic and obvious were not standard industry practice. This was an industry—and I use the word industry loosely—we could control.

PB: The true DIY.

DK: Yes, and some serious dollars began to be involved. I remember when a colleague at Rip Off Press told me they'd sold their millionth *Freak Brothers*. Guys like Gilbert Shelton and Robert Crumb were earning very, very good royalties that would have totally blown away guys working for Marvel or DC at the top rates. Somebody was working for one of the majors and I remember saying, "You should do stuff for the undergrounds sometime." He said, "You kidding? I'm making top dollar over there," which was in the $100 to

$200 range per page. And I cited Crumb's *Homegrown Funnies* that had been printed many, many times and I said, "I think to date, Crumb has made about $800 per page." We weren't out to convert people who worked for the big companies, but you would rub shoulders with them at conventions. And inevitably you compared things, and some of those guys who were really straight. Everybody makes their accommodations. Everybody makes their compromises, and not everybody lives in a commune and grows a beard.

PB: Did the mainstreaming of the counterculture hurt the creativity of underground comix?

DK: We knew from observation and history that the system or capitalistic forces co-opt everything, and that eventually it would have some effect on underground comix. But I think we were far less affected than things like fashion and music and film where much bigger dollars and audiences were affected. The underground comix stayed pretty weird and out there for quite a while without what I'd consider any outside corruption. It helped that key artists like Robert Crumb were pretty incorruptible. He turned down all kinds of opportunities to do Pepsi billboards and Toyota ads. And, let's face it, most underground comix were not capable of being brought into mainstream America. I'd argue that the essential creativity of comix only got better deeper into the 1970s. What affected the comix movement more than anything was the quick decline and disappearance of head shops. Distribution is everything, and periodical distributors wouldn't touch us.

PB: Are there any risks left for younger comic artists to take?

DK: Always. If you're talking about comic book artists, the new generation benefits from having censorship and subject barriers knocked down by an earlier generation or two. But every generation has its own hypocrisies and prejudices and inequities to address, and addressing them always has inherent risks. The graphic novel genre now permits cartoonists to break out of the relatively narrow head shop market or comic book shop nerd market that restricted my generation [and] into mainstream outlets, which is great on one hand but risky if you have to appeal to those outside a comfortably smaller and receptive audience, while new technologies and formats like iPads and Kindles are opening up a world audience. Sharp new cartoonists have an amazing opportunity now to aim at a niche audience or to reach out to potentially vast numbers of readers, and, in either case, there are risks to be taken creatively. I think we will see more literate comics and less masked, caped superpowered characters as both creators and audiences come to expect increasingly sophisticated combinations of words and pictures. It's an exciting time to be a young comic artist but still one fraught with creative challenges and risks.

Li'l Abner's Al Capp:
A Monstrous Creature, a Masterful Cartoonist

MICHAEL DOOLEY / 2013

From *Print* magazine online (March 4, 2013). Unpublished source interview. Printed by permission.

Michael Dooley: List whatever biographical details about yourself you'd like me to include.

Denis Kitchen: Denis Kitchen, a self-described very confused man, can't seem to pick a career and stick with it. He began as an underground cartoonist in the late 1960s, was a publisher for thirty years (Kitchen Sink Press), founded and oversaw the Comic Book Legal Defense Fund for eighteen years, and today is simultaneously a literary agent, art agent, book packager, and author. Oh, and he still draws comics and curates on the side.

MD: Describe the scope of the new Kurtzman exhibition and your role in creating and assembling it.

DK: Monte Beauchamp and I cocurated this for the Society of Illustrators in New York. It opens March 8 and runs through May 11. It's a career-spanning show of about 125 originals, from Harvey's solo art starting with a charcoal life study from 1941 through his own art for *MAD*, the E.C. war comics, *Marley's Ghost*, *Jungle Book*, and *Esquire*, plus collaborative work for *Humbug*, *Help!*, *Trump*, and *Little Annie Fanny*. Beyond that there are also wonderful obscure and never-seen pieces that even hardcore Kurtzmaniacs haven't seen. The Kurtzman family and various private collectors provided top-notch examples. I hope you can get to New York to see it, Mike.

MD: Describe any upcoming Capp-related events that you'd like plugged.

DK: Well, the fifth volume of *Li'l Abner* just came out from Dean Mullaney's IDW imprint. I recommend those highly for fans who appreciate classic strips. Andrew Cooke (Will Eisner documentary) and I are working on a screenplay

Harvey Kurtzman and Denis Kitchen, 1973. *The Art of Harvey Kurtzman: The Mad Genius of Comics* by Denis Kitchen and Paul Buhle won the Eisner and Harvey Awards in 2010.

based on Capp's life. I'm also hoping to place an Al Capp retrospective, but those and a couple of other percolating projects are premature to plug in any detail. Right now, I'm concentrating on promoting the brand-new Capp biography.

MD: Also detail any other upcoming Denis Kitchen projects you'd like mentioned.

DK: A week after the Harvey Kurtzman opening, I'll be in Lucerne, Switzerland, for the opening of an exhibit of underground comix art that I cocurated with James Danky. That one consists of about 175 originals; [it's] an expanded version of the *Underground Classics* exhibit that Abrams published the catalog for a couple of years back. I'm also trying to allocate time for the drawing board. I recently finished a five-page color comics-style minibiography of Dr. Seuss for an anthology about famous cartoonists that Simon & Shuster will be publishing next year. My primary partner John Lind and I are on the precipice of announcing something new that I'm especially excited about, but I'll have to bite my tongue for the moment. A press release will be out soon enough on that.

MD: What was it about Capp's work that first attracted you to him?

DK: As a kid in the 1950s I eagerly grabbed our newspaper's comics section and devoured every strip. But *Li'l Abner* was always my favorite. His clever cliffhangers were part of what kept me turning to his strip first, but it was also the style. I loved the way he drew: the bold but delicate brushstrokes, the distinctive lettering, the heavy use of blacks and silhouettes. And probably the moment puberty kicked in, it was Capp's beautiful and voluptuous women. At the same time the grotesque villains and inventive character names were a big appeal.

MD: Prior to Fearless Fosdick's appearance in 1942, what other strips were exploring similar "cartoon take-off" territory? Were there parodies in other media that may have influenced Capp?

DK: Nothing stands out as a particular influence. In the case of Fearless Fosdick, Chester Gould's *Dick Tracy* is the obvious source, but there was a hitherto unknown inspiration: a 1941 Columbia serial, *Holt of the Secret Service*. The protagonist Jack Holt has both the Fosdick hat and the mustache. He's a human dead ringer for Capp's character. So we're pretty certain that Fosdick was initially an amalgam or simultaneous parody of both Holt and Tracy, but no one remembers Holt.

MD: The best of Capp's satires attacked the injustices of the rich and powerful; what shared sensibilities do you see between him and Harvey Kurtzman? Is this commonality characteristic of a type of Jewish humor? Could you cite specific examples?

DK: Attacking injustice and hypocrisy and the foibles of the rich and pow-erful are the hallmarks of satirists. "Exposing the truth" was the way Kurtz-man put it, and both he and Capp were among the best satirists ever during their primes. That was their commonality. Their Jewish family upbringing and early neighborhood influences are undeniable. But neither was religious at all, neither practiced Jewish traditions in any meaningful way, and neither injected overt Jewish humor into their comics. With Harvey you do some-times get Yiddish-sounding phrases in strips, but largely because they just sound funny. Harvey worked for much of his career in comic books, an indus-try populated overwhelmingly by Jews during the industry's early decades, and he collaborated with largely Jewish cartoonists, notably Wolf Eisen-berg—Will Elder—who delighted in adding what he called "chicken fat" into their stories. Capp, meanwhile, was quickly a star in the syndicated newspa-per strip world, and that was a distinctly more WASPish world. Capp moved to Boston, hung for a long time with rather patrician Harvard crowds. His coworkers were more often Italian than Jewish. I'm sure some would argue this, but I don't see much Jewish humor. When I've discussed this topic with Harvey's widow Adele and Capp's daughter Julie, they seem to agree.

MD: What was their relationship like? Had Kurtzman acknowledged Capp's satires as precursors to the *MADs* of the mid-1950s?

DK: They didn't have a relationship per se. When Harvey's *Hey Look!* sales to Stan Lee and Marvel trailed off in the late 1940s, Harvey began contribut-ing similar filler pages and more developed stories like *Pot Shot Pete* to Toby Press, the publishing arm of the empire Al Capp had carved out with brothers Elliot and Bence. Harvey worked closely with Elliot and liked him. Elliot even let Harvey retain his copyright, and they later collaborated on a syndicated strip pitch that failed. But Harvey was a huge admirer of Al Capp's work. He probably parodied *Li'l Abner* more than any other comic strip, not just in a full-blown parody treatment but in countless ongoing details in *Hey Look!*, *Trump*, *Humbug*, and *Little Annie Fanny*. Harvey acknowledged his deep debt to Capp as well as Will Eisner, for their pre-*MAD* parody work.

But Capp was such a huge figure that by the time Harvey acquired some fame in his own right, as editor of *MAD*, he was still too cowed to even ask Capp directly for a simple favor. When he was writing and laying out his graphic adaptation of "The Face Upon the Floor" for *MAD* #10, Harvey wanted the very last panel—the image that strikes the artist dead—to be *Lena the Hyena*, Basil Wolverton's prize-winning entry in Capp's famous 1946 contest judged by Frank Sinatra, Salvador Dalí, and Boris Karloff. But instead of ask-ing Al directly, or via Elliot, he instead wrote to Capp's clueless and careless syndicate, which summarily rejected the request. So, for better or for worse, Harvey had Wolverton create a new hideous face for that *MAD* story. But it's a small example of how Capp's bigger-than-life persona intimidated Harvey.

MD: One way Capp differed from Kurtzman was that he was motivated by personal jealousy and revenge. You describe Capp's long and intense feud with *Joe Palooka*'s Ham Fisher in great and often chilling detail, such as his boast that he considered Fisher's death in 1955 "a personal victory," and "that driving Fisher to suicide was his greatest accomplishment." Were there aspects of Capp's life that his heirs would have preferred to be excluded from the book? And if so, how did you handle such conflicts?

DK: Hah! I'm afraid there were a good number of things that key members of his family resisted having us include. In some cases, out of genuine respect for their feelings, we truncated excerpts from letters, in particular a discarded suicide note, because Capp's invective was so bitter and personal. We also agreed, for example, to eliminate a raunchy story that Frank Frazetta once related to me. In some cases, the evidence for certain alleged events was not enough for us to be comfortable stating as fact, so such elements didn't make the cut for evidentiary reasons, but in most cases, we included fact-based controversial material over their objection. I've known the family for many years and felt we had become friends. So when I started this biography with Mike Schumacher, I assured them that we were very serious and that it would be a "warts and all" biography. To their credit, they cooperated fully and provided access to most of the surviving papers and correspondence. But I don't think they realized what other people had on Capp. When they finally read our draft manuscript, it was clear they were hoping we had far fewer "warts" to reveal.

MD: As Capp rose to fame in the late 1930s, you note that he "couldn't understand why Fisher didn't seem to realize that there were plenty of room for both strips in the comics universe. . . ." Capp was a smart man; how could he remain unaware that he'd become the "monster" he saw in Fisher with his later attacks on other cartoonists whose popularity began to overshadow his own?

DK: That's a very good question. It's apparent to you, . . . myself, and some others that Capp evolved very much into a miserly egomaniac, one with the crude lusts for women and the insatiable need for fame and attention that marked Ham Fisher. Capp deeply resented how Fisher had treated him as an assistant, with good reason, and Capp, by and large, treated his own assistants very well. But in his later years Capp turned on some of them with a vengeance. He even stoutly denied to an interviewer that Frank Frazetta, a decade-long employee, had ever worked on *Abner*. Capp was exceptionally smart and an astute observer, so I suspect he had at least some awareness he

Cover, *Al Capp: A Life in the Contrary* by Kitchen and
Michael Schumacher (Bloomsbury, 2013).

was becoming a mirror image of his monstrous enemy, but, if so, I don't think
he cared much. After his youth he didn't seem eager to make close friends; he
was misanthropic and self-loathing, so what did it really matter? That he had
defeated or destroyed his enemies was the point.

MD: And similarly with Capp's 1968 ridiculing of Charles Schulz's com-
mercialization of *Peanuts*, how could he ignore the fact that, during his own
heyday, he'd likewise cashed in on the *Abner* "brand" with everything from
Shmoo merchandise to hair oil and underwear ads? Or was he somehow able
to reconcile his double standard?

DK: Exactly. No one in the comic strip business had commercially exploited
his property like Capp. And in his case, after 1947, his own family corporation
controlled licensing, cutting out the middleman. The 1968 *Peanuts* parody to
me was a sign of Capp's awareness that he was inexorably slipping from top
of the heap. As *Peanuts* and other strips began to gain and surpass *Li'l Abner*
in popularity, Capp had a very difficult time coming to grips with his waning

influence, not to mention diminishing licensing revenue. That particular parody was not funny, it was downright mean, even suggesting that Schulz had no cartooning talent. Schulz, in turn, had said that having Li'l Abner and Daisy Mae marry in 1952 was the biggest mistake any cartoonist had ever made.

MD: Where might Capp have gotten the idea to collaborate with other creators to create phony feuds, as he did with Allan Saunders's *Mary Worth* in 1957?

DK: I don't know what specifically might have sparked the notion, but he was masterful at publicity stunts in general during his long career. He had learned to manipulate the media as masterfully as anyone of his period. And he didn't rely on a paid press agent to generate ideas and pull things off. Capp and his core assistants were notorious for their wild brainstorming bull sessions with loud guffawing. The fake feud concept could have easily come out of such back and forth or from Capp alone during his often-solo all-nighters. And, as you no doubt know, he was also capable of arranging a fake cartoonist feud and then reneging on his end, as he did with Will Eisner. Eisner drew a wonderful parody in *The Spirit* called "Li'l Adam, the Stupid Mountain Boy," on the premise that Capp would reciprocate. Not only did Capp fail to keep his end of the bargain, he muscled in on the subsequent *Newsweek* feature story that was supposed to be on Eisner himself.

MD: Although you've been associated with Capp for quite a few decades, are there any ways in which your views of Capp changed in the process of writing this book?

DK: At the start of the commitment to the book, I was already a longtime fan of his work. I thought Al Capp was a flat-out genius. That said, I had also known for many years that Al Capp had quite a dark side. I'd been collecting every article and scrap for years and interviewing any associate I could find, so I fully expected our biography to depict a deeply flawed and even tortured man. And we did. So in that sense my views were largely pre-formed going into this biography with Mike. Certainly, we learned a good many subtleties as the contrarian and complex man emerged. The "monster" discussed earlier was also a devoted son and father, an often-generous man with assistants and strangers, a man capable of great charity, a man who wouldn't tolerate a racist or homophobic joke. But I was surprised in one particular and unexpected area. I was very cynical and even judgmental about his relationships with women. He certainly initially loved his wife Catherine, but the humiliation she had to endure for many years was, I thought, a form of cruelty. She lived well into her nineties but consistently refused to be interviewed about Al, but in one 1974 diary entry we had accidental access to, she called Al the "worst creature I ever could have spent my life with." I had heard and read so many distressing stories about Capp's serial "womanizing"—to put it in polite terms—and later the kind of aggressive behavior that today we would call sexual predation or attempted rape that I had effectively concluded Capp was an irredeemable pig of a man.

Then a few years ago a woman contacted me whose mother had died and left a pile of love letters wrapped in a blue ribbon. They dated from the early 1940s and were from Al Capp. They revealed a previously unknown relationship with a nightclub singer named Nina Luce, but most importantly, they revealed what had been a true and intense love affair. Capp wrote remarkably revealing and tender letters to her, punctuated, I should add, by sometimes crass and thoughtless statements as well. Capp had long before destroyed her letters to him of course, along with an entire storage unit full of potentially incriminating materials, but the surviving letters to Nina showed a side of Capp we never would have otherwise seen. Emotionally wrenched and torn between choosing Nina or staying with his two young daughters and then-adoring Catherine, Capp fatefully chose not to break up his family. That traumatic break up possibly marked his last romantic love. Afterward, with the exception of a lengthy affair with William Saroyan's wife Carol, Capp's "relationships" with women was comprised of paid companions, countless one-night stands, and predatory behavior. But after carefully reading those 1940s love letters, I can never again see Capp quite the same way. He was, for a while at least, a real, emotional, head-over-heels in love man. Before he became Ham Fisher.

MD: Capp's often inexcusable behavior, particularly with regard to women, can easily overshadow his enormous creative talents; how do you hope he's remembered?

DK: Ultimately, it's usually the work that endures. I hope he is recognized for a long time as one of America's great cartoonists and satirists. He was without doubt the most famous cartoonist of his era, but as we see in so many high-profile areas of culture and politics, even the most famous of the once famous tend to fade quickly into oblivion. Dogpatch USA, not all that long ago a thriving [*Li'l Abner*–themed] amusement park in Arkansas, is already abandoned and decrepit. Aesthetically I think *Li'l Abner* will remain a great example of what makes the comics medium effective and appealing. However, I fear that *Li'l Abner* will have it tougher than some other great strips standing the test of time. Capp-coined terms like "double whammy" may permanently be fixed in the lexicon, but the occupants of Dogpatch and their hillbilly dialect seem increasingly bizarre and undecipherable to younger readers. A good deal of Capp's humor and targets were topical, which will require considerable annotation for context and comprehension

and patience from would-be future readers. Sadie Hawkins Day was a liberating idea in its day, so much so that it spawned literally hundreds of annual
campus dances for many years in which the girls could (gulp!) ask the boys
for a date. How quaint. Now we watch *Girls* on HBO and anything goes. But
assuming comics in some form continues as a popular medium, I think Al
Capp was so prominent in his time and so fascinating and controversial a figure that he, and perhaps to a lesser degree his work, will continue to hold a
good degree of fascination. Of course, it'd help a lot if the movie Andy Cooke
and I want to make about Capp is made and is a big hit!

Denis Kitchen on Harlan Ellison

NAT SEGALOFF / 2017

From *A Lit Fuse: The Provocative Life of Harlan Ellison*, NESPA Press (2017). Unpublished source interview. Printed by permission.

Nat Segaloff: What's your first contact with Harlan?

Denis Kitchen: Way back in 1975 director William Friedkin optioned *The Spirit* from Will Eisner, and one of the people he tapped to write the script was Harlan. That may have been my first connection to Harlan. Friedkin told Will that pulling the script out of Harlan on deadline was impossible. Harlan kept putting him off and putting him off and finally—I'm trying to remember if it was false pretenses or not, but he got him into some hotel room and he literally locked him up until he delivered the treatment. That was in 1977. You may have heard that before.

NS: No, I didn't hear it before, and it's odd, because I wrote Billy Friedkin's biography for William Morrow.

DK: I have the manuscript because it was suggested by Will that maybe we publish it. The combination of Harlan's name and Will's name and so on. It turns out that Friedkin rejected Harlan's script and also, I believe, he got Jules Feiffer to do one that he rejected, and then Will said that he got Pete Hamill to do something. Finally, he got Will himself to do one, and Friedkin rejected all of them. Harlan, of course, insisted that his was fine and ought to be published but, for various reasons, we did not, although it was considered. I think part of it that came up was the legal status. Harlan insisted that he owed it, and Will counseled me that probably Friedkin owned it, or the studio. So I think that may have been my earliest connection. The funniest story, though, that I can recall, would have taken place in around 1985. I was in central Wisconsin at the time. When I moved there, I was originally in Milwaukee, and for low overhead when the underground comix business got a little shaky in 1973, I bought a farm and set up my business there and slowly remodeled it into my offices and carved them out as I needed to. At one point I was hiring a new assistant. The downside of being in the country is you don't have the number and, typically, the quality of applicants for jobs, but generally speaking that wasn't a problem. I hired a really sweet young woman named Paula, but she was somebody who was not at all plugged into the popular culture, certainly not comics and film and fiction. I basically had her screening calls and doing minimal things. Shortly after she started the phone rings and she answered it and, in her perky voice, she said, "Hello, Kitchen Sink Press, this is Paula, may I help you?" And the voice said, "Denis there?" She goes, "Who's calling, please?" Voice said, "Harlan!" And she said, "Harlan who?" to which he said, "Harlan fucking Ellison." So she buzzed me and said, "Denis, there's a Mister Harlan fucking Ellison." She had no idea who he was.

NS: Yeah, that's Harlan.

DK: You're expected to know. It's one of those one-word names.

NS: Have you spoken with him lately?

DK: He would call out of the blue. A while back I was representing an artist, Pete von Sholly, a storyboard artist in Hollywood who loves to do monsters, and he came upon the idea to do all the most famous republicans really monstrous and creepy, and the title for it was "Repuglicans" with "ugly" in the middle of it. He went to Harlan, who he knew somewhat, to get a quick blurb, with some temerity because he felt Harlan would be mean or something. Harlan not only gave him a blurb, he loved it and wrote a lengthy introduction, and to anybody who'd ask, he'd tell them how great it was, because these were people he hated. These were really mean portraits; nothing was held back; these were truly repulsive characters, and he thought they should be depicted in a really repulsive way. So he became a real champion of that.

NS: His fascination with comic art eludes me. He hardly ever talks about it, but he wants to possess all of it.

DK: Tell me about it! I'm a generous guy by nature, but when I was a publisher, one day he said, "Put me on your comp list." I said, "Sure, I can do that." I figured there'd be mutual favors—I wasn't sure how—but I put him on the comp list. Once a month we would consolidate comic books and books, and the books we published might have been soft cover or hardcover or both. I don't remember if it was the first package, but it was the first package in which there would have been two editions of a book, and we just sent him the soft cover. He called me, very testy, and he said, "You didn't send me the goddamn hardcover." My first thought was, "I also didn't charge for it; you're on the comp list." No one had ever complained [to me] before about getting free books that weren't of the best edition. He basically explained to me that he was a serious collector and everything in his library had to be the best edition, so if there was a hardcover, he had to have it, and if there was a signed cover, there better damn well be a signed hardcover. I remember thinking, "Wow, that's pretty brazen," and he kind of intimidated me, but I put in a note to whoever was in the shipping room that, for this particular recipient, be sure they always get the best edition when there's a choice. He wasn't someone I wanted to argue with. And also, some part of me simply realized that he probably had a super library and, yeah, I want to be represented in it and what does a best edition cost me, an extra couple of bucks? But that was another example of his being demanding because he has high standards.

NS: He's very much a completist—

DK: —yes—

NS: —have you ever been to the house?

DK: I have seen pictures, but, no, I have never been there.

NS: The only way to describe the inventory is "one of everything." Even back to when he was a kid because his mother *didn't* throw his away. I think he likes to have them, but I'm not sure how much he uses as reference or lays there with a box of Fig Newtons and goes through them.

DK: I remember the time—I think I heard this secondhand—somebody was there in his library and asked, "Gosh, have you read them all?" and he said, "You fucking moron, how could anybody possibly read them all?" As for his house, I remember from the pictures, and from Will's telling me, there's a round window with the lines across that replicates the window on the Spirit's cemetery hideaway. Have you seen that?

NS: I've seen it, but I never made the connection.

DK: It comes from Will Eisner's *The Spirit*. It shows how much Harlan obviously loves it and told his architect to mimic it.

NS: I just don't understand how he can know so much and amass so much. His mind is a living card catalog.

DK: I get that impression. One of his other favorite things was Al Capp—not for political reasons, but as a cartoonist—who did *Li'l Abner*. When Harlan was growing up, that was one of his favorites, as it was mine. I published it, in nearly thirty volumes, and I didn't quite finish; it's kind of an encyclopedic set. When I got to volume 14, it was the year of the Shmoo, 1948. [Harlan] had told me, "Hey kid"—he used to call me "kid"—"Hey, kid, when you get to that volume, that's my intro." I said, "Yes, Harlan, yes." I made sure he had plenty of time, and we paid him, and he delivered this wonderful intro. The only problem from my perspective as a publisher—I ran it word for word—was that it included more than a few four-letter words. Capp was dead, but his daughter ran his estate and was, I would say, a little on the prudish side, and apparently, she had a tradition of, every time one of our new volumes would come out, she would sit with a couple of her grandkids and would read aloud to them so they would learn about their grandfather. So she's reading the intro for the first time and started running into F-words. I'm sure she delicately stepped around the expletives while reading it aloud, but I got a very nasty note from her saying that she was appalled by the language that we used, that it was disrespectful to her father and blah-blah-blah and henceforth all volumes had to be preapproved by her and her attorney. Suddenly, assembling the volumes got complicated, thanks to Harlan's irrepressible vocabulary.

Gay Comics—Unearthing the History of the Seminal LGBTQ Publication *Gay Comix*

RYAN CAHILL / 2020

From *WePresent* (October 4, 2020) Unpublished source interview. Printed by permission.

Ryan Cahill: What made you want to launch and publish *Gay Comix*? How was the idea conceived?

Denis Kitchen: I was involved in the underground comix movement starting in the late 1960s, first as a cartoonist and then primarily as a publisher (Kitchen Sink Press). My "hippie" generation was caught up in the caustic politics of the time, primarily in opposition to the Vietnam War, but also encompassing the ongoing civil rights movement, women's rights, efforts to legalize marijuana, and the growing gay rights movement. Mainstream comic books had traditionally been aimed at a largely juvenile audience, but young activist cartoonists were pushing back at that industry's self-censorship, unfair economic structure, and seeming inability to create relevant comics for a rapidly changing culture. So creating our own freewheeling "comix" was the answer. Four primary publishers evolved and hundreds of titles proliferated for quite a while, some selling in six figures.

As a publisher in a field dominated, like so much, by white men, I encouraged work from women and minority cartoonists, but by the late 1970s it was still very rare to see work by openly gay cartoonists. I had been publishing *Barefootz Funnies* by Howard Cruse, and for some years he'd been a regular contributor to my anthologies like *Snarf, Bizarre Sex*, and *Comix Book*. I had noticed a gay artist named Headrack appearing in *Barefootz*, and it occurred to me that Headrack might be an autobiographical element. In those pre-internet days I wrote to Howard, who I think was still living in Birmingham, Alabama, deep in America's "Bible Belt." Paraphrasing, I said, "Howard, no offense intended, but might you be gay?" He wrote back that

he was, but professionally closeted. I proposed a comix anthology by gay cartoonists and asked if he would consider editing it. He initially responded that
he'd love to see such a publication but feared that coming out would harm his
primary career as a freelance illustrator. But after thinking it over for a while,
he agreed to tackle the project.

But then Howard confessed that he didn't know any other gay cartoonists.
Neither did I. So we agreed that I'd send out a form letter on Kitchen Sink
stationery to every artist in my Rolodex, announcing *Gay Comix* and asking
any gay men, lesbians, and bisexual cartoonists to send submissions to Howard. A few recipients were not at all happy to get such a letter. I'll never forget a growling phone call from S. Clay Wilson, who ranted about even being
on such a mailing list. But much positive support came back and some very
pleasant surprises.

RC: Was it challenging to publish it at the time? Were you faced with any
restrictions or pushback?

DK: It was challenging in practical ways that I hadn't really anticipated.
The first issue of *Gay Comix* came out in 1980. At that time the larger American culture was still far from accepting gay people as social or legal equals.
There was a great deal of homophobia. I had somehow thought the comics
community would be more embracing, but I quickly learned otherwise. In
the late 1960s and through most of the '70s, underground comix had been
primarily distributed via "head shops," where pot paraphernalia was sold,
because undergrounds for the most part were too outrageous to be sold on
newsstands or traditional periodical outlets. But head shops were increasingly being driven out of business by local ordinances, and by 1980 my distribution had shifted to comic book shops whose primary customers collected
superhero titles. There was considerable resistance from many of the retailers, or at the very least, the vast majority simply declined to carry it. So I was
forced to create a completely separate distribution method for *Gay Comix* in
order for it to be viable. My staff and I, again in the pre-internet era, located
all the specialty gay bookshops we could in the US and Canada, along with a
couple of gay book distributors and a handful of European outlets, and we did
special mailings to all of them. There was a high enough response rate that
the combined markets made *Gay Comix* sustainable, at least for a few years.

RC: What were your initial thoughts on the publication?

DK: I thought Howard did a wonderful job. His own contributions were
first rate, and he conscientiously put together solid anthologies. I was happy
to add it to Kitchen Sink's family.

RC: The topics covered were arguably "ahead of their time." Do you think it was a brave decision to cover topics like the AIDS epidemic and safe sex?

DK: I don't know that I'd call it "brave," necessarily. The idea from the start was for the series to deal with topics of interest to the gay community, and certainly AIDS and safe sex were vital issues.

RC: Do you remember what the cultural impact was at the time? Particularly on the gay community?

DK: As a straight guy I was never exactly plugged into the gay community, so my feedback came indirectly via Howard, some contributors, and the direct and wholesale customers who reached out to us. I know that we had almost universally positive responses from people we heard from. Everyone seemed to love the concept and the content, and most thought a venue for gay cartoonists was long overdue. We also started to see encouraging and even rave reviews in some gay publications and occasionally reviews in general publications about comics. I've always thought of comics as a kind of universal language and hoped the *Gay Comix* format could connect people using humor, satire, and heartfelt autobiography in ways that more strident publications might not. As another example, when I published Howard's *Wendel Comix*, a compilation of the feature that ran for years in *The Advocate*, it never occurred to me that it was just for gay readers. Wendel and his friends are gay, sure, but the stories and humor have universal appeal, and that's how we marketed it.

RC: The publication also featured work from women. Why was it important for the comics to also feature lesbian presentation?

DK: From the very beginning Howard decided that half of each issue would be by men and half by women. That was an editorially sound idea, though we found that—in those days—there seemed to be quite a few more male cartoonists and readers. We also found that none of the lesbian and feminist bookshops at the time would carry *Gay Comix*. That was a source of frustration from a sales point of view, but Howard, to his credit, didn't vary his formula. I think Robert Triptow and Andy Mangels, the subsequent editors, also tried to maintain the gender balance among contributors.

RC: How did it then come into the possession of [publisher and activist] Bob Ross?

DK: After a few years and five issues, I found that the cost of producing *Gay Comix* was disproportionately higher than any other title, because I had to maintain the dual distribution system and create distinct mailing devices and marketing tools completely separate from the rest of the line. It was also difficult, if not impossible, to stretch my limited advertising budget to effectively promote *Gay Comix* to its primary reader base when everything else I published could be efficiently promoted and pushed via the comics industry's "direct market" system. I increasingly felt that *Gay Comix* would best benefit from being with a gay publisher who knew that specialty market far better. I forget how I connected with Bob Ross, who owned the *San Francisco Sentinel*, a weekly gay paper, but when he expressed interest in acquiring the title in 1984, it seemed like a good match. I sold him the trademark, the only thing I owned, since the copyrights, like all undergrounds, were retained by the respective creators.

RC: Did you keep an eye on how Bob Ross progressed the comics or observe the direction that he was taking it in?

DK: I was on the comp list for a while but other than that had no insights into his operation. But because he published the *Sentinel*, I just assumed he'd regularly advertise *Gay Comix* in his own newspaper. After all, "house ads" would cost him nothing, and it seemed like a win-win strategy in a city known as the capital of underground comix. But I heard from Robert Triptow and others, to their dismay, that Ross "never" advertised the comic book in the *Sentinel*. Ross continued to publish *Gay Comix*, but with what seemed like a certain benign and puzzling neglect. That approach kind of astonished me as a fellow publisher, but it was the way he handled it. I much later learned that in 2009, the *Gay Comix* trademark was signed over to Triptow in a quit-claim letter from Bob Ross's heirs.

RC: Do you have any fun anecdotes linking to *Gay Comix*? Any interesting memories you want to share?

DK: Comics conventions for me were always informative marketing surveys: rare opportunities to see fans firsthand, and in those days probably 90 percent of attendees were guys. I'll never forget the Chicago Comic Con in 1980 or maybe '81, the first one after *Gay Comix* was published. I always had a big display there, three or more tables and a big backdrop, because it was a short drive from Wisconsin, where Kitchen Sink was located for over twenty years. Stacks of all of our newer titles were prominently displayed. *Gay Comix* was there right alongside the latest *Snarf, Bizarre Sex, Snappy Sammy Smoot, Dope Comix, Omaha the Cat Dancer, Corporate Crime, Death Rattle,* Will Eisner's *Spirit,* various R. Crumb titles, and so on—a truly disparate lot of comics. *Death Rattle* was a creepy horror comic, but evidently it was not the scariest comic on display. Standing behind the table that long weekend, I observed as fan after fan would pick up the Kitchen Sink titles one by one, typically giving the comic a quick flip through, then the adjoining title, and so on. Then— almost always—when *Gay Comix* was the next in line, they'd kind of freeze.

Very, very few would even pick it up, even though it had a beautifully drawn and hilarious cover by Rand Holmes, a very popular artist. It seemed they were almost afraid to touch it—that someone might see them looking and conclude they were gay. That was my introductory witnessing of the deep-seated aversion that title—that word—provoked among average comic book fans. I remember thinking, "What's wrong with these people!?!" Of course, that was forty years ago. Today there's a remarkably diverse abundance of comics and graphic novels being produced by equally diverse creators, and the audience now—certainly the younger audience—is majority female. Clearly a lot has changed.

RC: Can you remember a particular storyline or story in the comics that you admired the most?

DK: I was always a huge Howard Cruse fan, so I usually loved anything he did. I think the story that jumps out the most for me is his "Jerry Mack" in the second issue, a quite touching piece. It's especially meaningful because of its autobiographical content: A young cartoonist and the main character is a minister from Alabama, like Howard's father.

RC: Looking back, are you proud of what the comic has achieved and the positive impact it had on the LGBTQ+ community?

DK: Absolutely. I felt especially proud when I was invited to participate in the first Queers & Comics Conference in NYC in 2015, organized by Jennifer Camper. It was great to feel welcomed as part of the community, to participate in panels, and to see so many of the *Gay Comix* contributors [and] all three of its editors, and to meet Alison Bechdel and some other luminaries for the first time.

Interview with Denis Kitchen

L'ESPRIT de WILL EISNER / 2021

From *L'Esprit de Will Eisner* [exhibit catalog], *10th Biennale du 9th Art de Cherbourg-en-Cotentin* (2021). Reprinted by permission.

Question 1: Why were you attracted by comic art in the first place?

Answer: As a young boy in America in the 1950s, comic books and newspaper strips were my favorite forms of entertainment. I would immerse myself in the daily paper comic section. When I received my allowance of fifty cents a week, I would typically rush to buy five new ten-cent comic books. I regularly traded comic books with neighborhood friends, and so my tastes and collection both expanded. I had a certain talent for drawing and writing, which first emerged by making illustrated stories for classmates. At the age of thirteen I created a satirical newsletter called *Klepto* that often poked fun at the school and administration, so the single copy was circulated out of sight of my teachers. That was my first experience with the "underground press" [*laugh*]. Soon I began using a hectograph duplicator to produce fifty or sixty copies with primitive color, stapled together, and I sold them to classmates. This lasted for about twenty-five issues. *Klepto* gave me very early hands-on experience drawing cartoons, writing to entertain, publishing, and distribution. It proved much more valuable to my eventual career than the classes!

Q2: What means being an underground artist or editor for you?

A: Two very separate things. As a cartoonist I wanted the freedom to express myself without censorship or restriction. Underground comix developed in the late 1960s as the Vietnam War was a huge issue, as were burgeoning movements like civil rights, women's rights, gay rights, legalizing marijuana, and free speech. Underground comix allowed cartoonists of my generation to use our favorite medium to satirize the establishment, to express anger, or to explore taboo themes, often while using humor or shock value that older generations did not understand. But when wearing my publisher's or editor's hat,

Program cover, *L'Esprit de Will Eisner* exhibition at the *10th Biennale du 9th Art de Cherbourg-en-Cotentin* (2021).

I had to curate content, deciding which stories, which aesthetics, and which ideas best deserved to be in certain issues. It was sometimes a thankless task that cost friendships. I always wanted to give opportunities to new artists and fresh ideas while also needing popular cartoonists to balance sales and to keep the company going. It wasn't always easy being a hippie businessman!

Q3: When did you understand the power of comics? What do you like the most in comics? What is the force of comics that literature or fine arts do not have?

A: At an early age I began noticing educational comics. I observed advertisers using the comics format to sell products. I saw that the combination of words and pictures could be very effective communicating messages in ways that neither words alone nor images alone could do. So the "power" of comics can sell a product as well as political ideas—propaganda in its worst form. But in its purest form comics entertain and enlighten us and, for some, it is an aesthetic pleasure in deeply satisfying ways. When comics are both beautifully drawn and well written, they are on par with the best of their cousins, novels and film, yet uniquely different. I especially appreciate that I can read a comic or graphic novel at my own pace. I can linger over background detail that might enhance a storyline, admire an artist's crosshatching or brushwork, or revel in a skilled artist's realization of a landscape or a particularly appealing face. A film moves at its own pace. Of course I can stop a digital version and rewind to study stopped frames, but that's not the same. Likewise, one can reread certain passages in a novel, but the comics experience is ultimately most satisfying in my view because I can simultaneously savor the written and visual elements in my own comfortable timeframe.

I'm also enthralled and fascinated by the endless variation of drawing styles and storytelling techniques. I can appreciate wildly varying styles—from minimalists like Jules Feiffer or Charles Schulz to the *ligne claire* of Hergé, or the magnificent brushwork of Eisner's *Spirit* to the complex compositions of François Schuiten, among countless examples—but their storytelling can be equally impactful. With certain exceptions where trademark styles must prevail, like Disney or many assembly-line superheroes, I love that I can automatically recognize hundreds of distinctive cartoonists and their idiosyncratic styles and unique manner of rendering.

Q4: How was your first meeting Will Eisner? I heard you both liked to speak about all aspects of the industry of comics—the techniques, but also the publishing and the commercial sides.

A: My first meeting was totally unexpected. I was attending my first comics convention in New York City. The French curator-slash-comics historian Maurice Horn was there. Maurice was doing some business at the time with Will. Maurice saw the name on my badge and said, "Mister Will Eisner wants to talk to you!" I told him he must be mistaken, but he insisted, and he took me to Will's room in the hotel. Phil Seuling, the impresario of the convention, was a fan and distributor of undergrounds and told Will about the growing alternative comix phenomenon, and [he] mentioned that one of the young publishers was in attendance, so that's how Will knew. When we met it was probably a curious sight: Will was dressed in a three-piece suit and tie. He was in his mid-fifties and nearly bald. I was twenty-five, tall and skinny, with hair past my shoulders, unshaven, and wearing bell-bottom pants and a leather vest. The classic businessman and prototype hippie were an odd couple. As Will described us years later, "Denis and I both smoked pipes, but with different substances!" The funny thing is, we found we were also kindred spirits, bound by a common passion for comics.

Q5: What interested Will Eisner in underground comix and in the underground publishing field?

A: As soon as we began talking, it was apparent that Will was intensely curious—a lifelong trait. He peppered me with questions about my "underground business model," which fascinated him: artists owning their copyrights, artists getting paid royalties instead of flat page rates, artists keeping their original art, no censorship, and comics distributed on a non-return basis. These were all the opposite of the comic book business he had grown up in. I tried to ask him about the old days, which fascinated me, but he kept coming back to the present. Before long he was ready to leave his educational and instruction comics businesses to return to actively producing comics for a new generation of fans.

Q6: What is your favorite *Spirit* story and why?

A: I have two favorites: the two-part "Sand Saref" episodes from January 1950 (actually drawn in 1948 for an ill-fated *John Law* comic book). It's the first real glimpse into the young Denny Colt and the first love of his life who has become a dangerous femme fatale. The splash pages and certain other panels are Eisner at his best. The other is "Li'l Adam," a 1947 parody of *Li'l Abner* as well as *Dick Tracy* and *Little Orphan Annie*. As a fan of those strips and their creators, especially Al Capp, it has a special resonance with me. It also begins with a classic "Eisnshpritz" splash page, and Jules Feiffer draws the "Fearless Fosdick" parody panels. The originals to this story hang on my office wall, so I get to see them every day.

Q7: *The Spirit* series belongs to several genres; it is pretty difficult to locate. Would you say that the Spirit is more a superhero or a private detective?

A: I never think of the Spirit as a superhero because he has no superpowers and his "costume" is minimal. I see it as the detective–adventure genre with a dash of humor. I also love that the Spirit himself is often a minor character and others periodically take over.

Q8: Is there something "underground" in *The Spirit* for you?

A: Hah! Yes, it is in a way. First, the Spirit sections were not created as either traditional newspaper comic strips or as comic books. It was an entirely new format: a short story inserted in Sunday papers. So that alone makes it something of an outlaw. There is also the notable lack of a standard trademark. Will deliberately changed the logo on the splash page of every story, something I don't think any other cartoonist had done. Eisner took advantage of the unique format to craft unusual stories, often defying the norms of comics to that point, so I think you could say it was underground in comparison to every other comic of its time.

Q9: Eisner's *Spirit* is full of leitmotifs, of recurring graphic patterns, such as what Kurtzman called "Eisnshpritz" (but we can say the same thing for the windows that we find everywhere and the gloved anonymous hands). Would you say that Will Eisner has an obsessive nature?

A: Absolutely. The pervasive presence of water, as you note, is most obvious: rainstorms, puddles, scenes at waterfront docks, and on boats and the ocean. And always the play of shadow and light, whether from the flick of a match in a blackened room to subtle moonlight to searing sun in a desert. My favorite is broken rays of light coming through window blinds or similar unconventional sources. I love that his "camera eye" is everywhere: bird's eye views, worm's eye views, and even stories where you see the action literally through the eye sockets of a character. He utilized so many inventive storytelling techniques. I don't know if I'd call certain recurring motifs "obsessive," but I think he enjoyed the challenge of drawing things like water and light and shadow—these are things less talented artists avoid. For Will a few simple brush strokes—instinctive for him—could create an evocative atmosphere that most artists could only painfully resolve.

Q10: It seems that yet in 1941, Eisner has the intuition that *comics* are an art form. But he also demonstrated that *comics* are an educational tool or medium. Was it so rare at the time? What was your own vision of comics at this period?

A: Will Eisner was the first to articulate the literary and artistic potential of comics. Thankfully an article survives from a 1941 Philadelphia newspaper that interviewed him, and it's remarkable how prescient Will was, with a clear vision of how comics could evolve. But at the time no one seemed to take his views seriously. He told me he once discussed his theories at a meeting of the National Cartoonist Society in the early 1940s. After listening impatiently Rube Goldberg finally said, "We're just here to sell newspapers, kid!"

With regard to the educational potential of comics, we have to remember that there was a deep prejudice against comics in general from educators and intellectuals, at least in America, with very few exceptions. When Will joined the army, he was soon producing educational posters, but it took quite a while before he was able to do instructive comics. The generals thought comics were for kids. But when Will pushed hard, they agreed to have comparison tests done with the University of Chicago. The resulting data showed that the soldiers studying the same material in a comics format retained more informative and performed tasks better with the comics-style instruction than soldiers tested with dull text and photo manuals. After that the top Pentagon general in charge of training approved what became *Army Motors* and then, later, *P.S.* magazine, which Will produced for many years as a civilian, along with other educational comics for corporations, medical groups, other branches of the government.

Q11: When you first reprinted *Spirit* stories in 1973, what was the editorial line? Then, in 1977, when you continued *The Spirit Magazine* started by Warren, what was your purpose? Why didn't you follow the chronological order of *Spirit* stories' first publication? There are a lot of additional contents, such as essays on comics, one-page stories by Will Eisner, chapters of Will Eisner's graphic novels, interviews of comic artists also by Will Eisner. . . . I believe this kind of publication in a comic book was very rare. How was this idea born?

A: All of Kitchen Sink's publications prior to *The Spirit* were underground comix. But I loved Will's 1940s work, and I had a strong feeling that other fans would too. So after getting to know him following the 1971 convention meeting, I took a bit of a gamble. Will was skeptical that my generation would care about this "dated" material, but it did work via my head shop network, and we were both happy. It worked well enough that Jim Warren saw the opportunity to sell many more copies via conventional newsstands, and he made Will an offer Will couldn't refuse! Later, of course, Eisner and Warren split, and Kitchen Sink resumed publication of *The Spirit Magazine* at a time when my distribution was much stronger.

We published the stories out of order because that's the way Will and his brother Pete sent them to us. Keep in mind that there was no database of stories; there was no place in those days where my staff and I could go to see all the stories. It was largely a mystery what existed. So we received them in whatever random order Will or Pete selected them. Pete would mail the original art—which was so wonderful to hold and examine—and we would make Photostats and return. In retrospect that was not the smartest way to do it [*laugh*]. But I wanted to augment the stories with the articles and history of Will's career and the "Shop Talk" interviews so the magazines would have a broader appeal. Eventually the "Shop Talk" material was collected in book form. In fact, there is a French edition of *Shop Talk* coming soon from Komics Initiative.

Q12: Why have you taken over from Warren and not just started another series? Was it your choice to keep the "magazine format" used by Warren, instead of using the standard comic book format like you did for the 1983 series?

A: At the time my feeling was that Warren had established a large fan base that would support a familiar format. It was as simple as that. At a certain point (issue #41), I discontinued *Spirit Magazine* and created two separate publications, *Will Eisner's Quarterly*, which focused on serializing his new graphic novels and instructional essays and the interviews with other artists, and a new *Spirit* series in comic book format, with the postwar stories in chronological order.

Q13: What was the print run of each *Spirit Magazine* for the first 1977 series, and then for the 1983 series?

A: In 1977 the *Spirit* magazines regularly sold about 20,000 copies. By 1983 the comic book circulation was in the 13,000 to 15,000 range.

Q14: When [did you start] printing and selling posters of Will Eisner's art? You still have some for sale, but others are sold out. Did you sell a lot immediately?

A: Posters and trading cards and postcards and that sort of thing was a natural element of Kitchen Sink Press, which had a merchandise side to it. We even produced chocolate candy bars in "cigar boxes" featuring R. Crumb's Devil Girl, Gilbert Shelton's Freak Brothers, Jeff Smith's Bone, Betty Boop, etc. We had Spirit candy bars on the drawing board when the company finally ended in the late 1990s. I just personally loved producing a sideline of products, and Will was happy to see such items as well. We also did several limited edition signed lithographs and serigraphs with Will, some in partnership with Bernard Mahé.

Q15: After a long period of shame, comic books are finally becoming something one is proud to show in his bookcase. In France, 2020 was dedicated to comic art, and there were lots of events (fairs, exhibitions, shows, etc.) related to comics. There still are. And there are also lots of events dedicated to Will Eisner. In 2020–2021, no less than four events have been scheduled: the exhibition of the Jewish Museum of Florida, the *Will Eisner: Graphic Novel Godfather* exhibition in Dortmund, the sale of *A Contract with God* original pages in Belgium, and the *L'Esprit de Will Eisner* exhibition in Cherbourg, France. You were Will Eisner's agent. Do you think there is a resurgence of interest for his work? And why this enthusiasm? Is it just him, or do other classical artists know this renewed interest?

A: As the agent for the Eisner estate I can say that there have never been so many exhibits, events, and catalogs and books happening at once around Will's career. I think we have finally come to the point where the very best comic art is recognized by a good number of art museums and in university studies, and that gradual acceptance—which has been slow but steady—is very gratifying to see. It's not just Eisner, though he is recognized as one of the primary creative geniuses of his era. On a more commercial scale we also see prices for some comic art skyrocketing in auctions in America and Europe. It's astounding to see, for example, what a Hergé page—or even a single panel—can bring. It's a new era.

Q16: You have reprinted lots of "classic masters" of comics (Al Capp, Bushmiller, Caniff, Hamlin, Herriman, Sterrett, Raymond . . .) during the 1980s and the 1990s. Why at this time? Were they personal inspiration for you, or was it a general interest for them in the underground-slash-alternative comics field? Is there one other master you wish you could have reprinted at the time?

A: It was basically the same reason I wanted to publish *The Spirit* in the early 1970s: It was almost impossible to find any book collections of these comics masters, or at least to find *quality* books. I knew how curious I was personally, and I assumed there were thousands of others who shared my passion for this material and felt confident they would support such books if published. It was another gamble that proved successful. The difficult part often was finding great source material. Sometimes I would locate syndicate proofs and even original art. But sometimes we had no choice but to work from printed newspaper pages. In every case we did our best to make the comics collections look as wonderful as possible and the package designs first rate.

Q17: What do you think of Frank Miller's *Spirit* movie adaptation?

A: Very little! There is a scene in the movie where Denny Colt is in his coffin digging his way out of the grave with his badge. I turned to the friend next to me in the theater and said, "That's Will Eisner digging his way of his grave to kill Frank Miller!!"

Q18: How did you meet Bernard Mahé, and what was the nature of your collaboration?

A: Will introduced as at a convention, as I recall, and encouraged us to cooperate. I quickly took a liking to Bernard and saw that we shared similar tastes and aesthetics. As noted earlier we partnered on four lithographs and produced Will's very last serigraph, dividing the costs and the print runs. We have another thing in common too: We are both passionate collectors of original art, but Bernard's collection next to mine is like the *Titanic* next to a tugboat.

Q19: When did Will Eisner start working on his graphic novel project? How did he first explain it to you? Did he use the term "graphic novel" at the very beginning of his project?

A: He did not use the term "graphic novel" with me. I didn't see those words till I saw his cover of *A Contract with God*. While he was working on it, he referred to the project in conversations in 1977 rather mysteriously as "something very different," but he would not elaborate. Of course, when I saw what he had created I wanted to publish the book, but Will for this one wanted "a New York publisher with a Park Avenue address, not no. 2 Swamp Road," which was my very backwoods address in central Wisconsin at the time, very far from Park Avenue. As it turned out, Baronet eventually went under and in a few years, I inherited the book . . . despite my rural address!

Q20: Graphic novels are often seen as the second or third career of Eisner, but the fact is that there is a real continuity between the postwar *Spirit* and the graphic novels, especially when you look at stories like "The Killer" (1946), "Gerhard Shnobble" (1948), "Two Lives" (1948), or "Ten Minutes" (1949), for example. So it seems that "graphic novels" is only a term referring to a liberating format with less narrative and formal constraints. What do you think?

A: I would agree that Will's experimental *Spirit* stories are precursors of what would come later. Any of the stories you mention could be the basis for longer works. One of my favorites, the two-part "Sand Saref" story from January 1950, is only fourteen pages, but it could easily have been expanded into a graphic novel with rich layers of additional plot detail.

Q21: In the *Eisner/Miller* interview [book] published by Rackham, Eisner tells that the reader of his graphic novels is a sixty-year-old man who has just been robbed of his wallet in the subway. Do you agree? Is it still true today?

A: *Hah!* He also frequently said that comic book readers were "fourteen-year-old cretins from Kansas City." The truth is none of us could say at that time who was reading his graphic novels, or anyone else's graphic novels. There were no comprehensive marketing surveys. It was anyone's guess based on some anecdotal information or limited observations. Today you could argue convincingly that women make up more than 50 percent of graphic novel readers. There is very little hard data that I've seen. I'm skeptical that the typical readers of Will's books are sixty-year-old men. But if they *are*, they will need their wallet . . . graphic novels are not cheap.

Q22: Which one of Will Eisner's graphic novels (or short story published in [his] graphic novels) is your favorite? And why?

A: *A Life Force* is my personal favorite. I think it is the most richly plotted of his efforts, with characters that I care about. It has that great segment with the protagonist Jacob Shtarkah in an alley, suffering from a heart attack, talking to an upside-down cockroach about life and death. The preamble to "The Enchanted Prince" chapter, on a second level, is about Will's son, someone he never talked about publicly because his son suffered from a mental illness. In this passage he is able to talk about his son's pain without being open about the real meaning. I also like that Jacob, unhappy in his marriage, works to bring his one-time love from Germany. He assumes they will finally be a couple again. But it doesn't work out, which is both realistic and unexpected. I think Will constructed something quite wonderful here, one that even Robert Crumb—never a fan of *The Spirit*—called a "masterpiece." My second favorite is *To the Heart of the Storm*, an overtly autobiographical account of his and his family's experiences with antisemitism that I found very revealing and touching.

Episode 190: Politics of the Funnies Part 2, with Denis Kitchen and Kerry Soper

ERIC MOLINKSY / 2021

From *Imaginary Worlds* podcast (2021). Reprinted by permission.

Eric Molinsky: You're listening to *Imaginary Worlds*, a show about how we create them and why we suspend our disbelief. I'm Eric Molinsky, and this is the second of a two-part episode about the politics of the funny pages. In the last episode, we looked at the career of Walt Kelly, who created the strip *Pogo*. This time, we're looking at the comic strip artist Al Capp, who created *Li'l Abner*. There are a lot of similarities between *Pogo* and *Li'l Abner*, but *Abner* had many more readers than *Pogo*, and the characters went way beyond the comics page.

[*Clip from a* Li'l Abner *trailer*]

Announcer: From the creative genius of cartoonist Al Capp, the fabulous characters of his world-famous comic strip . . .

EM: By the way, did you read *Li'l Abner* when you were a kid?

Denis Kitchen: Absolutely. It was my favorite.

EM: Denis Kitchen is a legend in the comics field. His company has published artists from R. Crumb to Art Spiegelman. And he wrote a biography of Al Capp.

DK: This was a strip that at its height was read by 80, 90 million people every day, or at least that was the newspaper circulation.

EM: The characters from *Li'l Abner* also appeared in animated shorts . . .

[*Montage of lines from clips*]

Character: "This statue of Hairless Joe and Lonesome Polecat is almost done. I hope it pleases them!"

EM: A live-action movie from 1940. . . .

[*Dialogue from clip*]

Character: "Howdy, fellers!"

Character: "Howdy, L'il Abner!"

EM: Another one from 1959. . . .

[*Dialogue from clip*]

Daisy Mae: "Abner, let's stop and talk for a while."

Abner: "This ain't time to do any talkin'."

Daisy Mae: "But Abner, don't you realize what you done? You finally asked me to marry you!"

Abner: Yeah, I know!

EM: And that movie was based on a Broadway musical.

[*Music from clip*, "The Matrimonial Stomp"]

When the characters Li'l Abner and Daisy Mae finally got married in the strip, after almost two decades of courtship, the story was so big it was on the cover of *LIFE* magazine. Al Capp himself was also on the cover of *Time* and *Newsweek*.

DK: He was also a regular on *The Tonight Show* and *Jack Paar* and *Merv Griffin* and so on and so on. He had his own radio show. He had for a while his own TV game shows.

EM: He was on other game shows too, like *Password* in 1965.

[*Dialogue from clip*]

Host: "Al, how long has *Li'l Abner* been a comic strip?"

Al Capp: "Actually, *Li'l Abner* been running for thirty-one years."

[*Applause*]

DK: He had his own amusement park. He was the only cartoonist besides Walt Disney who had that. He was everywhere. He was huge in the culture. And now if you're under fifty, you probably don't know who he is.

EM: In looking at the career of Al Capp, it is hard not to compare him to Walt Kelly. Both strips are mostly forgotten today, but they were titans of the comics page. And, like Walt Kelly, Al Capp was one of the few cartoonists who was able to fight for the rights to his own strip, which meant that he had a lot of creative freedom. He didn't have to worry about being censored or replaced. So both he and Walt Kelly broke new ground incorporating satire into story-driven entertainment. Both men were from the Northeast but set their strips in fictional Southern towns where fantastical things happened. But the characters in *Pogo* were talking animals, while the characters in *Li'l Abner* were mostly human—specifically, white Appalachian stereotypes with names like Mammy Yokum and Hairless Joe.

Kerry Soper teaches comics and literature at BYU. He says the main characters of *Pogo* and *Li'l Abner* also had a lot in common, even though *Pogo* is a cute little possum, and *Abner* is a very buff young man with a pompadour.

Kerry Soper: They're both fools, Pogo and Lil Abner, but Pogo was sort of like a wise fool in the Shakespearean tradition. And then, with Li'l Abner, he's like a hapless fool, and it's almost like Capp has contempt for him and uses him sort of as just a stand-in for a foundational American type that's uneducated, easily manipulated—kind of like a sad version of a Huckleberry Finn, if he grew up to be this kind of tall foolish guy.

EM: Their drawing styles were also pretty different. Before he created *Pogo*, Walt Kelly had been an animator at Disney, so his characters looked Disney-esque. Al Capp was more of a caricaturist. The people in his strip looked a little grotesque but funny at the same time, and that reflected their different outlooks on life. Kelly was gentle and indirect in his satire. Most of the characters in his imaginary swamp were good at heart. Li'l Abner himself was good at heart, and so were many of the characters in Dogpatch—the fictional town where Abner lived. But the world around them was more of a dog-eat-dog kind of place.

And Al Capp's worldview partially came from his childhood. When he was nine years old, he lost his leg in a trolley car accident. His coping mechanisms were learning how to draw and developing a dark sense of humor.

DK: In his candid moments Capp would talk about how he thought cruelty was at the base of all humor. . . . But I think it was a way to show man's inhumanity to man in the most obvious way, because these were the neglected citizens who always got dumped on by government bureaucrats or rich people of one kind or another who were there to exploit whatever Dogpatch had, which wasn't much. And if it wasn't bureaucrats or rich people, it would be the turnip termites who would destroy the only crop they had. Like every year with his Sadie Hawkins Day race, when these desperate old maids would have to chase these mostly scrawny hopeless guys.

EM: Yep, Al Capp invented the idea of Sadie Hawkins Day, where girls ask boys to a formal dance instead of the other way around. In the real world, that became an all-American tradition. But in the strip, the storylines were not as wholesome.

DK: There was a scene where these bachelors are running from the women on Sadie Hawkins, and they hide in a glue factory and they get rolled together in a ball of glue, like a handful of bachelors. And then they get set on fire, and they're squealing in pain. There's like a fireball of humans burning to death. And he made it funny because of the way he drew it.

EM: One of my favorite recurring bits that Al Capp did was a hilarious takedown of *Dick Tracy*, which exists as a comic strip within the world of *Li'l Abner*. The Dick Tracy character is called Fearless Fosdick, and he fights ridiculous villains that were parodies of the already ridiculous villains in *Dick Tracy*. And we even get to see the creator of *Fearless Fosdick*. His name is Lester Gooch, and he's depicted a deranged comic strip artist who fetishizes violence and mayhem. Chester Gould, the creator of *Dick Tracy*, was a good sport about all this, and he thanked Al Capp for the free publicity. But I just have to say one more fascinating thing about Fearless Fosdick. The character may have been a parody of Dick Tracy, but he became so popular—in the real world—he got his own TV show, starring marionette puppets.

[*Clip from* Fearless Fosdick]

Character: "Fosdick, you're gettin' too big for your britches!"

Fosdick: "I'm not too big. The pants just happen to be a little too small, that's all."

EM: But I think the best example of how Al Capp used comics to convey his world view came from a totally bonkers storyline about these creatures called Shmoos. Now eventually, Hanna-Barbera got the rights to the Shmoos, so you may have seen the Shmoo cartoons in the 1970s and '80s, but the characters were originally created by Al Capp in 1948. They were these white creatures with bulbous bottoms and then their bodies shot up into a long, curved shape with a smiling head on top.

DK: They're, they're phallic symbols, without question. If you look at some of the panels where he draws the Shmoo, sitting on Li'l Abner's lap, stretching its neck, and it's like, "Oh my God, there is an erection in a newspaper today read by 90 million people. Am I the only one who sees this?" And Capp got away with it.

On another level, take away the sexual element, I think what he was saying is even if humanity had a panacea for all of its ills, it would find a way to fuck it up. When people got a Shmoo, and it would lay eggs and Grade A milk and turn into a steak if you looked hungry, its whiskers were toothpicks. All of that stuff, it was basically a way for a family to be self-contained. And so people would quit work and society fell apart. And basically, the strip was indicating you'd have anarchy unless the government came in and, with their Shmooicide squad, literally exterminate the Shmoos because it was too much of a good thing.

EM: The Shmoos were apparently not too much of a good thing in the real world. They became a merchandising bonanza. The Shmoos were on every kind of toy or consumer product you could imagine. And in the 1948 election, Thomas Dewey said that Harry Truman was promising everything to the American people, including the Shmoos. After Truman won, the president appeared alongside Al Capp to promote a savings bond with the Shmoos on it.

With that much cultural power, Al Capp liked to push things. He didn't depict real politicians in his strip, like Walt Kelly, but Capp created original characters that were based on real people. Like General Bullmoose, a ruthless businessman who had too much influence over elected politicians. And then there was the character of Senator Phogbound.

DK: So you had this Southern senator who was incompetent and corrupt. And so periodically editors would complain to the syndicate and say, "Hey, we're going to drop the strip because you're making fun of senators. That's not something we like." And Capp would scoff at it because, you know, the guy had anywhere from 800 to 1000 newspapers, and if one or two threatened to quit? To him, any publicity was good publicity.

EM: And where Walt Kelly used his strip to go after the KKK, Al Capp used his strip to promote civil rights. And he did it in a way that could get into Southern papers.

DK: After Rosa Parks's incident on the bus in Alabama, within I think six weeks of that happening, he had rushed into print a Sunday sequence of three or four episodes where Mammy is involved with the Dogpatch society women. "Sass-iety," she said. And they were upset to see that a new family moved into Dogpatch and they had square eyes, and they were all indignant. And they said, "There ain't gonna be no square-eyed people in this town." And so they started making it very difficult for those people to live in that town. And then the next week Mammy looks out her window, and she sees a little square-eyed boy [who] trips and skins his knee, and the square-eyed mother runs over and caresses him and tries to make him feel better. And Mammy starts tearing up and she says, "Well, that mammy's treating her boy just like I would treat mine. She loves that little boy." And basically comes to realize "them people has square eyes, but they's people just like us."

EM: And Kerry Soper says in the 1940s and '50s, Al Capp's politics were more progressive than Walt Kelly.

KS: We're celebrating Walt Kelly for achieving real clout as an artist, you know owning his copyright, but he was actually against advocating for a union that cartoons could belong to or helping out younger cartoonists with artists right issues. Whereas Al Capp was more about unionizing, giving fair kind of compensation to female artists.

EM: In fact, when the first woman applied to join the National Cartoonists Society—an artist named Hilda Terry—she faced fierce resistance.

DK: It was an all-male club, and they liked it that way. And Capp stood up and said, "It's time to let women in. She's a professional. And I won't be a member of an organization that won't admit her." And when they voted her down, Al Capp quit.

EM: By 1960, Capp and Kelly were both seen as heroes on the left for different reasons. They were using their cultural power to break an unwritten rule that the comics page was supposed to be a neutral zone, free from politics or satire. And despite the pushback, they were getting away with it. Their strips were more popular than ever. And that is where their careers went in very different directions. There's a lot more about Al Capp after the break.

[*Commercial*]

EM: Denis Kitchen had been a lifelong fan of *Li'l Abner*. And in 1966, he was in college. He opened up the funny pages and he was shocked to see that Capp had introduced a new group of characters to the strip—an unruly mob of student agitators called SWINE, which stood for Students Wildly Indignant about Nearly Everything.

DK: And it was pretty obvious he had a chip on his shoulder about students who were protesting the Vietnam war. And I was one of those students, so I started taking it personally

EM: Afterward, Capp introduced a new character called Joanie Phony, who was an unflattering caricature of Joan Baez, the folk singer. And this really stood out because Al Capp didn't usually do caricatures of real people in the strip.

DK: Somebody chased down Joan Baez. And they said, "Are you aware of what Al Capp is doing in his strip?" And she said, "I certainly am. I have my lawyers looking into it." And then of course, they went back to Capp who was waiting for them. He anticipated this. And I—as much as I was not happy with him at the time—I thought what he said to the reporters was spot on, because first he said, "Well, Joanie Phony in my strip is hideous looking, has no talent, never bathes, rips off her fans, is a hypocrite, and so on. I can't imagine why Miss Baez sees a similarity with herself." It was mean, but it was brilliant. But then he said, "Gentlemen, she protests for a living. Am I also not allowed to protest?" And that got me because I realized the left and the counterculture I was a part of, we didn't, we didn't own satire [*laughs*].

EM: In many interviews, Al Capp was asked why he turned to the political right. He said he didn't go anywhere. It was the left that changed.

DK: He lived in Cambridge and so he was right next door to Harvard, and he saw, in his view, overprivileged kids with mostly rich parents sending them to the best schools. And in his view, instead of getting an education, like he would have loved to have had—he wanted to go to college; he couldn't afford it—he saw them squandering their parents' money and in his jaded view not bathing and all that other sidebar stuff.

EM: He wasn't just offended by the long hair, and beards—although that did bother him. Al Capp would often mention this one incident from 1966. Robert McNamara was the secretary of defense—and the architect of the Vietnam War. McNamara came to speak at Harvard, not far from where Capp lived. A hundred students swarmed McNamara's car, preventing him from leaving. McNamara tried to have a dialogue with them, but the students shouted him down. The police had to intervene and get McNamara out of there. Capp was furious. He said the students were denying McNamara's freedom of speech and putting him in physical danger. He was also mad that the university didn't punish the students.

Capp thought he was doing what he always did, using his artistic platform to speak out against something he thought was outrageous. But it also brings up a question that a lot people are wrestling with today when it comes to entertainment. There's an old rule in comedy and satire that you need to make fun of people that are more powerful than you—politicians, industry leaders, people who have the power to send teenagers off to war. It's called punching up. You're not supposed to punch down and make fun of people who don't have the same platform that you do.

But from Capp's point of view, the counterculture was a swarm, an unstoppable movement that was taking over the culture at large. In his mind, they had more power collectively than any single person with power. So when he aimed his satire not just at celebrities like Joan Baez, but college students and hippies, he turned the idea of punching up upside down—which was groundbreaking in its own way.

Now that Denis Kitchen is older than Al Capp was at this time, he's tried to understand where Capp was coming from.

DK: Yeah. I've tried my best to put myself in his shoes. It would be easy to say it was cynical, but the fact that I think it was genuine I think you have to take into account. Now that said, I still can't forgive that he became close friends with scoundrels like Nixon and Agnew and was literally among the handful of friends Nixon had. I interviewed Al's grandson.

EM: His grandson Willie lived in the same house as Al Capp, and he told Denis the White House often called in the late 1960s and early '70s.

[*Clip from Nixon's "Address to the Nation on the War in Vietnam"*]

Nixon: Tonight I want to talk to you on a subject of deep concern to all Americans. . . .

DK: A number of other times [Willie] would be in the room, and it would be like one time Nixon gave a speech, and right after the speech, he called Al and he said, "What did you think of my performance?" And Al critiqued his performance and said, "You should have done this. You should have done that." This is the kind of confidant he was in a way that certainly, I don't think any other cartoonist was ever that close to a president.

EM: And here's another big difference between Al Capp and Walt Kelly. For Kelly, the strip was everything. He was such a perfectionist, he lost opportunities to push his characters beyond the strip into merchandising and other types of media. Al Capp went in the opposite direction. At this time in his life, he became less hands-on in creating the strip. He went on speaking tours around the country. And instead of appearing on game shows, he was now appearing on political talk shows.

DK: I also think you have to put his political change in the context of a guy who had been the king of the hill in his profession for many years. By the time, and I can't remember exactly, there was a point when *Peanuts* by Charles Schulz was beginning to catch up and basically pass him. And *Peanuts* became the most popular strip. And I think there was something about Capp where he had to be king of the hill. And so he was getting suddenly a lot of attention from the conservative side of the fence, which he never did before, because he had been a liberal darling for decades, but I think he enjoyed the new attention from a new audience. And as he was losing his old crowd, I think he thought, consciously or unconsciously, "Here's a new area. And they like me a lot."

EM: But he may have met his match when John Lennon invited him to John and Yoko's bed-in for peace. Now the first thing that amazes me about this video is that here is a comic strip artist, walking into a room with rock stars—actual rock stars—and people are starstruck by him. Someone says, "Oh, you're *the* Al Capp!"

[*Dialogue from clip*]

Ono: "Oh, you're the Al Capp."

Capp: "Yes, I'm the dreadful, Neanderthal, fascist, how do you do?"

EM: It starts out kind of friendly, but soon he and Lennon are going at it.

[*Dialogue from clip*]

Capp: "I could make a lot more drawing people like you than confronting you, and I must say it's much more appetizing drawing them because I can leave them."

Lennon: "I prefer singing to doing this."

DK: That was a publicity stunt that both sides knew what they were doing. And John and Yoko knew when they invited him that there would be a confrontation and that's what they wanted. They wanted press. And so Capp was there to be the villain. He certainly was the villain.

EM: Here's the problem for Capp. That moment happened over fifty years ago, and people are still talking about John and Yoko. But until I began to research this episode, that was the only video I had ever seen of Al Capp because it was in a John Lennon documentary that I watched in high school. And I remember thinking at the time, "Who is that guy?!" Denis says behind the scenes, behind this public persona, Capp's feelings were a little bit more complicated.

DK: And in talking to his grandchildren, they saw a very different man than I saw in press accounts. They saw a very loving grandfather. In fact, one of them who is about my age said that she was also one of those students. And when he talked to her privately and she stated her position, why she was protesting, he looked at her and he said, "You know what, maybe you're right." And he could privately say that to her. He could not publicly change his stance because he was already very steadfast in what he was doing.

EM: But I've read that you think that the strip itself kind of suffered during that period. It wasn't as good.

DK: It's not just my opinion. He said that himself. When he retired in 1977, in his last interview, he said, "The strip hasn't been funny for years."

EM: But he didn't retire just because the strip wasn't funny anymore. His health was failing. And also, Al Capp was a womanizer. He went after much younger women—including a young Goldie Hawn. The accusations of sexual harassment, indecent exposure, and other charges piled up, until newspapers started to pull *Li'l Abner* from their comics pages. Way before cancel culture was a thing, he was literally being canceled. So he quit.

Denis may feel disgust and disappointment towards Al Capp, but he still has respect for him as an artist. In fact, Denis went out of his way to preserve *Li'l Abner*, which he thinks was brilliant in its heyday, even if he felt stung as the subject of its satire.

DK: I can tell you, in terms of reprints, my own series, Kitchen Sink Press, published twenty-seven volumes of *Li'l Abner*. And I only got halfway before my company went under, or I would have finished. We had planned to do fifty-four volumes, which was truly encyclopedic. Another company tried doing it not very long ago. And they got up to about eight volumes, and they had to cancel it because there just wasn't enough of an audience for it to be even marginally profitable. And that tells you everything: A strip that was read by 80 or 90 million people as recently as the 1970s now can't even sell a few thousand book collections. It's staggering.

EM: Also, the comics page does not have a lot of cultural weight anymore. I mean, of course, there are still comic strips—and web comics are really popular—but those audiences are limited. It's hard to imagine today several panels of cartoon characters, printed in a newspaper, having that much influence over the imaginations of millions of Americans.

Although in pushing the boundaries of what this supposedly nonpolitical art form could do, Al Capp and Walt Kelly helped create the process that led to our culture breaking up into subdivisions and echo chambers. And the questions that they began to ask through their comic strips—What is political? What is fair game? When should storytellers use their fantasy worlds to comment on the real world, and can they do it in a way that doesn't lose sight of the storytelling itself?—we are mired in those questions today. There are no easy answers. Every storyteller and every fan have to make those choices for themselves.

That is it for this week; thank you for listening. Special thanks to Denis Kitchen and Kerry Soper.

The 3D Work of Denis Kitchen

LAWRENCE KAUFMAN / 2022

From *Stereo World* [National Stereoscopic Association, Inc.] (May/June 2022). With assistance from Denis Kitchen. Reprinted by permission.

Denis Kitchen was an original member of the "Underground Comix" movement in the late 1960s and '70s, equally well known as the founder and publisher of the pioneering publishing house Kitchen Sink Press (1969–1999). He also founded the Comic Book Legal Defense Fund (1986–), is the author or coauthor of numerous books, a literary and art agent, a longtime editor, and a curator of comic art exhibitions in America and overseas. A monograph of Kitchen's artistic career, *The Oddly Compelling Art of Denis Kitchen*, was published by Dark Horse in 2010. With partner John Lind he created the Kitchen Sink Books imprint in partnership with Dark Horse Comics in 2013. He was elected to the Will Eisner Hall of Fame in San Diego in 2015. A few years ago, Columbia University Libraries acquired 60,000 letters, along with production files, comprising his Kitchen Sink–related archives. His life story is prime for a Netflix limited series. Check out his website: deniskitchen.com.

Denis is an iconic artist and publisher. For more than fifty years, he has navigated the many twists and turns and hills and valleys of publishing. His biography is online on his website and on Wikipedia. In addition to the previously mentioned *The Oddly Compelling Art of Denis Kitchen*, you can read about his many triumphs and challenges in several other books, including *Kitchen Sink Press: The First 25 Years* (1994), *Comic Book Creator* #5 (2014), and *Everything Including the Kitchen Sink: The Definitive Interview with Denis Kitchen* (2016). A free bonus pdf to *Comic Book Creator* #5 is available online at twomorrows.com/freestuff.

Stereo World: I know you didn't go to many movies when you were growing up, but do you have any recollections of any of the 3D movies or any of the 3D comic books which were released in 1953 or '54?

Denis Kitchen: I have a vivid memory of buying *Whack* as a young boy. I think it was my introduction to 3D. At twenty-five cents, it cost half a week's allowance, but I was very impressed. It had to me, at the time, a kind of *MAD* feel to it, and the three-dimensional effect was mind-blowing. I also recall having 3D versions of *Mighty Mouse*; the *Three Stooges*; *Sheena, Queen of the Jungle*; and *Superman*. I swapped comic books regularly with neighborhood friends, but the 3D comics were in my no-trade stash.

SW: You collect vintage postcards and group them together into stories. Have you considered how similar those are to stereoview cards of the same time period, which were sold in sets from the early twentieth century, with similar subjects, such as the wife waiting for her husband with a rolling pin?

DK: I haven't collected stereoscopic cards with the same fervor as vintage postcards, but I've certainly seen enough to know there were strong parallels. It's amusing to see how much joy folks a hundred plus years ago seem to have gotten from certain repeated motifs, like the roller-pin-waving wife and drunken husband. In fact, I'd love to acquire stereo cards with those kinds of humorous themes, so if any readers are amenable, I'd be open to swapping postcards, comics, whatever, to obtain.

SW: Not only did you publish the first underground 3D comic book, *Deep 3-D Comix*, but your artwork appears on the back cover and it was the first new 3D comic book in over sixteen years. The book was dated summer 1970, with a seventy-five-cent cover price. It sold out and at that time, your print runs were smaller, probably due to the upfront printing costs and the quantity of copies you could pick up from the printer and haul in your personal vehicle. It had a second printing and at least a third in 1972, when the cover price was increased to one dollar. Did the second printing have a printing problem and need to be thrown out? How many copies do you estimate were printed and sold of this title?

DK: You know too much, Lawrence! But the vehicle early on was a hearse, so it hauled quite a load. The printer did a bad job on the reprintings. Ink coverage was too light, as I recall, and I was too inexperienced at the time as a publisher to demand a do-over. That said, our largely stoned hippie audience didn't seem to object. As to numbers, I don't have to estimate: Each printing was ten thousand copies, so thirty thousand total.

SW: Thirty thousand is an impressive number. It is too bad that *Deep 3-D Comix* #2 never made it to print.

DK: A pretty good number, yes. Many people think underground comix were more marginal than they really were. The really popular titles, like Crumb's, could sell in six figures. The *Freak Brothers* cumulatively hit a million before too long. I would have loved a second issue of *Deep 3-D*, but artist Don Glassford took a bad turn not long after that comic. Drugs took their toll on him. No one else in undergrounds bothered to figure out the anaglyphic mechanics, or had the patience to.

SW: Over fifty years have passed, so any other questions may test your memory, but I wanted to see if the information on the *Grand Comics Database* website is correct. I always believed the price was increased with the third printing, but Comics.org states the second and third printing had one-dollar cover prices. The one-dollar copies which I have in my collection all state "printing number 7 6 5 4 3," so I assume that is printing number three. Comics.org states that the third printing glasses are attached at the centerfold, but all of mine are stapled to the cover. This also brings up the question about having the glasses printed. You must have printed extra glasses, since you offered replacement glasses with a self-addressed, stamped envelope. Do you recall if glasses were printed with each additional print run of the comic? In 1953, Harvey Publications made so many extra glasses that you can still purchase lots of them on eBay.

DK: Correct [that both the second and third printing were one dollar]. I just checked my file copies. Correct [that printing number 7 6 5 4 3 designates the third printing]. The glasses should have been in the centerfold. I suspect your copies had glasses stapled on by a dealer because they became loose? We would never have had our printer staple anything on a cover. Yes, we definitely printed extra [glasses]. We must have had a hunch they'd frequently get separated from the comic and lost. Presumably yes, [we must have printed extra glasses] because we couldn't have predicted there'd be three or more printings. I did not know [about Harvey trying to corner the market on 3D glasses in the 1950s]. That's hilarious. But then I'm pretty certain I still have a carton of *Deep 3-D glasses* in the warehouse!

SW: It would be another almost thirteen years before another new 3D comic book was published, when 3-D Cosmic Publications, a division of 3D Video Corporation, put out *Battle for a Three-Dimensional World*. That book was copyright 1982 but not available until May 1983. Ray Zone wrote that book, and it would start him out on a very prolific publishing and conversion career. By 1984, Ray was doing conversion work for several publishers and 3D comic books were selling very well. Kitchen Sink Press had several successful classic comic reprint series, including Will Eisner's *The Spirit* and Milton Caniff's *Steve Canyon*. Both of these series had one-shot 3D issues, with 3D conversions by Ray Zone. Did Peter Poplaski edit both of those, and whose idea was it to produce these 3D titles? Do you have any interesting recollections about these two books?

DK: Pete Poplaski oversaw both books and designed the covers. As you know, I love 3D, and I just thought it would be great to convert those two classic properties by true geniuses who also happened to be real gentlemen to work with. Neither strip had appeared in 3D before. I remember getting a call from Milt Caniff after *Steve Canyon* 3D was printed, telling me how much he enjoyed seeing his characters in three dimensions. Just to hear that old pro exhibit some enthusiasm was alone worth the effort. Will also loved the conversion. His *Spirit* splash panels and layouts in particular were perfectly suited for 3D. I know we had planned a follow-up *Spirit 3-D*, having identified a good number of visually dramatic stories as candidates, but I think the market must have shifted—perhaps a glut of 3D titles? But in any event that intended follow-up never materialized.

SW: In 1990, Rip Off Press, Inc., published *Underground Classics #12: Gilbert Shelton in 3-D*. The 3D was by Roger May and the printing was by the 3-D Zone. While you weren't involved with this title, Kitchen Sink was one of the largest distributors of Rip Off Press items by mail order and in their retail outlet. Do you have any recollections of this 3D title or perhaps any of the other 3D titles which were released in the 1980s 3D comic book boom?

DK: I remember enjoying seeing Gilbert's work in 3D. I still have a 3D Freak Brothers poster that someone issued around then too. Of course, Gilbert's stuff is hilarious in any dimension. I was certainly following the 1980s 3D revival with interest. I loved some of the reprints like *Sheena* and *Seduction of the Innocent*, mainly because of the gorgeous Dave Stevens covers, and several *Three Stooges* in 3D. Eclipse did an "explosive" issue called *Destroy* that was a fun plotless excuse for dimensional mayhem. There were also a couple of very cool Basil Wolverton adaptations someone came out with and a couple of 3D *Tor* by Joe Kubert. But a lot of the stuff being converted to 3D during that revival period was pretty pedestrian and much of it only converted, I presume, because it was public domain and the publisher could avoid licensing fees.

SW: Larry Welz had a very popular adult comic series with *Cherry* (originally *Cherry Poptart*), published by Last Gasp through issue #13. Kitchen Sink Press published issues #14 and #15 and reprinted eight of the previous issues. Welz's Cherry Comics continued publishing at least seven more issues and reprinted the previous issues. *Cherry* #11 was a 3D issue, first by Last Gasp in 1990 with a $3.50 cover price, 3D by Roger May, with printing by the 3-D Zone. Kitchen Sink reprinted it in 1994 with a $3.95 cover price. The paper quality in your reprint is great and looks a lot better than the original version. I am curious why Kitchen Sink only reprinted eight issues. Was Kitchen Sink involved in the later issues, and is it possible the 3D issue had additional reprints? Can you tell us about this partnership and any other recollections?

DK: Kitchen Sink published new issues #14 through #19, along with several *Cherries Jubilee* and quite a few reprints of the earlier Last Gasp issues. My file copies show only two KSP printing of the 3D *Cherry*. I'm afraid my recollections of this particular "partnership" are not fond. Larry called me in 1992, expressing unhappiness with Last Gasp—accounting issues, he said—and asked if I'd publish *Cherry*. I was already publishing the long-running *Omaha the Cat Dancer*, an erotic anthropomorphic soap opera, and *Melody*, the autobiographical account of a Quebec-based exotic dancer, so it seemed like it might be a good fit in our "sexy department." The difference was that *Omaha* and *Melody* were what I'd call literate and artistic comics, whereas *Cherry* was more in-yourface porn without any subtlety whatever. At that time Kitchen Sink had about fifteen employees, the majority of whom were women. Concerned that *Cherry* might be offensive to them, I held a staff meeting and passed around copies. I stated that if there was discomfort among the staff that I'd turn down the opportunity. Someone asked if it would sell well. I said it was likely to be a very good seller and would help Kitchen Sink's bottom line. When I eventually asked for hands, all the women voted yes and the only dissent was my brother James, our head of production. So I moved forward.

There were two wrinkles. First, I had to pay Last Gasp for all of their film and ship the heavy flats to Wisconsin. Last Gasp publisher Ron Turner warned me about Larry, but I was already committed and had no way of knowing which complainer was right, if either. The second wrinkle was that Larry insisted on a guarantee of $3,000 a month, a considerable sum for me to commit to in the early 1990s. After running the numbers we determined it would be a good investment if Larry produced three or four new issues per year. He claimed to be very prolific, assured me that was no problem, and we made a deal. We paid his monthly advances regularly. Not long afterward I merged with Tundra and moved to Massachusetts. Larry proved incapable of staying anywhere near the promised schedule, and back issue sales were not what we expected. At a certain point he was overpaid by about $35,000. I told him his advance had to stop or be significantly reduced until his sales caught up with his royalty earnings. He bristled, immediately lawyered up, threatened to sue me (!!!), and abruptly left to self-publish, or whatever he ended up doing. So I ended up stiffed for thirty-some thou[sand], not to mention legal costs. I'd been stiffed by various distributors and retailers over the years—par for the course in publishing—but this was the only time in my long career a creator did so. So I'll just say I have no warm memories about that relationship.

SW: Kitchen Sink had a home run with Mark Schultz and his *Xenozoic Tales*, with fourteen issues from 1987 to 1996. *Cadillacs and Dinosaurs* was a 1989 one-shot by Schultz from Kitchen Sink. In July 1992, there was a 3D *Cadillacs and Dinosaurs* issue, with 3D By Roger May. This book included a 3D one-page ad for Roger May, with a 3D cartoon by John Pound that showed Roger May, Denis Kitchen, and Ray Zone discussing 3D. *Cadillacs and Dinosaurs* became a CBS Saturday morning cartoon show and a line of Tyco toys. There was a 3D *Cadillacs and Dinosaurs* CBS variant cover copyright 1993. Can you tell us anything about the decisions to make this 3D issue and how Roger May was picked to do the 3D conversions?

DK: The folks at CBS and our merchandise licensing agent thought the novelty of a 3D comic would get the attention of merchandising people outside of comics fandom, so they encouraged it. My recollection is that it did help, though nothing could ultimately save the property from an ill-fated time slot. We originally had offers from both Fox and CBS. Since CBS had for several years dominated Saturday [morning] animation programming, we went with them. But the upstart Fox launched a then-unknown *Power Rangers* in the time slot opposite *Cadillacs and Dinosaurs*. The rest is history. Had we gone with Fox, [*Cadillacs and Dinosaurs*] would have either led into *Power Rangers* or followed it and almost certainly shared the exceptionally strong ratings. We can only speculate, of course. You can't win 'em all.

Selecting Roger for the 3D conversion was an easy one. He was truly enthusiastic about Mark's work, and also just more available than the busy Ray Zone. Roger was a real character: an archetypal hippie with flowing beard, and he typically wore an Uncle Sam–like stovepipe hat. He was also super serious about his craft. In those days anaglyphic 3D required meticulous hand-cutting of often minute sections of a duplicate photostat with an X-acto blade and repositioning left or right vis-à-vis the uncut image, as most of your readers know well. He loved all the detail in Mark's work and was up for the challenge of layering the elements as best he could for dramatic effect.

SW: You explain in *The Oddly Compelling Art of Denis Kitchen* that in 1992 Michael T. Gilbert asked you to do a pinup page for his *Mr. Monster Triple Threat 3-D* comic, published by the 3-D Zone in 1993. At that time, you had never created an image for anaglyphic 3-D. You produced the 2D art, and Ray Zone did the conversion. This was one of the final 3-D Zone titles, and several others artists did art for this title including Dave Stevens, Alan Moore, Ken Brunziak, Paul Ollswang, Jeff Bonivert, Terry Beatty, Bill Messner-Loebs, Tom Sutton, Paul Chadwick, Brian Buniak, Kim and Simon Dietch, Lyndal Ferguson, and Mark Pacella. Do you remember anything else about this 3D comic?

DK: I was really happy to get the invitation from Michael. When Don Glassford created his *Deep 3-D* comic for Kitchen Sink twenty years earlier, he asked if I wanted to do a guest page, like Jay Lynch. But Don expected me to do my own 3D overlays. I was stymied by the process—or the time involved—and bailed, doing the non-3D back cover instead. So knowing that Ray would convert my Mr. Monster image was a relief and something of a thrill. I created an image where a stream of tiny demons escape from a test tube, designed so that they formed a corkscrew spiral. I naively thought I needed to explain to Ray the intended spiral effect, but he rather abruptly assured me it would be child's play for him. I was delighted with the results and hope to reprint it in a future collection or as a small print.

SW: You had previously told me that *The Land Before Time 3-D Adventure Comic* (1996) was a scarce title. It was one of only two titles issued under your short-lived KS Kids imprint and was not distributed through regular channels such as Diamond Comic Distributors, but only via an MCA Treasure Chest assembled to promote *Land Before Time* videotapes. I finally found one in Australia. The book was written by Steven Utley and illustrated by Douglas Potter. I had known Steven Utley from the Dallas area science fiction groups in the 1970s. The 3D conversion was again done by Roger May. The cover states 3D glasses included, but mine does not have 3D glasses. Were these bound-in or separate? What else can you tell us about it, and [do you have] any idea why it wasn't published on its own, separate from the videotape promotion? My comic shop has nine users who have placed it on their want lists.

DK: Sorry you had to chase so far for your *Land Before Time in 3-D*! My file copy has no bound-in glasses, so I think generic ones must have been packed separately in the little "treasure chest" of goodies. The cartoonist Doug Potter was also from the Dallas area—I met him in Dallas too, at the annual Fantasy Fair where the Harvey Awards used to be held. That 3D comic was done exclusively for MCA's distribution, with no additional copies printed for the comics market. We may have been able to carve out an exception for that, but in the 1990s there was virtually no interest in kid's comics via the direct market used to reach comics shops, so I suspect we thought the numbers would not be sufficient. In retrospect it makes sense that this title would be one of the very scarcest Kitchen Sink comics.

SW: Let's move onto your 3D posters—you have done a number of these now and you have many 3D and 2D posters for sale on your website, so they must sell pretty well. In 1992 writer Don Baumgart, artist Gilbert Sheldon and Roger May had produced 187 *The Fabulous Furry Freak Brothers* 3D posters, which you mentioned earlier. These were available signed at comic book conventions. Roger May was also selling a *Xenozoic* 3D poster with art by Mark Schultz online. You are currently selling a 14.75″ × 25″ limited quantity poster as produced, but never released due to technical reasons, available from deniskitchen.com. Is this the same poster that Roger May was selling?

DK: It is the same one, yes. The "technical" reason Kitchen Sink did not distribute it had nothing to do with the 3D effect, which was excellent. The problem was that Roger insisted we use his West Coast printer so he could "supervise" the production, but he never ran the specs or proof past us. He made the credits way too large in the lower right corner. KSP always gave credit, but more discreetly, so as not to distract from the image. Plus, the paper was thinner than we'd have used. I still had to pay his printer and was very annoyed with Roger at the time. We never reprinted it and only fairly recently I found the remaining small stack that is currently being offered in Steve Krupp's Curio Shoppe.

SW: Jason Little had done a 3D conversion of *Little Nemo in Slumberland* in 2014. This 18″ × 24″ poster was your interpretation of Winsor McCay. You have signed (heavier card stock) and unsigned versions available from deniskitchen.com. You had done this art in 2D for the oversized *Little Nemo: Dream Another Dream* (2014). Did Jason Little do the 3D conversion at about the same time? What else can you tell us about this poster?

DK: First, it was just very gratifying and a lot of fun to do my take on McCay. For the book you cite, it appeared in full color, like an old Sunday newspaper page. Afterward it occurred to me that the panels—with the clown doll hurtling toward the reader in the nightmarish dream—could be ideal for a 3D conversion. So that's when I reached out to Jason, who I knew was seriously into 3D and could handle the technical side. Then Josh O'Neill, the book's publisher, asked if they could use the 3D poster as a Kickstarter incentive. I consented, but 18″ × 24″ was too large for their custom packaging. From my files they printed a somewhat smaller version. So, for the record, there's a variant size out there.

SW: *Major Arcana* is a record album cover you drew in 1975. You also recycled the art into a three-page story in *Mondo Snarfo* (1978). That story was also reprinted in *El Vibora* #8–9 (1980). Roger May did a 3D conversion in 1999 of a record album cover. That poster was 13″ × 17″ and sold out. In 2016 Jason Little produced a 16″ × 17.5″ enhanced version, which is available from deniskitchen.com. What else can you tell us about that?

DK: I would have reprinted this in the original size, but the irresponsible printer did not save the film negatives. So I reached out to Roger, who eventually found his digital files and supplied them to me not long before

Kitchen's most popular 3D poster, based on his surreal 1975 cover for Jim Spencer's psychedelic/ folk rock album *Major Arcana*.

he suddenly died. Roger had suggested some enhancements, so I asked Jason to make those modifications for the somewhat larger image for the second printing. Jason added a third color, yellow, that he felt would add to the dimensional experience. I've found that some people like the added yellow effect and some find that it distracts from the 3D. And I just found out this past month that the original album, out of print for nearly fifty years, is being re-issued in standard vinyl format by Guerssen Records, a Spanish label. I was never happy with the original album cover color, which printed darker than intended, so Guerssen is letting me provide a newly colored version for its edition. I'll then use that newly colored version for a limited edition giclee, so this image has found itself transformed far more than ever anticipated.

SW: You produced a 3D *The Road to Wealth* poster in 2019, a 17″ × 12″ Harrison Cady (1877–1970) illustration with 3D by Jason Little and available from your website. You and your daughter Violet also wrote an impressive art book monograph about Harrison Cady in 2020, *Madness in Crowds: The Teeming Mind of Harrison Cady*. There were 250 signed and numbered slipcase editions produced, which included a *Road to Wealth* 3D print (13″ × 9″) and glasses, which is still available from the publisher Beehive Books. Am I correct that the 3D print was only in the slipcase edition? What can you tell us about the poster and the inclusion of the print in the book?

DK: Yes, it was only available via Beehive as a bonus with the deluxe book edition, but it's now also available in our web store (Steve Krupp's Curio Shoppe) along with the other 3D posters you've mentioned. I clearly love Harrison Cady's work and was struck with how deeply dimensional and layered so much of his work for the old *LIFE* magazine was. So it just seemed obvious to adapt something to 3D, and I picked this carousel image which satirizes wealth disparity. Though drawn more than 110 years ago, it still pointedly attacks the same kind of disparity we still have with us. Some things never change.

SW: You also have a 3D *Road to Hell* by Harrison Cady (2021) poster available. This 1910 parody of a *LIFE* magazine centerfold with 3D by Christian LeBlanc is 12″ × 18″. Are you going to do other Cady art in 3D, and what else can you tell us about this poster?

DK: *Road to Hell* is one of my favorite Cady drawings. It's featured and discussed at the very beginning of the *Madness in Crowds* book. The jam-packed cartoon skewers the silly religious notion that "sins" like cussing, flirting, betting on horses, playing cards, and dancing would lead mortal souls to eternal perdition, all depicted via a winding staircase into the gates of Hell itself. Like *Road to Wealth*, this deeply layered image simply demanded a conversion to 3D. I would love to see Cady's reaction to this anaglyphic version of his art. Perhaps I'll have the chance when I meet him and most other cartoonists in Hell.

SW: You have another 3D poster in production. Anthony Smith drew a one-shot *Acid Head Arnie* in 1994. Smith asked you to do an illustration for his *Acid Head* anthology. Charles Barnard is doing a 3D version of your *Acid Head* # 1 art for a poster. What else can you tell us about this, and when will it be available?

DK: The background for this is a swap that Anthony and I made, so long ago that neither of us remember what he initially traded me, but I knew I owed him an original custom cover in return. Years literally went by. I developed a mental block about the debt. At one point in the 1990s, to hopefully break through my impasse, I told him that he could take fifty dollars' worth of merchandise from my web store every month until I delivered. So here I was, effectively paying someone so I didn't have to draw! He happily accepted the benefits of my selfguilt for at least a year or two, but I still didn't deliver, and eventually he became guilty. Then a few years ago Anthony mentioned wanting to do an anthology called *Acid Head*. That title itself enticed my imagination, and then he suggested an aquatic composition. Suddenly I felt a jolt of inspiration and quickly fulfilled the roughly twenty-fiveyear-old debt. When I showed the color version to Charles Barnard in early 2019, he said he'd love to create a full-color 3D version, a jump above our usual two-color 3D collaborations. Charles got maybe halfway through it when he became super busy and hasn't been able to get back to it. I know it'll be wonderful when he completes the conversion. It is no doubt karmic justice for me to now be the one waiting.

SW: We have been promised *Denis Kitchen's 3-D Chipboard Portfolio* for a while now. I think it is a publisher delay more than anything else. With 3D by Charles Barnard, you and Charles have really enhanced the 3D on these images by adding white elements. Are we going to see that any time soon?

DK: Yeah, originally Beehive Books was up for it, but their lineup got congested, including another big monograph my daughter Violet and I are doing for them on Boris Artzybasheff, and they just didn't think the portfolio was viable for them. I'm now looking at a format much closer to the heavy card stock *3-D Frank* book Charles Barnard did with Jim Woodring. It's just much easier to market a book than an art portfolio. So now it's just a question of scheduling the remaining pages and lining up a new publisher. It's possible I'll be doing it with Tinto Press in Denver. They're publishing *Creatures from the Subconscious* this year, a square hardcover collection of 170 or so of my surreal "chipboard" drawings. One way or the other, the 3D project will get back on track. The conversions Charles did are simply too spectacular to stay on the back burner. Your *Stereo World* readers will have a sneak preview.

SW: I wanted to thank you for your time to answer all these questions! I had one more comment. I am so glad that in *The Art of Harvey Kurtzman: The Mad Genius of Comics* by Denis Kitchen and Paul Buhle (2009) that you included the original art for *3-Dimensions!* from *MAD* no. 12, June 1954. While I enjoyed the short intro to Kurtzman's five-page story lampooning 3D, after its short cycle had come to an end, the intro does contain a couple of factual errors. If you should reprint the book, let me know, and I can put you in touch with a 3D historian.

DK: Good to learn! We should have consulted with you in 2009!

Denis Kitchen has produced, published, sold, and appeared in numerous 3D comics, and he continues to produce many 3D items. He was recently featured on an episode of *NYSA Presents!* discussing much of his 3D work.

Withstanding the Heat: Denis Kitchen on Comics, Curiosity, and Censorship

CHLOE MAVEAL / 2022

From *The Gutter Review* (November 22, 2022). Reprinted by permission.

For every comic you've ever touched that someone else got upset about, that contained a story that was a little beyond the pale by normal comics standards, or simply made it through the days of the Comics Code unscathed, there's a pretty solid chance that there's one man to thank: Denis Kitchen. From helping to found the underground comics movement in America as we know it in the 1960s to publishing countless talented creators through his iconic company Kitchen Sink Press, helping give voice to marginalized creators, and generally bolstering the comics medium as we know it through fair and careful curation, there are few things in the industry that Kitchen hasn't touched in some way or another . . . and made better as a result.

If you've read this site for longer than five minutes, it's pretty clear to see that Denis Kitchen is one of those people in comics that has not only struck an chord with me personally with his ethos, but has helped to shape the way in which I view comics history as a whole—through a careful lens of caring in the now and an unquenchable need to learn more about where it all comes from, for better or worse. What better way to pay homage to that then by talking to the man himself.

After our initial meeting at New York Comic Con of this year, I was fortunate enough to stay in touch with Kitchen and conduct this interview over Zoom last week.

Chloe Maveal: How was Lucca? I know you just got back from Italy not long ago.

Denis Kitchen: It was wonderful. Only five days. I wish it were a couple of weeks instead of a few days, but it was great.

CM: When you do international shows like that, do you bring any of the American underground comix like what you were doing at New York [Comic Con]?

DK: Oh, I don't exhibit. No, I was there as a guest and did some panels and events. I curated a Will Eisner exhibit for them last year. I was going to go the year before as well but because of COVID my wife and I couldn't go.

CM: Of course. The case for so many things, right? Is doing panels different over there?

DK: Well, generally, yes, because I don't speak Italian, so there has to be a translator. It just slows things down a bit. It always seems to be really well-attended, and the fans are super knowledgeable. The questions for the Will Eisner panel were all very smart. But yeah, it just takes twice as long [*laughs*].

CM: Well, internationally or not, I wanted to kick this off with something that's probably relatively basic but seems like a broad place to start considering the breadth and depth of your career. Do you still like comics?

DK: Hmm. . . .

CM: I mean, you've worn damn near every hat in the business. Even for one person who wears one or two of them during the course of their career, the answer is often a "no" by this point [*laughs*].

DK: No, that's actually a good question. I'm very jaded about mainstream comics in general, I think. I haven't read a Marvel or DC comic in more years than I even would guess. They just don't interest me. But I'm always on the lookout for good graphic novels, something by generally younger creators. I get a lot of recommendations, and the one I'm in the middle of right now is Noah Van Sciver's [*Joseph Smith and the Mormons*], and otherwise I've just got a stack of graphic novels. My daughter gave me a copy of *Gender Queer* that she recommended, and the CBLDF, of course, was defending that one.

CM: Of course, yeah. Y'all played a big role in keeping that on the shelves.

DK: Right, exactly. So I have a special interest in it. That'll probably come up next. I was at SPX [the Small Press Expo] this year, and I bought three or four things that looked interesting. They're all on the table next to my lounge chair, but I don't read as much as I used to when I was really actively in the business and publishing. Back then it was a never-ending stream. And the other factor is, as you know, there's so much coming out today, you can't possibly stay on top of all of it. I do look for reviews, though, and references from people I trust. In Italy, I bought two or three books that were more visual just from browsing the show floor, so the library's always expanding. I definitely still love the medium after all these years. So, except for not looking for a new *Spider-man* or *X-Men*, I'm good.

CM: I was about to say, how do you keep that relationship fresh? Because honestly, it is hard to pick up a Marvel or a DC book right now and find something that's really engaging in a way that many graphic novels and independent comics are. Does browsing shows rejuvenate that more than shopping in a bookstore or comic shop?

DK: Well, yes. If I go to a bookstore, they tend to be dominated by the major publishers. And again, I don't want to denigrate people's favorite superheroes, but they just don't speak to me. When I was in college, I was hooked on them, but tastes change and evolve. They're very different stories now.

CM: So with that relationship kind of evolving, then . . . what's your key role right now? I know that's something of a broad question.

DK: Well, I'm trying to come full circle back to drawing and writing, and I'm semi-succeeding. [*Laughs*] I'm slowly kind of extricating myself from other commitments. As an agent, I still have clients who I represent and advise, and slowly that's changing. So I have a new book that's literally on a boat coming from China now called *Creatures from the Subconscious*, and that is from Tinto Press in Denver. It collects a lot of what I call chipboard drawings. A chipboard is that on the bottom of a notebook, it's the cardboard kind of paper at the bottom here. I'm always flipping over notebooks and drawing on that part . . . so I finally bought a carton of just plain chipboard from a printer.

CM: You can do that?!

DK: Well, sure! You can buy any kind of paper, right? Well, if you want a carton, they'll just sell it to you. But I love that surface. I've been doing it for many years. I don't know anyone else who loves it like I do. But anyways, I start with a Sharpie marker and no thought whatsoever of what I'm going to draw, and a few lines appear and suddenly it just evolves in a way that's personally satisfying because spontaneity is the key. If I were drawing a comics page on an assignment, I would have my illustration board and pencil it all out and letter it carefully, and then finally ink it and it would be fine because that's the formal way of doing it. The chipboards are the opposite. They're very liberating, and I never know what's going to come out. I'm not sure I'd want a psychiatrist to look at them though [*laughs*].

That's why they're called "creatures from the subconscious," though, because more often than not, they are creatures of some kind. Sometimes, they're regular humans, but the humans have horns, and things like that. I never know where it's going to go. So that's one aspect. I'm also working on a couple of books. My youngest daughter, Violet, and I did a book a couple years ago for

Cover, *Creatures from the Subconscious* by Denis Kitchen
(Tinto Press, 2022).

Beehive Books about Harrison Cady, a now largely forgotten illustrator, who we both love and thought deserved to be rediscovered. So we're following up on that with one on another guy, also largely forgotten, Boris Artzybasheff. And for any of your [audience] who aren't familiar with him, if you do a quick Google search, I think you'll go, "Wow," because it really is amazing.

He was an illustrator-slash-cartoonist-slash-surrealist who did the absolute best anthropomorphic machinery of anyone ever. I don't think anyone can touch him. He's probably most famous for stuff he did during World War II. He did a lot of anti-Axis cartoons, and he also did scores of *Time* magazine covers that were portraits of famous people, but they're really also unusual, because the backgrounds often were kind of surrealistic and just very inventive in a way that the average boring *Time* magazine cover would not be. He always brought something extra to what he did, and he's got a fascinating backstory. So we're writing his monograph. I'm also working on a book about the *Nancy* cult . . . well, the Ernie Bushmiller cult—

CM: Which is still miraculously strong!

DK: It's amazing, isn't it? It's multigenerational, so it's hard to exactly explain what's going on, but there is something going on. I'm sure of it. So, anyway, I keep busy, Chloe.

CM: I can see that! Talk about a full workload.

DK: Every day is fresh, and in a way it's good to wear several hats because you don't fall into a rut. There's always new directions, new challenges, but I am trying to slow down now that I'm getting kind of ancient [*laughs*]. I'm trying to smell the roses, too.

CM: Going back to drawing on chipboard for a moment . . . it's kind of funny you say that you just make a lot of markings until something happens. I've actually heard similar things from several other artists recently. As someone whose brain just does not work like that, I'm kind of fascinated. The idea of letting the subconscious just sort of fall out like that . . . it almost ties back to your roots with the underground. Is that something that still resonates with you a lot, making sure that creating something where your id can flow through?

DK: Well, speaking for myself, yes. You have to put yourself in a certain state of mind. I know other artists can do that. Some don't or don't try, but even doodlers can do it. I mean, you might say you can't draw, but you might find—if you are in the right state of mind—your doodling will take unexpected directions. But you have to be in that . . . I'm not sure what to call it . . . a zen state or something? [*Laughs*] I do it so often now it just comes naturally. But I think for anyone starting out, you may have to just free your mind in a way that a lot of other people might have to put some effort into, but I think it pays dividends.

The underground cartoonist is still there long after underground comix have ceased to exist as they were; they've evolved, as you know. But the kind of person who went into underground comix is probably the kind of person who was already unconventional or seeking an unconventional route. And that's not something tied to any particular generation, I don't think. I mean anybody— no matter what age you are—can say, "I'm not going to think mainstream. I'm not going to do what people expect of me. I'm going to do whatever I want to do." Now, usually, you can't make a living doing that. Even back in the underground comix days, it wasn't easy to make a living at it if your name wasn't Robert Crumb or Gilbert Shelton. That's why I quickly became a publisher. So I never stopped being a cartoonist, but I had a wife and children and—

CM: You gotta find a way to pay the bills! Tale as old as time for artists.

DK: Absolutely, and publishing was the way I was able to do that. But I think it's the most rewarding if you're able to do that. And if you can't do it for a living, at least you can do it in your free time or part time. So there shouldn't be any excuse if you say, "Well, I can't just let it all go and let my id explode, for better or worse." I think everyone has free time, and you can experiment, and you never know what might come out.

Recent cover art by Kitchen: *Jack the Radio* (George Hage
Publishing, 2022).

CM: Speaking of what comes out, you're very much a champion for these
older works that hone in on that skill. When you're looking for things to
curate and bring back into the spotlight, what exactly makes for good curation for you? It seems like you're willing to do it for anyone who's willing
to try. . . . Your style of curation is more about the abstract thought behind
making sure everyone has a voice in creating this kind of art and less about
personal taste.

DK: It really is a combination, Chloe. You can't eliminate your personal
taste, but if I'm curating—whether it's literally an art exhibit or it's curating
an anthology or anything else where you have to select—if you don't have
personal taste, there's probably something wrong and you shouldn't be curating. But at the same time, you know, you have to think about the audience. I
guess there's no easy, quick answer to that. I try to take each of those opportunities seriously and give it a lot of thought. I mean, I think that's the only
responsible thing to do, right?

CM: Sure, of course.

DK: I mean, here you are curating guests for your website. We all curate. When I go to dinner, I'm curating the menu. You do your best with the choices you have, and not to make light of it, but when I first started doing this, and the first time I think I realized, "Oh, I'm getting credit as a guest curator or whatever," that's one of those words that's kind of rarefied because you think the fine art museum curators, and it's a pretty snooty, highfalutin crowd. But the truth is it happens on many, many levels. In the comics field in particular it's pretty rich, so if I'm doing an exhibit, I find it a great challenge, and also, it's a great deal of fun. But then also, if you do an exhibit and maybe the crowd is grumpy, maybe you guessed wrong or your choices were unpopular—that doesn't happen very often, but it gets down to you can't please everyone. You've got to basically trust your instincts.

CM: In that case, how difficult is it to exhibit or curate or collect the particular creators that you do for the audience that is the primary viewer now? Is that increasingly difficult?

DK: Well, I would say yes, just because now it's more political. You can't escape the fact now that let's say I'm asked to put together a show for some college in six months. There's definitely going to be an expectation that there'd be a sufficient number of women, people of color, LGBTQ people, and other variables that I wouldn't have thought about ten years ago when I did a show. And of course, I would have still included all of those groups ten years ago regardless, but it wouldn't have been with the kind of conscious pressure that you have now.

I used to do shows for the Society of Illustrators, for example, and with each passing year, not naming names, I would be told, "Well, make sure you check off the list." I don't like that, even though I understand that these things need to be more diverse and it's making up for the time when everybody was pretty much a white guy. I get that, absolutely, but at the same time it takes the pure curation out of it because suddenly there are asterisks, and you'll be second-guessed if you seem low on some area where you were expected to do more. It just complicates things.

CM: I get that, I think. I'm sure it can be limiting when you're trying to base things solely off of the merit of the history in relation to the art.

DK: Yeah, but I also understand, you know? For a long time, comics was a field that was dominated by men, and generally white men. And there's a lot of reasons for it. I remember talking to Trina Robbins about this exact thing one time, and she said when she was in high school and she wanted to pursue cartooning, her advisors, teachers, friends, they all said, "No, no, no.

You should go into fashion design. That's what women do. Comics are not for young women."

So it was a perception that was shared by the entire culture, and so you had to overcome that pressure. I remember meeting Dale Messick, the cartoonist who did [*Brenda Starr, Reporter*], and she had to change her name from Dalia. Dale was a male author name in the same way a famous female author in England changed her name to George a century or so back. [Editor's note: George Eliot, who was originally Mary Ann Evans.]

CM: Oh sure, sure. There's so many women assuming male pen names throughout publishing history.

DK: Exactly. So the point is that you have to recognize the voices that haven't been heard sufficiently in the past. Probably—hopefully—at some point, our society will be such that you don't have to think so consciously of it. That's what we're all striving for.

CM: I'm sure that in itself is difficult on a new level. You're wanting to present the work for what it was in the time period that it exists in while still being conscious. Feels like you're going to be butting heads with someone no matter what.

DK: Right.

CM: So how do you reckon with that? Putting out work that can really be difficult to come to terms with in its own context—or, for that matter, work that's often really difficult to teach about right now?

DK: Yeah, it's tough. I mean, I've not been in the academic area, so I can't really speak to any personal experience there, but I know it's the same kind of politically charged arena that we have in the other areas we're talking. Phoebe Gloeckner, as you know, is a perfect example, who brought up Robert Crumb in teaching her comics course and came under fire, and it's a controversial incident. I mean, Crumb is always kind of a lightning rod when you talk about these things because he's a guy who—you talked about the id earlier—he has no lid on his id, so to speak.

CM: Sure, that's kind of his whole deal.

DK: I mean, I know Robert well. I don't believe he is a racist. I don't believe he's inherently a misogynist. He certainly has healthy relationships with his wife, his daughter, and other women. The things he draws inflame some people, though. I know my own daughter, Violet—who is an aspiring cartoonist—she will admit that he's an amazing draftsman, but she will not look at his work because she finds it highly offensive.

As you probably know, at SPX maybe three or four years ago, Derf Backderf and Carol Tyler got in trouble when they brought him up as an influence on their career. I wasn't there, but I understand they were hissed and booed. I don't like it when there's an environment when you can't even talk about who your influences are or talk about somebody without automatically getting piled on. It's a touchy and controversial area, but I think like with everything in life you have to have a rational discussion, you know? If you don't like it, like my daughter, don't look at it, but there are people who will look at it, enjoy it, because again, Crumb doesn't just do images that inflame people. He's also done some extremely thought-provoking, historical, autobiographical work that I think will stand the test of time.

He's never ever going to be loved by everyone—in fact, he's probably going to be hated by more than he is loved. And again, it's the test of time. But in the current era, that's the situation. And I don't envy the Phoebe Gloeckners of the world who have to teach comics history and be very careful who they can even bring up. I don't know how you talk about comics history without at least touching on somebody like Crumb, for better or worse.

CM: I suppose. It's a kind of tightrope walk, right? Because it's so much of wanting to understand where people are coming from and—to an extent— understanding the anger and offense that people get seeing some of these images. But when you put them in context with a bunch of variables or as a genuine piece of satire calling things out for what they were and saying the quiet part out loud . . . I mean, it's hard to explain that context against a feeling, isn't it? It's hard to make people want to understand it in context, especially when they bring up extremely personal and valid points about some of these comics.

DK: Right. But that's why we have lots of trigger warnings in advance and things like that. If people don't want to hear about it, I guess they don't attend the class or whatever. But yeah, it's certainly a societal challenge. I can tell you, as someone who was with the CBLDF from the very beginning, we were very accustomed to defending comics against what I would say are religious zealots and right wingers and just a lot of, generally speaking and—totally using generalized terminology—"the right." The conservative, the Bible Belt, you know. But in recently years—

CM: It's coming from all sides?

DK: Yes! It's coming from—again, very generalist terminology—"the left," as well. Almost as much as the conservative right, the left is where many of the criticism and attempts at censorship are now coming from as well. That's what worries me the most.

CM: We do have a bizarre wave of puritanism coming from different angles right now, sure. I've gotten really into the underground branch of comix history in the last few years, and if it's one thing I've noticed in talking to people about them, it's that either you get met with the conservative die-hards who call you a chump for questioning or critiquing anything about it, and you get called a sympathizer for wanting to connect with them and their problematic content at all. There's an occasional phenomenon of being written off as being a piece of shit for even wanting to bother either way [*laughs*].

DK: Right, yes. And the underground comix you're referring to really were actually the opportunity that opened the door to a lot of female cartoonists, people of color, gay cartoonists. That was the beginning of it! So when you write off underground comix as being sexist, racist, whatever, right from the jump—well, that's just not the facts. Underground comix were, themselves, widely diverse, as were the creators and the topics as they evolved. I suppose it's easy to get typecast. You look back at any era and you generalize because it's the easiest way to approach things. But critics of underground comix on either side should also at least acknowledge that some great stuff came out of it. And, perhaps most importantly, opportunities to people who were previously unwelcome in comics.

CM: That's sort of the nature of that era's particular rebellion, though, isn't it? "Let's push back." I mean, the queer community alone, even if they couldn't directly identify with the comics themselves—or were put off by them—could go, "Well, wait a minute. This is pushing back. That's really important. Let's do this, too, in our way." I mean, just look at everything Howard Cruse did!

DK: Absolutely! I'm a straight man, but in the late 1970s, I thought there ought to be gay comics, and Howard was the only gay cartoonist I knew at the time . . . and even that was not something that was even spoken of. Howard was closeted like a lot of his peers. So when I proposed the idea of *Gay Comix* to him, he said, "I'd love to see it." And then, when I said, "Well, would you edit the series?" he was hesitant at first.

First of all, he lived in Alabama, and he made a living as a commercial artist and was rightfully concerned that he would lose gigs if it became known that he was gay. But he gave it some thought, and I remember it didn't take too long before he said, "You know what? I will do it." And then the next challenge came when I said, "Do you know other gay cartoonists?" And he said, "No, do you?" [*Laughs*]

CM: Oh no! [*Laughs*]

DK: Yeah, so we kind of sat down and said, "So what do we do next?" So again, in 1979, I believe it was, the game plan we came up with was that I would take my Rolodex and I would send a form letter that he and I would write to everybody in my Rolodex because we didn't know who else was closeted.

CM: . . . like a gay Bat Signal?

DK: [*Laughs*] Exactly. And we ended up with ten or twelve or so artists raising their hand, saying that they'd love to be on board. I also got a handful of nasty notes or phone calls back from people—like S. Clay Wilson called me up and said, "Why the fuck did you send me this letter? Do you think I'm a queer?" and I was just like, "I don't know. . . . are you?"

CM: Always worth asking.

DK: Well, back then, it was kind of awkward because, again, it was just the state of the society. But I think we've largely overcome that. And the series ended up then being a magnet itself that attracted gay cartoonists who first discovered the comic, like Alison Bechdel, for example.

Sometimes you just have to instigate something if that's your instinct. I remember one time back then Trina [Robbins] was complaining to me that the so-called erotic comics we were doing were offensive to her and some other women. I said, "Well, why don't you do your own erotic comics?" And she said, "Oh, great!" And so we started a new series.

CM: [*Laughs*] That's kind of brilliant. Everyone gets what they need in their own way, I guess.

DK: Sometimes you have to find a way to make it work. And again, being a publisher who didn't have to answer to stockholders or anybody—I could just make a decision on my own. It wasn't a huge-scale business. More often than not, the things that my instinct told me was right to do also proved to be commercially successful, so it wasn't just charity. It was just looking at the market more objectively than others were, perhaps, but it certainly wasn't charity.

CM: So . . . how do you go about explaining to people how to be more curious in that way? Because I think that's such a key factor in what you've done and what you still do—you go with your gut and stay curious. How do you teach people how to stay curious in that way so that it's a trend that can continue on in creating these spaces in comics and creating comics history?

DK: . . . I'm a little stunned by that question. Hmm.

CM: Sorry. [*Laughs*]

DK: No, no. I just . . . I don't think we should have to. Maybe you're right.

CM: It just seems like it's not something that's done in the same way anymore. The passion is there, but certainly not everyone is curious.

DK: Is it parenting? Schools? Where does lack of curiosity come from? Aren't we all naturally curious?

CM: One would think so. The envelope is pushed in some really great ways and is very much now lacking in others.

DK: Yeah, I think for lack of a better term, the current state of culture tamps down on that curiosity because maybe if you're too curious in some areas, then some of your peers will come down on you. I don't know. I can't speak as a twenty-something anymore. My own experience comes from a different era, and I'm sure I'll be criticized for some of the things I've already said to you, but I've got to speak my mind as well.

CM: Sure. All perspectives are important in these conversations surrounding art.

DK: It's just like we started to touch on earlier—censorship is censorship. It doesn't matter which side it comes from. I don't care if it's the church or the government or my neighbor telling me what I want to read and see what I want to read and see. And that is also part of natural curiosity. I mean, I occasionally turn on Fox News because I'm curious. I'm usually repelled entirely, but I'm curious because I want to know what other people are hearing. Is that curious or stupid?

I remember first hearing that from Harvey Kurtzman. I went to visit him one time, and he was on an exercycle, and he was watching the Jimmy Swaggart show. And for those who are too young to know, Jimmy Swaggart was a televangelist who actually got busted with a prostitute, and then he cried a thousand tears and was magically forgiven and welcomed back by part of his congregation. But that's not the point. The point is, I did not expect to see Harvey watching a televangelist while he was on an exercycle. And so, when he was done, he turned off the TV. And I said, "What's going on? Why would you watch that?" he said, "I want to know what other people are seeing and thinking."

CM: Kind of like "I want to see what's on the other side. I don't agree with it at all, in any way, but man, I want to see what's over there"? Like a "know your enemy" mentality?

DK: Exactly. I mean, you may hate the politics or the religious view or whatever, but you got to understand people are people, and some of these people may disagree with you, but there's still a humanity to explore. What makes them think what they think? What is the draw? What are the core differences here, and how do you talk about them? Well, you'll never know if you don't look at what their influences are. This is, I think, the issue of our day. We're so fucking polarized.

I mean, I was talking to someone recently who was at a bar and two people were arguing about Trump, and the pro-Trump guy turned to him and said, "What do you think?" And he said, "I was going to jump in, but I realized," he said, "I didn't want to escalate an argument. What I would like to have had was a rational argument between two people with opposing views. And that wasn't going to happen right then with this person." We need more rational dialogue. Comics are an ideal place for that sort of thing, I think.

CM: You'd think that.

DK: Yeah, sure. But it's just a medium. And someone was telling me about. . . . What's that frog that was embraced by the right wing? Pedro?

CM: Pepe the Frog?

DK: Pepe the Frog, yes. So somebody apparently did a Kickstarter comic a couple years back with that character, and it had a six-figure sum, like very quickly.

CM: No shit, six figures?

DK: Yes, and it was so demoralizing on one hand because it was lousy art, the politics were extreme and awful, and so on. But it did prove that if you are a right-winger, and you want to do comics, you certainly will find an audience. The cartoonists I know, and most of the comics fans I know are on the left side of the fence . . . but we don't own comics.

And now that schools and educators are embracing comics more than ever, it's a good sign, but it also means there has to be a real carefully curated neutrality, because any educational comic you do has to go through the Texas Board of Education because they're kind of the gatekeeper for other states.

CM: Which is insane.

DK: But that's the way textbooks work, unfortunately. So everywhere you look, it comes back again to curation and to the power of comics, and the way they overlap with comics is . . . I mean, comics and politics is a fascinating area. And I think we on the left side have to get used to the fact that conservatives are going to understand it's a very effective medium, and they're going to employ it more and more, too.

CM: That's kind of been harnessed for ages already, hasn't it? I mean, combining art and text has been around in as far as things like political cartoons for centuries. It seems surprising that it surprises people that it's something that can be harnessed for both purposes and all sides.

DK: For sure. And you bring up editorial cartoons, which are a distant cousin, but they're still part of the family. So you perhaps have noticed that editorial cartoonists are dying out. There are fewer and fewer every year. And that's partly to do with the fact that newspapers are sadly dying.

CM: Sure. Which is incredibly sad.

DK: But there's also that the newspapers who are desperately trying to stay alive are much more timid about hiring an editorial cartoonist because they're a very vocal, visible symbol of that paper. If you've got a liberal editorial cartoonist and even a quarter of your readership is more conservative, you're going to go, "Well, I don't know. That cartoonist isn't really helping us retain our readership." So in a way that we never had to deal with before in journalism or cartooning, editorial cartoonists are probably going to be extinct before long.

CM: Isn't that something that will be kind of extended to like zines again? Or indie comics and web comics and things like that? Makes me think of *The Nib*, who still do great editorial cartoons.

DK: Hmm. Perhaps that's true. Online presence definitely makes a difference. Really, *The Huffington Post*s of the world need to hire editorial cartoonists. That's the real answer. To be an effective editorial cartoonist, you have to be extremely topical; you have to do your cartoon for tomorrow's audience today based on what just happened, generally speaking. That's a special kind of artist and a special kind of vehicle. And if it's not a paper, then it has to be an online counterpart. I just think, again, it's part of that polarization that's affecting everything, including our favorite industry.

CM: Looping back really quickly to kind of where we started all of this: Does that contribute to part of what keeps you interested in comics, but also what kind of jades you to them?

DK: Well, I'm finding the ones that I probably enjoy the most at this point are well-researched, historical comics like the one I'm just reading about Joseph Smith. I know the basic Mormon story, but I know that Noah grew up as a Mormon, and I know that he did his research very carefully. He's not a Mormon anymore, but he wanted to be sensitive to that faith, including his own core family. It's fascinating. And I find myself attracted to the kind of artists who are willing to do that research because it takes them longer. If you want to do something autobiographical, the research is within you. But if you're doing something about the War of 1812 or something, you have to be a proper scholar, or no one will take it seriously.

And I first saw this sort of thing with Jack Jackson, who was one of the underground cartoonists who did mostly histories of Texas and the Southwest. He was a true historian who was also a cartoonist, and he was highly effective, I thought. I wasn't particularly interested in Texas history, but he certainly made it fascinating. And we all have a superficial knowledge of, say, the Alamo, but all the forces behind it? He showed the Mexican side of that in a way that I hadn't seen in an American textbook.

He's another example of if you try to pigeonhole underground comix. Jackson was doing both science fiction kinds of comics, but he was also doing historical comics that I think will stand the test of time. He's a guy who influenced even somebody like Will Eisner, who certainly acknowledged the undergrounds. Like Justin Green was another one who influenced Will. The autobiographical stuff started in the underground, and that seems to be a dominant genre these days. I like a lot of it, although—I mean, correct me if I'm wrong—but I think there are a lot of younger cartoonists who maybe ought to live life a little longer before they tackle autobiography. Not to say you might not have a fascinating life story at twenty-two . . .

CM: I get what you mean. Everyone has a unique story, but in order to write about life, it's important to really live it.

DK: I think so. Anecdotes and short stories from young people are so important and insightful—I have to be careful not to be too broad with this sort of comment. It's all very important, but so is living before you write about living.

CM: I guess that, too, comes back to that curiosity then, doesn't it?

DK: Yes. And if there are members of your generation or peer group that you think need some education, maybe that's part of what you're doing as a service. It's important to keep that going. That's what we do.

INDEX

Numbers in **bold** refer to figures.

ABOUT THE EDITOR

Portrait by Darick Robertson

Kim A Munson is the editor of the Eisner Award–nominated anthology *Comic Art in Museums* and the forthcoming *Conversations with Trina Robbins*. She has contributed to many publications, including *The Cambridge Companion to Comics*, *The Comics of R. Crumb: Underground in the Art Museum*, *International Journal of Comic Art*, *Source: Notes on the History of Art*, and *Places Journal*. She curated the art exhibits *Women in Comics* (with Trina Robbins, New York, Rome, and Napoli), *Colleen Doran Illustrates Neil Gaiman* (New York and San Diego), and *Beautiful Monsters: The Art of Emil Ferris* (New York).

www.ingramcontent.com/pod-product-compliance
Lightning Source LLC
Chambersburg PA
CBHW060352030726
47497CB00003B/687